BRANDING TEXAS

BRANDING TEXAS

Performing Culture in the Lone Star State

LEIGH CLEMONS

UNIVERSITY OF TEXAS PRESS
Austin

Portions of Chapters 2 and 3 first appeared in "Your Mission, If You Accept It: 'Texan' Culture and the Performance of the Alamo" (*Theatre Survey* 41.1 [May 2000]: 23–46).

Printed in the United States of America
First edition, 2008

♾ The paper used in this book meets the minimum requirements of ANSI/NISO Z39.48-1992 (R1997) (Permanence of Paper).

Library of Congress Cataloging-in-Publication Data
Clemons, Leigh, 1967–
Branding Texas : performing culture in the Lone Star State / Leigh Clemons. — 1st ed.
p. cm.
Includes index.
ISBN 978-0-292-73937-6
1. Texas—Historiography. 2. Texas—Civilization. 3. Popular culture—Texas—History. 4. Group identity—Texas—History. 5. Folklore—Texas—History. 6. Performing arts—Texas—History. 7. Theatre—Texas—History. 8. Texas—History—Revolution, 1835–1836—Drama. 9. Texas—History—Republic, 1836–1846—Drama. I. Title.
F385.2.C64 2008
306.09764—dc22

2007038706

CONTENTS

PREFACE vii

ACKNOWLEDGMENTS ix

1. INTRODUCTION: TEXAS AND THE PERFORMANCE OF REGIONALITY 1

2. "DEEP IN THE HEART": THE ARCHITECTURAL LANDSCAPES OF TEXAN CULTURAL MEMORY 14

3. TEACHING "TEXAN": THE PEDAGOGICAL FUNCTION OF THE TEXAS REVOLUTION 37

4. "WHAT'S THE MATTER WITH YOU PEOPLE?": THE PERFORMANCE OF AUTHENTIC BEHAVIOR IN SMALL-TOWN TEXAN PLAYS 71

5. SELLING TEXAS: THE POLITICAL BRANDING OF TEXAN CULTURAL IDENTITY 95

6. CONCLUSION: "OUR FLAG STILL WAVES PROUDLY FROM THE WALLS" 120

NOTES 125

INDEX 157

PREFACE

If you ask me who I am, I will tell you that I am a Texan, born and raised. What does it mean to say this? Where does my "Texan" identity come from or, for that matter, what does the concept of Texan identity mean? This idea of what it means to be Texan, or to associate anyone or anything with that quality, appears to have a deep and iconic symbology and may even qualify as an archetype. And what does the image of the Texan as seen by the rest of the United States and, these days, the world, entail? How was it formed, and how does it continue to be formed, and performed, in contemporary society?

This book considers these questions and offers possible answers. It examines how theatre and other representational practices have helped to create and maintain a sense of "Texas" as a distinct national and cultural identity more than 150 years after it ceased to be a separate nation. It looks at how the various representational practices present in historical and contemporary performances of the Texan intersect with the history, myth, and memory of the Lone Star State.

As a distinct cultural identity, the Texan is grounded in the history of Texas' years as an independent republic (1836–1845). The events of these years, and the Texas Revolution that preceded them, laid the groundwork for a complex web of performed identities that distinguished between those who were Texans and those who were not. Furthermore, there is a complex set of mythologies that stretches far beyond the Texan, defining, more or less, the qualities that are associated with the people, places, things, and traditions that constitute the practice of Texan identity. These distinctions continue to this day, as contemporary political and social issues are colored by the events of Texas' past.

The performance of Texas' history and culture is contained in such diverse forms as plays, films, television shows, museums, and battle reenactments. These sites form a complex web of identity that makes up the performance of a Texan and separates those who identify as such from those who fall outside the popular or institutional definitions, including women, African Americans, and Hispanics. These groups form their own narratives, which complicates the notion of Texan identity, further enriching the history of the region.

In his dystopic novel *1984,* George Orwell writes that "who controls the past, controls the future, and who controls the present controls the past." In this book, with an eye toward determining the future of the state's history and cultural memory, I attempt to determine not only how Texas' past is controlled, but how it was, and is, represented, contested, and, often, inverted.

ACKNOWLEDGMENTS

I would like to thank the following people and groups for their assistance in making this book a reality:

The late Dr. Richard "Doc" Hossalla of Southwestern University, Georgetown, Texas, for convincing me to get a Ph.D. in theatre;

Jill Dolan, who first launched this project during a visiting lectureship at the University of Minnesota in 1993, when I wrote a paper on *Greater Tuna*. She first encouraged me to explore exactly what a "Texan" was in performance;

Profs. Richard Rudolph and Mary Jo Maynes, for introducing me to the concept of national identity and allowing me to explore its usage in performance;

Michal Kobialka, my dissertation advisor, for keeping my work honest;

The staffs of the Southwestern Writers Collection at Texas State University and the Daughters of the Republic of Texas Library at the Alamo for their help in securing hard-to-find documents;

Newton M. Warzecha, director of Presidio La Bahía, and the reenactors of the annual Battle of Coleto Creek/Goliad Massacre for giving of their time to answer questions about both Texas history and battle reenacting;

The annual meetings of the American Society for Theatre Research, the Mid-America Theatre Conference, and the Historiography Working Group of the International Federation for Theatre Research, for allowing me to present various parts of the book as they developed over the years and giving me valuable feedback;

Guillermo Gómez-Peña, Pocha Nostra, and Jump Start Theatre Company, for including me in *Epcot: El Ala-MALL,* which provided an opportunity for me to participate in the reshaping of Texan cultural narrative through performance and to reflect on that process;

Prof. Robin Roberts of Louisiana State University, who read early drafts of the chapters and provided support during the highs and lows of the process;

The reviewers of my manuscript, who provided helpful insights in their reports, which helped to strengthen my argument;

William Bishel, Megan Giller, and Kathy Bork of the University of Texas Press, for seeing me through the publishing process and answering my many questions;

My colleagues in the Department of Theatre at Louisiana State University, for their understanding and support;

Milo S. Fisher, performance artist, who will always be my inspiration;

Prof. Rosemarie K. Bank, for both her friendship and her valuable and insightful feedback on the book;

Patrick Lichty—collaborator, colleague, best friend, and husband—for being there every step of the way and helping with the little, but important, details;

And finally, my parents, Clara and Ray Clemons, to whom this book is dedicated—they not only raised me, they were the backbone of this project. They introduced me to Texas history and made me aware of its importance in my life. Over the years, they accompanied me to countless battle reenactments and numerous visits to the Alamo, helped me search out historical markers, took photos, sent me local newspaper articles, and kept me going throughout the long journey that has resulted in this book.

BRANDING TEXAS

ONE

INTRODUCTION

Texas and the Performance of Regionality

I was raised in the West. The West of Texas. It's pretty close to California. In more ways than Washington, D.C., is close to California.

GEORGE W. BUSH

What exactly is this "Texas" of which George W. Bush speaks in the epigraph?[1] Is it a place? A culture? Does Texas actually exist anymore, or has it been obscured under layers of myth and iconography until whatever was real about it is no longer visible?

Texan cultural identity is a complex set of performances that creates and maintains the *idea* of the state as a distinct entity and as a site of identity for its inhabitants. These performances include cultural behaviors, historical events, and architectural spaces and objects. They occur in historic sites, pageants, festivals, and other forms of performance integral to creating and maintaining the "Lone Star" brand, or consumable, commodified image, of Texan cultural identity. This brand is then consumed by a willing public through visits to historic sites such as the Alamo, the viewing of films and television shows featuring Texan characters, or attendance at plays and other live performances which bill themselves as representing Texans or Texan-ness. The contestation of exactly what constitutes Texas and the nature of these Texans provides a site in which to analyze or interrogate the construction and performance of a unique regional identity.

The performance of regionality is not unique to Texas; one can find similar processes in play in various areas of the United States: Manhattan, Minnesota, California, Louisiana, Maine, to name but a few. Texas, however, deserves study because of its paradigmatic construction of a regional identity, and the importance of this identity to American identity.

THE NEW/OLD REPUBLIC

On April 27, 1997, Richard McLaren, the ambassador of the Republic of Texas separatist/militia movement, and several other members of the group barricaded themselves in the Republic's headquarters in the West Texas town of Fort Davis.[2] They took two hostages after breaking into a nearby home and wounding one resident. Although the hostages were soon released, the standoff lasted until May 4, when McLaren and three others surrendered to authorities.[3]

The Republic of Texas movement, which is still in existence,[4] professes that Texas was illegally annexed by the United States in 1845 and, therefore, is still an independent country.[5] To much of the American media, the Republic of Texas movement was no different from any other militia-type separatist group operating within the United States. In fact, it was even less well known; a *U.S. News and World Report* article on the rise in militias dated exactly one week prior to the start of the siege does not mention the group.[6] To many of its members, however, the group's identification with the state's heritage as a formerly sovereign nation—a status among the states shared only by the Kingdom of Hawai'i[7]—provided a unique angle to the standard rhetoric of many militia groups in the United States and their issues with federal bureaucracy, eminent domain, and other issues. Texas, however, had a legal claim (though dubious) that other states did not: having entered the United States under treaty, it retained rights that other territories ceded to the federal government upon annexation, such as control of its public lands.[8] The Republic of Texas movement seized on this provision and twisted it into a tool for antifederalist rhetoric grounded in supposedly Texan notions of freedom, independence, and the struggle against a tyrannical government.

Yet the Republic of Texas movement did not invent these associations; they are part of a larger field of relationships which circumscribe Texas as a historical space once separate from the United States—as a former nation with its own unique identity. In this sense, the Republic of Texas represents an extreme performance of what I call "Texan cultural identity," and national identity in general, since the Texas Revolution. The history of the Texan cultural identity must be viewed not as a story but as a structure, one that seeks to keep its foundations firm and level even as dislocating forces swarm around it. For as Francis Barker states, it is that careful balance which is the key to achieving changes in the way history is constructed, both then and now:

> And notwithstanding those who confuse memory with nostalgia—they are committed to the charm of the bad new days—it will have to be a historical practice, deploying—in practice—the sense which is not anecdotal but structural to both history and the possibility of thought, the sense that things have not always been like this nor need remain so. Where "this" and "so" are not as much particles of grammar as the diacritical sites of historical signs. The sense, in other words, that if historicity is lost, so too is the capacity to formulate (not just to desire and embrace, but also to know and shape) change.[9]

The process of maintaining a cultural identity, while most often associated with reductive conflicts over perceived geographic boundaries that separate territory claimed by one group from that of another, is a complex set of performances that creates and maintains the *idea* of the nation-state. These practices, drawing on myths, beliefs, behaviors, geographies, and ideologies, form a field of relations that defines the boundaries of history and performance for Texan cultural identity. Examining Texan identity reveals how regional identities in general are created through performance.

Often, these performances appear to produce representations of specific local practices within larger global practices. For example, the story of the Alamo, site of the most famous battle of the Texas Revolution, was used by John Wayne in his 1963 film *The Alamo* to personify the "American" heroic spirit. This spirit is posited in the geographic space of Texas, imbuing that space with performative power. This invocation of the Texan as one of the strongest, most extreme instances of a greater American identity gives insight into the role of geographic location in the construction of identity.

This concept of national identity formation rests not in the ability to document an actual, lived Texan past, but in the way that events are reconfigured into pedagogical historical narratives that grant primacy to the authors of the history. National narratives may work within the spheres, rhetoric, or other strategies of nationalism, but their continuous movement and redefinition are based on shifts in the opposing side's perspective; this is, in the words of Homi K. Bhabha, the "Janus-faced discourse" of national narration.[10]

While, as this book will demonstrate, Texan cultural identity has many faces, not just two, it is in the interplay between the major forces that we see the struggle for control of the creation, preservation, and promulgation of the identity. These moments of contestation over exactly what constitutes

"Texas" provide an illuminating site in which to explore the use(s) of performance for identity construction.

The process of regional and national narration includes not only the performance practices of cultural behaviors and historical events but also architectural spaces and objects. While it may seem odd, initially, to think of space as having the ability to contain and perform identity, the construction of historical and cultural spaces as unique performative sites comes from shifts in the fields of ethnography and cultural geography. What Barbara Kirshenblatt-Gimblett calls "ethnographic artifacts" or "objects of ethnography" are key to the study of performance culture. These artifacts "become valuable . . . not because they were found . . . but by virtue of the manner in which they have been detached" from previous contexts and given new ones. She asserts that, through these practices, "disciplines make their objects and in the process make themselves."[11]

Material objects examined in this book include historic sites and historical pageants, festivals, and other forms of performance practices in which the performance site itself is integral to the experience and understanding of the material. In the case of Texan performance, these practices revolve mainly around historical events and architectural monuments.[12] These sites of engagement give the performances a permanent archival function that modern-day Texans can reference through visitation, pictorial representation, or verbal evocation. The struggle among the various performances—political, aesthetic, or cultural—illustrates the importance to the various ethno-political groups within the state of having a claim to Texan cultural identity. LULAC (the League of United Latin American Citizens) and prominent Hispanic residents of San Antonio often protest the Daughters of the Republic of Texas (DRT) and their single-handed control of the Alamo shrine and, by extension, the story told by the space. At other times, the Texas government has attempted to intervene in the DRT's ownership of the Alamo site by attempting to return it to a more "authentic" framework.[13] As a result of each of these confrontations, Texas' national narrative shifts, travels, and, from time to time, even ruptures, creating ever more fragmented representations.

Factors besides history and memorialization play a key role in the creation of Texan cultural identity. Diana Taylor asks, "How does expressive behavior (performance) transmit identity, memory, and culture?"[14] While some of these practices can be traced, like the Republic of Texas movement, to specific pieces of Texas history (however interpreted), many are more elusive. Shifting interplays of perception between the performer/resident and the audience/tourist within a Texan cultural field create a conflicting set of

Texan features. The continually shifting relationships between "staged" and "real" identity create a simulated Texan cultural identity interwoven with aspects of Texas history, behavior, and other cultural forms. Out of actual events and re-created objects, the Texan has now emerged as a brand, a commodity, which can be constructed, maintained, and sold to the public.

Marketing the Texan as a brand grew out of both the desire to remember important historical events and the maintenance of architectural repositories of cultural memory like battle sites and museums. The pedagogical practices of Texas' national narrative strive to establish the "Lone Star" as the primary image of Texan cultural identity.[15] This façade allows Texans of a certain historical background (direct descendants of original settlers or revolutionary soldiers), ethnic heritage (primarily Anglo), or gender (primarily male) to engage with and profit from the pedagogical national narrative of the Texan and Texas' cultural heritage while consigning those outside of this narrative, for whatever reason, to outsider or "tourist" status. Ironically, as the percentage of such individuals grew smaller in relationship to the state's population, they nonetheless solidified and maintained the fiction of the Texan as unilaterally white and male.[16] For a Lone Star who exists within the complex forces of national narration, being able to connect with the heritage is everything; it provides historical grounding, legitimates cultural behaviors, and provides a geographic frame of reference. Some Texans connect through geographic location; others connect with historical events; still others identify with certain behaviors or attitudes associated with Texan characters in popular media, like John Wayne's or Fess Parker's Davy Crockett at their respective Alamos.

Finally, there are those Texans whose idea of cultural identity stems from the marketing of the Texan as a distinct brand for consumption: the Lone Star. Yet the primacy of the Lone Star brand is constantly in flux, as those voices typically obscured or downplayed by the façade—Hispanics, African Americans, and women, to name a few—strive to ensure that their own representations are included.

Because this book analyzes the dominant branding of Texan identity, my focus is the historical emphasis on white, male Texans and the importance of whiteness in the construction of Texan cultural identity. The activities and resistant performances of those outside this construction (nonwhites, nonmales) will be dealt with in Chapter 5. Texas provides one of the more obvious and complex manifestations of the "performance of regionality"—representations produced by a complex field of identity discourse—national, racial/ethnic, gender, and historical—which varies from location to location within the American cultural landscape.

TEXAN CULTURAL IDENTITY

The relationship between performance and everyday life in America is central to the formation of Texan identity. Early discussions about the performance of everyday life, such as those of J. L. Austin and Erving Goffman, posited that the daily representation of self was inherently performative and followed a one-to-one equation, in which to state that one was doing something was, in fact, to do it, and in which to be perceived as behaving as a certain type of character in public was, in fact, to be that type.[17] Later, ethnographers like Victor Turner and Dwight Conquergood made visible a shift in research focus from looking at the "world as text" to looking at it "as performance," in which ethnographers could begin "thinking about fieldwork as the collaborative performance of an enabling fiction between observer and observed, knower and known."[18] Michel de Certeau reified this notion of performance with his concept of "the practice of everyday life," in which individuals created and moved through a field of practices, using tactics and strategies to construct distinct performance identities.[19] At the same time, theatre scholars like Marvin Carlson warned of the inherent preconceptions of casting all societal interactions as "performances," even though the use of performance-oriented language in these situations invited such comparisons.[20]

The diverse performances analyzed in this book all share formal characteristics: they are representations of an(other) designed to elicit certain responses from the viewer. A museum curator may mediate his or her performance through the use of cultural artifacts, but he or she is still constructing a performative space for museum audiences to consume. Battle reenactments, though largely unscripted, draw heavily on performances by the participants to lend to the authenticity of the event.

The complex interplay of attitudes and behaviors present in both theatrical and everyday performances creates a performative cultural identity in all of the senses mentioned above. As Judith Butler says, "the performative 'works' to the extent that *it draws on and covers over* constitutive conventions by which it is mobilized."[21] Analyzing specific examples of such performances allows us to see how their formation, maintenance, and reformation work in creating Texan cultural identity.[22]

The idea of identity representation as a tangible performance practice, however, has relevance for the understanding of Texan cultural identity precisely because there is no agreement on the parameters which frame this relationship. At first glance, it would seem that the geographic borders of the state determine the boundaries of the performance of Texan cultural identity. Yet those borders have shifted in the over 150 years since the Texas Revolution, changing the actual boundary lines between Texas and other states. In addition, much of Texan cultural identity is grounded in the events of the Texas Revolution, which took place in a very specific part of the state, roughly along what is now Interstate 10 from San Antonio to Houston and south to the Rio Grande. Other parts of the state have their own distinct names—West Texas, the (Rio Grande) Valley, the Panhandle—which points to a plethora of identities within the state's geography. Within Texan cultural identity, then, there are competing spaces and groups which vie for a dominant place in that identity.

Once so characterized through formal and "everyday" performances and behaviors, Texans can be created through historical plays. These representations are then exported to the rest of the world, creating a Texan character recognizable outside of the United States as well as inside it. In his 1897 novel *Dracula,* for example, Bram Stoker chose a "Texan" to round out his band of heroic vampire hunters: Quincy Morris, a romantic savage. Much like Cumberland's West Indian (in the play of the same name) of 150 years before, Stoker's character carries a Bowie knife and a Winchester rifle, uses language rich with western American dialect and colorful analogies. If one can take Stoker's use of the character as evidence of a broader representation of social strata,[23] the Texan identity performed by Morris serves a valuable, if somewhat sacrificial, function in the larger context of the novel by serving as a counterpoint to the stereotypical British characters of the landed aristocrat (Arthur Holmwood), the physician (John Seward), and the middle-class London solicitor (Jonathan Harker). Yet, in this sacrifice, Morris embodies the same Texan behaviors found later in representations of Crockett by John Wayne and Fess Parker, not to mention representations of the other men who died at the Alamo. Finding a literary representation of Texan identity several decades before the appearance of the Alamo as a central icon in Texas history in the late-nineteenth/early-twentieth century suggests that a Texan cultural identity was already coming together in the years following the Texas Revolution and the entrance of the state into the union.

The area of "cultural geography" (also a recent addition to the field of historiographic research) interweaves the study of cultural landscapes with their configurations as sites of commemoration and (often) tragedy. Battle sites like the Alamo are of particular interest to cultural geographers because their visitors "seek environmental intimacy in order to experience patriotic inspiration."[24] This reinforces the pedagogical function of such sites as agents of national narration, as the thousands of Texas schoolchildren—black, white, and Hispanic—who visit the Alamo and San Jacinto battle sites every year can attest. According to Kenneth E. Foote, the presence, or absence, of such sites "play[s] an active role in their own interpretation . . . the evidence of violence left behind often pressures people, almost involuntarily, to begin debate over meaning."[25]

Yet, because of their history, the study of these site-specific memorials as ethnographic objects revolves mostly around the story, rather than around the space of the performance. Like Civil War sites throughout the South, all of the major battle sites of the Texas Revolution—Gonzales, the Alamo, Goliad/Coleto, and San Jacinto—have either preserved architectural landmarks from the period or erected memorials and monuments at those locations that serve to mark and perform the site as a repository of history and Texan cultural memory. Many of these sites also sponsor annual commemorations that include some form of reenactment of the historical events which took place there, further marking the space with ethnographic (and performative) significance.

Yet these sites also mask profound absences: the bodies of those who died on both sides, military and civilian, men and women, Texian, Tejano, and Mexican. The absence of actual remains can foster a sense of immateriality within the discursive performance practices of the battle site, creating a hyperreal,[26] a field of simulations that masks the absence of the "real" and can, over time, become more real than the real ever was. While Baudrillard focuses on ahistorical Las Vegas, his description of America as a place of hyperreality also helps us understand Texan cultural identity, which insists on following the mantra of "bigger, badder, better."

The presentation of violence as romanticized spectacle is particularly relevant to Texan performance because of its grounding in revolution and battle. Battle reenactments are a popular form of entertainment at the town of Gonzales' annual "Come and Take It" celebration, commemorating the first shots fired in the Texas Revolution. Not all of the reenactments, however, center around the original historical event; some re-present already sanctioned representations of the event. Happy Shahan's Alamo Village was originally constructed as the set for John Wayne's *The Alamo* and then was used as a tourist attraction commemorating the making of the film, complete with museum and tours of the site (which still functions as a working movie set). Alamo Village also has attracted scores of reenactors, who represent scenes from Texas history books as well as from Wayne's film. As with Civil War battle reenactments, these performances strive for historical accuracy and claim to be "authentic" ethnographic representations, complete with time period–correct costuming, weaponry, and properties.

Not only historical events but also contemporary culture help keep the idea of the Texan alive and in performance through incredibly diverse, somewhat contradictory, contested representations. Anecdotes that illustrate Texan performance also abound in literature and film throughout the twentieth century. From J. R. Ewing of *Dallas* to Hank Hill of *King of the Hill,* Texans have been performing for audiences throughout America and around the world since the 1936 Centennial Exposition, when Texas began marketing itself as a place not only for cowboys and oil fields but also as a haven of culture, prosperity, and social progress suitable for national recognition. The current political climate and its attachment to Texan cultural identity emerged through the carefully constructed performances of Pres. George W. Bush as the Texan president. Similar tactics are in play when he presents himself as a self-styled Texan in his dealings with both the American and foreign governments by holding important meetings at his ranch in Crawford and when he doles out "honorary Texan" status to selected foreign dignitaries.

Texan cultural identity also exists on what Joseph Roach terms a "selvage," a border or frontier that works to segregate groups from one another while simultaneously forcing them together, creating paradoxical states of representation best indicated in public performance venues.[27] Members of various racial, ethnic, and gender groups vie for primacy in the national narrative of Texas as a republic-state. Hispanics struggle to have the history of Tejanos and their descendants included in the revolutionary narrative. Women insist on representation for their roles in the Revolution and for their efforts to preserve "Texas history" sites such as the Alamo. Blacks and American Indians, long excluded but with many historical ties to the state, struggle even to be acknowledged as part of the historical narrative other than as footnotes.[28]

In opposition to such practices, Texan historical performance is engaged in the replication of historical "Texian" identities such as Sam Houston, Jim Bowie, William Barret Travis, and, of course, Davy Crockett. The fact that none of these men were born in Texas bears no relationship to their ability to convey the innate qualities of the Texan, just as McLaren, a native of Ohio, was able to assume the performance mantle of the Republic of Texas' ambassador.[29]

While some nonnative Texans (as most of the revolutionary-era population was) could directly claim a Texan identity, others had to rely on representations of their Texan cultural identity in history, song, and story. Most of the nineteenth-century Texan population was functionally illiterate; the two survivor narratives from the Alamo—those of Moses Rose and Susanna

Dickinson—were dictated to literate persons decades after the event. Legend has it that Emily Morgan (or, sometimes, West), a young woman who might have been anyone from a mulatto slave to the housekeeper for one of the Texian officers, "distracted" Santa Anna in his tent and allowed Sam Houston's Texian army to sneak up on the Mexican camp at San Jacinto. Such "outsider" identities still had to be actively performed to reinforce the solidity of Texan historical discourse.

Texan cultural identity supports this "whitewashed" discourse, which places people of color at the margins. Characters represented as Texans are, on the whole, reflections of the traditionally dominant political and economic powers within the state. Architecturally, sites of Texan historical memory have been shrines to the deeds and exploits of Texians: the Alamo, Goliad, San Jacinto. History museums, designed to focus on or showcase famous people or important events, contain more content relevant to Anglo history than to Hispanic, unless specifically designed with that focus. Historically, Texian heroes have been more visible in films and historical pageants than have Tejanos like Juan Seguín and Gregorio Esparza; Santa Anna, the antagonist, has been the most visible Hispanic face, and representations of him on stage and screen range from the ludicrous to the barbaric. Attempts to re-present revolutionary narratives from the Tejano perspective have been criticized as inferior, inaccurate productions or farcical comedies.[30]

Finally, while J. R. Ewing and Hank Hill may be characters familiar to many television viewers, there have been no similar Hispanic figures in the national media to give descendants of the Tejano population and others of Mexican heritage living in Texas a visible media image. Their treatment in more recent live performances has not been much better than in the historical dramas previously mentioned.

The issues surrounding the gaps in Texan cultural identity further foreground the unilateral nature of its composition, despite the multiplicity of potential representations at its disposal. Some Texans hold onto traditions that have been removed from the historical narrative for being inauthentic, or at least highly contested, as in the case of David Crockett's death at the Alamo, rather than open the process to new interpretations.

There is racism inherent in defining the dominant Texan cultural identity as white, male, and (somewhat) wealthy. This character is perhaps best exemplified in the most famous Texan of the moment, Pres. George W. Bush. This book focuses on the exclusionary practices by which Texan cultural identity is created and claimed by various sections of Texan culture, including mostly white groups like the Republic of Texas. The Alamo provides yet another site for locating this identity by highlighting the "heroism" of the Texians over the "savagery" of the Mexicans. Battle reenactments play up the suffering of the white male victim or the triumph of the white male hero. Small-town Texas plays take white men as their primary focus; female and nonwhite characters either exist mostly to support and nurture the central characters or to provide comic relief. Each of these types of sites shows how dominant identity remains fixed and intersects with attempts to refocus the discourse on previously excluded groups.

Francis Barker writes that the historicizing of history turns it into a tool of the ruling classes unless it is undermined from below by revolutionary voices. There are questions involved in the debate over who controls the history and, by extension, the maintenance of Texan cultural identity; these questions create a crisis of representation as problematic images of Bush-like Texans are contested by narratives of oppression and disenfranchisement of the Hispanic population. In Texan cultural identity, the conflicting representations pose a crisis for the dominant control of history—a state of cultural emergency that calls for extreme measures to secure the safety of the Texan image.[31]

THE PERFORMANCE OF REGIONALITY

Texan cultural identity, with all its shifts, transformations, and paradoxes, is but one example of the power of regional performance in this country. Preston Jones' *Texas Trilogy,* the first trilogy ever to premiere on Broadway and a huge favorite at the Kennedy Center's Bicentennial Humanities Program in 1976, was panned by the most prominent newspaper critics of the time. New York critics Clive Barnes, Rex Reed, and William Glover gave the trilogy lukewarm reviews because of the "regional" nature of its subject matter and characters.[32] In the intervening thirty years, however, "regionality" has gone from being a condescending dismissal of (usually) noncosmopolitan mind-sets and attitudes to a legitimate, even trendy, form of expression. Texas has benefitted from this shift in regional status, as famous musicians and recording artists flock to the Austin music scene and Hollywood actors relocate to the Hill Country and promote their movies at the annual South by Southwest Film Festival, the heir to Sundance.

Even though recent biographies of Texian heroes like Sam Houston teem with discussions of their dark side and dubious choices,[33] even though political and cultural leaders have publicly stated that the traditional representations of Texas history do mostly exclude Hispanics, African Americans, and women, this does not mean that the representations supported by these pedagogical national narratives have been transformed in any way. Instead, these same limited, regressive notions of Texan performance influence representations of and attitudes toward residents in more subtle and, ultimately, less identifiable ways.

The performance of the Texan is a powerful example of how regionality melds discourses of history, race, gender, and culture into a powerful matrix of national narration designed to legitimate existence. Its performances, theatrical and otherwise, resonate not only on the local level of the state itself but also in the national and international arenas. Giving the space of Texas its own unique identity helps to mark that space as "known." The study of what makes a Texan provides insight into how people perform their regionality as well as how that concept of regionality performs them.

America's performances of regionality provide a way to group representations—theatrical, historical, or cultural—in ways which cast new light on the relationship between more traditional boundaries of theatre study. Race, ethnicity, gender, and class are still major issues, but they are seen through new lenses of a broad, cultural nature. Connections between Texas historical pageantry from 1935 and the plays of Preston Jones or Horton Foote are more easily presented when interwoven with the power of historical markers that shape the Texas landscape and film versions of the Alamo story.

The performance of regionality as represented in Texan cultural identity provides a valuable new insight into the ways in which American culture creates and maintains specific regional identities as a part of its national narrative practice. Analyzing Texan identity as a performance of regionality provides a site to explore the ways that physical spaces can function as an actor. From Susanna Dickinson to Peggy Hill to Miss Mona of the infamous Chicken Ranch, "the best little whorehouse in Texas," female representations reveal how gender shapes Texan cultural identity. Finally, the worldwide political use of Texas that appears in Pres. George W. Bush's performances shows the Texan identity's application to politics.

OVERVIEW OF THE CHAPTERS

Chapter 2 examines the role of physical spaces, including the Alamo, the battlefield at Goliad, the San Jacinto Monument, historical markers, museums like the Bob Bullock Texas State History Museum, and seasonal outdoor dramas such as *Texas!* at Palo Duro Canyon, in creating and maintaining the performance of the Texan. These memorial sites both encapsulate specific, sometimes contested, versions of the events that mark them and draw tourists to and perform for them various versions of Texas history.

The third chapter examines how the events of the Texas Revolution have been constructed and performed in film, on stage, and in physical spaces to tell particular stories of the Texan and his or her behavior. Particular emphasis is given to performances designated as "pedagogical," or designed to be performed for or by school-aged children because of a specific goal of educating young Texans in the proper interpretation of historical events. Films such as John Wayne's *The Alamo,* the IMAX film *Alamo: The Price of Freedom,* the Republic of Texas Museum, school pageants from the time of the 1936 Texas Centennial, historical outdoor dramas and other plays, as well as battle reenactments and yearly celebrations (like "Come and Take It" Days in Gonzales) are examined for their role in (re)writing Texas history for the benefit of the state's residents, children, and those unfamiliar with the story and its racial and ethnic parameters. Links to contemporary attempts to revise the biases within traditional representations by previously marginalized groups will also be discussed.

Chapter 4 looks at the representation of those behaviors and attitudes associated with Texan performance. Many of these examples are associated with the performance of an image of a geographic location, such as Preston Jones' *Texas Trilogy,* the *Greater Tuna* trilogy, television shows like *Dallas* and *King of the Hill,* and the "True Women" phenomenon. Emphasis will be on images of gender within regional performances.

Chapter 5 discusses how Texas markets its identity to the rest of the United States and the world, beginning with the 1936 Centennial and its central live-performance venue, the *Cavalcade of Texas,* as part of a concentrated drive to counteract Texas' identity as oil, rattlesnakes, and tumbleweeds so that investors would pump money into the state's Depression-era economy. The chapter reveals the hijacking of Texan cultural identity for a specific political purpose and the more insidious, subtle use of the Texan to construct and promote an ideology; George W. Bush makes explicit how such ideology is used in performance. Yet these practices, and the identification of them as specifically Texan in nature, are irrevocably affecting the creation and maintenance of the Lone Star façade.

TWO

"DEEP IN THE HEART"

The Architectural Landscapes of Texan Cultural Memory

If I owned Texas and Hell, I would rent out Texas and live in Hell.

PHILIP SHERIDAN

The Alamo serves as a memorial to the 185 men who died there during the 1836 revolution for independence from Mexico.[1] In 1994, an article in the *New York Times* focused national attention on the struggle between the Daughters of the Republic of Texas and state government over the historic Alamo site.[2] Several state legislators, led by Rep. Ron Wilson (D-Houston), wanted to wrest control of the Alamo from the DRT and return the site to its original form—a Franciscan mission founded by Spaniards from Mexico in 1718 and inhabited by the Indian population of the area. The "reclamation" process would restore the mission lands and the surrounding grave sites in their entirety. This would necessitate the demolition of several newer adjacent structures, including Uncle Hoppy's Barbecue Restaurant, a Hyatt hotel parking garage, and the Alamo Cenotaph, a 120-foot-tall monument located just in front of the grounds of the modern-day Alamo to memorialize those who died in the 1836 battle.[3] The attempt, was, ultimately, unsuccessful, but this struggle over ownership of the Alamo suggests the importance of architectural space in the creation of Texan cultural identity.[4]

The study of cultural memory (the process by which a society constructs a historical past for its members in order to maintain its present configuration) and its relationship to specific places has become an important facet of the work of cultural geographers, historians, and social scientists. Historical sites play a major role in the creation and maintenance of cultural memory.[5] Many historians now acknowledge that cultural memory manipulates the relationship of the past and the present rather than presenting a faithful record of events.[6] In order to ensure continuity in historical (re)presentation, most cultures use architectural spaces—museums, historic sites, and national parks or other specifically designated areas—to guarantee the continuous performance of "permanent" national narratives. The sites serve as archives in which past events can be stored, visited, and, when necessary, revisited for purposes of reinforcing or revising the social constructions they help maintain.[7] These constructions form the basis of cultural identity, for Texas as well as other regions.

The architectural representation of Texan cultural memory is a central element of Texas' narrative practice. Architectural settings become geographic repositories for the ideologies and interpretations of historical events that become part of the performance of Texan-ness. As the architectural spaces become commemorative sites, those reenactments, museums, and other memorials stake their claim as sources of Texan cultural identity. These performance representations expose the history of the space as it has been traditionally conceived, creating a pedagogical narrative. These same spaces can be outsiders when certain facets of the story (racial, gender, ethnic) are elided by those pedagogical representations. In each instance, the maintenance of the physical space as a site of Texas' national narrative, or the body of eternal "truths" which support the construction of a specifically Texan cultural identity for its inhabitants, separates Texas from the rest of the United States.

Battlegrounds are particularly powerful locations of cultural memory, for they provide a concrete place where visitors can come to reflect on past conflicts. This is accomplished not only through commemorative ceremonies, which "keep the past in mind by a depictive representation of past events,"[8] but also by the very performative nature of the location itself.[9] The designation—through living representation for the visitor—construction, and maintenance of any site (as in the case of "living history" sites like Colonial Williamsburg or Plymouth Plantation), recreation, or the visitor's individual interaction with the layout of the site (as with the Vietnam Veterans Memorial in Washington, D.C.) as historically relevant or culturally significant reinforces a specific type of identity. The Alamo, for example, provides a setting for both a specific historical interpretation and the reinforcement of the interpretation itself—the repository of that cultural memory.

The Alamo is not alone in providing this function; other battle sites, museums, historical landmarks, and historical markers aid in the creation of an architectural landscape of Texan cultural memory.[10] Some of these sites, namely, the Texas Spirit Theatre in the Bob Bullock Texas State History Museum and the outdoor drama *Texas!* in Palo Duro Canyon State Park, employ traditional theatrical practices as part of their overall performative processes. In addition, a number of greater- and lesser-known Texas museums use real, or even simulated, cultural artifacts, such as reproductions of the "Come and Take It" cannon or a Bowie knife, to ensure the continuous representation of Texan national narrative for visitors. Many of these objects and displays contain critiques of the narrative they are there to legitimate. The Bullock Museum merges high-tech spectacle to its narrative presentation to provide an indoor experience that references the outdoor grandeur of the Lone Star State; panoramic slides, photos, and film footage bring the outdoors indoors.

Such performances help to form an architectural façade, a cleanly defined look which immediately calls to mind some aspect of Texas history or culture. Even as the architectural façade of Texan cultural memory within each of these sites is continually set, visited, then reset and revisited, the paradoxical nature of these spaces, their contents, and the performance practices they embody provide counterdiscourses that problematize the Texan. This chapter examines how these landscapes, and the monuments which mark them, perform as archival spaces of Texan cultural memory. These archival spaces hold the meaning of what it is to be a Texan within their geography; their significance draws on the historical importance of the space, its natural beauty, or its sociopolitical function as a specially designed archive.

BATTLEGROUNDS

"Sanctified places arise from battles," states Kenneth Foote, "that mark the traumas of nationhood and from events that have given shape to national identity."[11] Americans use their battlefields—from Gettysburg to the Little Bighorn to Pearl Harbor—to memorialize, enshrine, and perform various aspects of the country's national narrative. Similarly, Texan Americans use three of their major revolutionary battle sites—the Alamo, Goliad, and San Jacinto—in much the same fashion. Using either the extant architecture or specially constructed memorials, these battle sites perform pedagogical narratives of the Texan for native Texans, descendants of the fighters, and tourists. Just as some people make pilgrimages to religious shrines to refresh their spiritual well, so do some travel to the Alamo, sometimes yearly (usually on the anniversary of the battle or on Veterans Day), to reconnect with their state's (or their own) cultural memory, ensuring that the Lone Star façade, and the Texan narrative which helps to construct it, remains secure.[12]

Many first-time visitors to the Alamo are surprised by its size and appearance, especially if their expectations were conditioned by the sight of Fess Parker swinging Old Betsy in the final moments of Disney's *Davy Crockett* or John Wayne staring out over the sagebrush in *The Alamo.* The current Alamo site encompasses less than a third of the original mission grounds and is located in the heart of downtown San Antonio, nestled, as one author puts it, "deep in the heart of Texas, across from Woolworth's."[13] Even with the enormous number of dioramas, paintings, and maps on display depicting the layout of the Alamo in 1836, it can be difficult to envision the site as it was then; skyscrapers tower above the high stone walls, tour buses rumble by spitting out black smoke, vendors hawk their wares, musical groups give impromptu concerts in front of the shrine entrance, and tourists abound (see Photo 1).

Despite the incongruous context of its contemporary surroundings, however, the Alamo serves as a site for national pedagogical narration of the past. Different forms of Texan cultural memory appear in various parts of the site. The lower part of the chapel and the outer wall of the Long Barrack contain the only extant pieces of the 1836 Alamo structure. They have been grafted together with similar pieces of rock in a façade that has a simulated historical appearance. Subsequent buildings also reflect this trend. The outside walls were built in the 1920's, the Alamo Museum in 1936, and the DRT Library in 1950, yet the entire compound simulates the age of the two oldest structures. This apparent seamlessness imbues every piece of architecture with the material authenticity of its oldest and most famous structures, the Long Barrack and the chapel, thereby making the whole site perform its role in the maintenance of Texan national narrative.

The chapel, with its anteroom displays of state and national flags denoting the homelands of the 187 men who perished during the March 6 battle, is devoted completely to the memorialization and veneration of bravery, patriotism, and sacrifice—the buzzwords of the Alamo. The Long Barrack museum tells the history of the colonization of Texas and of the events of the Revolution and the Alamo's place within them; it commemorates the heroes of Texas who were soldiers and statesmen. The Daughters of the Republic of Texas Library at the Alamo contains information about a variety of Alamo representations, from the history of the historic site to press releases from John Wayne's movie to the work of the DRT (whose membership consists of blood descendants of the original Texas settlers and participants in the Revolution) throughout the past century in preserving the Alamo as a shrine to Texas liberty and the men who died fighting for it.

Throughout the enclosed grounds, small monuments commemorate the contributions of specific groups to the historical events of the Alamo, like the "immortal Thirty-Two" from Gonzales—the only men to respond to Alamo commander William Barret Travis' call for reinforcements in 1836. Other monuments reinforce the significance of the site as a symbol of courage to fighting Texans in subsequent wars and to other soldiers in countries throughout the world.[14] Each of these monuments links its individual space of memory to the larger cultural performance of the Alamo. The concepts of liberty, heroism, and sacrifice are foregrounded in the text of the monuments, as these are the same ideals for which the Alamo battle is remembered. The smaller monuments draw from this association a sense of legitimation, an element of prestige, and some extra remembrance of their placement within the larger narrative.

One of the most fascinating shifts in the display's representation of the Alamo, however, concerns the sanctification of the Alamo *after* the Texas Revolution. Judging by the information given within the architectural site, the most important thing Texans need to remember about the Alamo after 1845 (when Texas became part of the United States) is its salvation from destruction and transformation into a shrine by the DRT. The Alamo site, then, functions to remind visitors not only of its centrality to Texas cultural memory and national narration but also of the heroic efforts of the DRT to ensure the existence of the space as an eternal monument to Texas liberty. The DRT communicates this effort through its Web site, http://www.drtl.org. Three of the specially linked sites featured on the DRT's homepage are to Alamo-related sites: the Alamo site itself; the gift shop; and the DRT Library at the Alamo. The brochures handed out by volunteers at the door to the chapel feature the DRT's official seal above the picture and name of the Alamo, much like a theatre program features the producer's name above the title and author of the play. Finally, the statement of purpose of the DRT clearly foregrounds the organization's commitment to and association with the shrine: "The Daughters of the Republic of Texas, by virtue of the authority delegated by the State of Texas, is the custodian of the Alamo, Shrine of Texas Freedom."[15]

The Alamo also reflects the culture of its rescuers and caretakers, the DRT, and the conflicts which surrounded the creation and maintenance of the Alamo as a memorial site in the early twentieth century.[16] This struggle was grounded in the ethnic tensions between Anglo and Hispanic descendants of the original Texians and Tejanos who fought in the Revolution.[17] In 1903, DRT member Adina De Zavala insisted that the Long Barrack, the sight of the bloodiest fighting within the compound, was a more historically significant site than the roofless chapel, which had merely sheltered the women and children. In the years between 1836 and 1903, however, the two-story Long Barrack was transformed from a U.S. Cavalry quartermaster's depot to a general store to a saloon and was known as the Hugo-Schmelzer building. The use of the Long Barrack for such common and vulgar purposes, claimed fellow DRT member Clara Driscoll, had diminished its potential as a shrine to the martyrs. She stated that the "Hugo-Schmelzer building [was] not historically sacred. The Alamo chapel [was] the real Alamo," and that this "whisky house" only obscured "the most remarkable building in the world."[18] After a ten-year struggle (during which, at one point, De Zavala barricaded herself in the Long Barrack for three days to prevent Driscoll from taking possession of the property), Driscoll's vision of the shrine prevailed and De Zavala and her DRT chapter were voted out of the organization.

The significance of this struggle is evident. Driscoll was not about to let the Alamo fall to the enemy again, even though, this time, the "Mexicans" opposing her were her sisters from the DRT.

Once vindicated by her organization and the local government (which removed De Zavala from the property), Driscoll was free to sentimentalize the Alamo by turning it into a combination memorial/shrine/archive for her vision of Texan cultural memory, a vision grounded in (Anglo) Texan supremacy over Mexicans of any time period.

Her extant writings—novels, a comic opera, and the short story collection *In the Shadow of the Alamo*—reinforce these beliefs. According to Richard Flores, Driscoll's representation of Mexicans in her stories "displaces responsibility for their beleaguered plight from the realm of the social to that of personal non-achievement . . . a realm insulated from Anglo-American influence and expressed as a cultural flaw, that is, stemming from the Mexicans' way of life."[19] De Zavala, on the other hand, worked from outside to insert stories, visions, and legends into the Alamo narrative that repositioned it as a Spanish mission.[20] Her contributions serve as a performative counterpart to Driscoll's pedagogical narrative by subverting the latter's image of the Alamo as a sacred shrine to "Texan" cultural identity. By placing the Alamo's role in the Texas Revolution within a larger field of relations that predated Anglo migration to Texas, De Zavala provides a means for Tejano descendants of revolutionary and contemporary Hispanic residents of the state to recast the Alamo as part of *their* cultural history, not a representation of ethnic enmity.

The impact of this formative struggle can still be seen. Numerous plaques and proclamations throughout the grounds hail Driscoll as the "savior of the Alamo" while completely ignoring De Zavala's contribution to the rescue and creation of the site as a repository of architectural memory. A single marker in the corner next to the Long Barrack honors both women, who "each in her own way" contributed to the rescue of the Alamo. This is the only recognition De Zavala receives within the Alamo grounds besides a brief note on the Wall of History.

Driscoll's attitude toward the chapel indicates her desire to construct the Alamo not only as a place of remembrance but also as a site of worship of fallen heroes. The fact that the chapel was at one time a Spanish mission only reinforced, to her, the site's historical significance and its position as sacred ground. Any representations, performances, or information conveyed there should reflect that solemnity and reinforce the role of the Alamo not only as a simple monument but also as a temple of worship and remembrance.

The rules which regulate the use of the chapel resemble those found in other sacred sites—no noise, no photos, no food or drink; gentlemen are to remove their hats; and only ceremonies which honor Alamo heroes are permitted within the shrine (i.e., the chapel). If a visitor ignores or is ignorant of these rules, one of the helpful docents—most of them members of the DRT—is quick to remind him or her to be reverent.

The completion of the Alamo Cenotaph in 1939 (a project begun during the Texas Centennial Celebration) capped the grandeur of this space of representation. An epic memorial/tomb for the dead defenders, it renders the images of the major players and the names of all Texans who perished here while performing their sacred duty in perpetuity.

There was perhaps an additional, less "historically sacred," consideration in Driscoll's championing of the chapel. Due to continued use in the intervening years, the Long Barrack resembled a contemporary turn-of-the-century building.

The unique mission façade was virtually the same as in 1836, save for some restorations and the addition of the portico over the main doorway. Why worship a regular old building, hardly recognizable, when such a distinctive-looking architectural façade was available? Indeed, the reproduction and marketing of this image is part and parcel of the Alamo's national narrative function. The Alamo museum gift shop, constructed to resemble the other buildings and located discreetly behind the chapel shrine, contains a plethora of Alamo-imprinted merchandise—plates, cups, shirts, belts, caps, posters, postcards—all of which market the image of the chapel as "the Alamo" and make it available for purchase—your own little piece of the rock, as it were. In addition, thousands of elementary school children from across the state draw, paint, or etch the façade (or their best approximations) onto paper, clay, or wood and, through this group practice, into their collective cultural memory. In this sense, the Alamo is a malleable site of national narrative engagement, subordinate to economic opportunism and practical visual considerations,[21] whose image is a reminder not only of Texan cultural memory but also of the state's booming tourist economy.

The Alamo may be the most famous memorial from the Texas Revolution, but it is not the only one; however, these other sites are under the control of state or local authorities, not the DRT. Monuments of various sizes have been erected at Gonzales, Goliad, and San Jacinto to commemorate the other three major battles of the Revolution. Whereas the Alamo was itself a remnant of the actual 1836 battle, the other spaces are literally open fields on which monuments have been constructed (mostly as part of the cultural and historical campaign during and after the 1936 Centennial Celebration). By far the largest is the San Jacinto Monument, a 570-foot tower topped with the Lone Star located just east of Houston off Interstate 10, near Baytown.[22] The carnage of the battle is downplayed—reduced to four words ("the slaughter was appalling"). The diverse national origins of the many soldiers who populated the Texian army are recast into a celebration of diversity in unity (the inscription lists twenty-five states and eleven countries from which they hailed).[23] Finally, while the initially liberal policies of Mexico toward Anglo settlers are mentioned, they are soon overshadowed by the rise of Santa Anna and his tyrannical treatment of the citizens of Texas (the tyranny he imposed on the other provinces of Mexico is never mentioned).

As with the more recently installed Wall of History at the Alamo, the goal of the architectural narrative is not to portray an ethnic "other" as inherently evil but to ensure that the national narrative remains focused on the "correct" interpretation of the outcome: freedom from Mexican rule and the establishment of the Republic of Texas. This interpretation is necessary to legitimate the preservation of the site as historic and sacred as well as the resulting sociopolitical structure which led to Texas' entrance into the United States under treaty in 1845.

These reinforcing tactics of Texan national narrative continue inside the space of the monument itself. The base of the memorial contains a small museum of artifacts brought back to the site (the battle site itself had long been stripped clean of souvenirs when the monument was built), the ubiquitous gift shop, and a theatre which runs a slideshow, *Texas Forever!! The Battle of San Jacinto,* narrated by Charlton Heston. It is, according to its press, "a riveting recreation of the Texas Revolution and the Battle of San Jacinto. Powered by rapid-fire computer technology, 42 projectors containing over 3,000 images and lifelike surround sound carry you into the saga and down the rugged roads of early Texas. The action is captured with motion picture sequences, brilliant illustrations and 35 original paintings created exclusively for this absorbing, multi-image trip back in time." [24] The story contains the necessary historical background—Spanish settlement; American immigration; Mexican rule; the tyranny of Santa Anna; the battles at Gonzales, San Antonio, and Goliad; the Runaway Scrape [25]—needed to educate one on the import of the Battle of San Jacinto. Through it all, Houston is portrayed as the hero, the Mexicans and Santa Anna are cast in dark colors.[26]

The task of constructing an acceptable version of the narrative was particularly difficult in the case of the Battle of Coleto, site of the Goliad Massacre. Unlike the Battles of the Alamo and San Jacinto, this event could be portrayed as neither heroic nor necessary to the cause of the Revolution; rather, it was the result of a series of overconfident blunders on the part of both Texian and Mexican army commanders. Texian colonel James Fannin allowed himself and his men to be surrounded at Coleto—an open, low-lying plain—by troops belonging to Gen. José de Urrea. Fannin negotiated a surrender; Urrea, who had no stomach for cold-blooded execution, promised to recommend clemency for the prisoners. However, Santa Anna, who had long since decreed death to all captured as part of what he saw as an American immigrant rebellion against the Mexican government, demanded that Fannin and his troops be shot. The men, who believed they were to be released, were grouped into three lines, marched out of the garrison at Goliad in three directions, and killed on the morning of March 27, 1836 (Palm Sunday), almost three weeks to the day after the fall of the Alamo.[27] Francita (Panchita) Alavez, the companion of Mexican army captain Telesforo Alavez, intervened and saved several members of Fannin's company from execution. For this, she is remembered and revered as the "Angel of Goliad." [28]

The ruthlessness of the executions and Santa Anna's refusal to grant clemency frightened many of the settlers who still remained in the area and turned Sam Houston's army of ragtag soldiers into an infuriated mob seeking revenge (which they got less than a month later at San Jacinto, on April 21, while shouting "Remember the Alamo! Remember Goliad!" as they routed Santa Anna's army).

Once the Revolution was over, however, Goliad became to the Texian army what Little Big Horn became to the U.S. Cavalry: a mistake to be blamed on the commander and, subsequently, obscured within overt representations of Texan national narrative. Goliad is the least-celebrated of the Texas Revolution's battle sites, even though no fewer than three architectural monuments exist to mark the major sites,[29] and, until recently, no large-scale commemorations were held on the anniversary of either the battle or the massacre.[30] In fact, most people who come to Goliad are there to see Presidio La Bahía and Our Lady of Loreto Chapel, a Spanish mission/presidio complex established in 1722 and a National Historic Landmark. La Bahía was used as the garrison headquarters during the massacre, and the Fannin Memorial Monument is located nearby. Because the defeat at Goliad reflects neither heroism nor sacrifice, however, it is not a cultural memory conducive to the maintenance of the Lone Star façade. As a result, the site is subtly marked and, then, silenced.

Through its status as a marked site, however, Goliad serves a powerful performative function within Texas' national narrative. It reminds Texans that heroism and freedom can be squandered, enemies can be sympathetic, and no historical event can ever be completely presented so as to obscure all of its "problematic" facets. It also foregrounds the idea that, during the conflict, ethnicity did not necessarily determine loyalty; the pedagogical narrative binary of Anglo Texian versus Mexican, so vividly reinforced in the architectural façades of the Alamo and San Jacinto, is problematized here. Panchita Alavez, as the Angel of Goliad, opens the door for consideration of the Mexicans and Tejanos who fought and died alongside the Texians for independence from Mexico (e.g., Gregorio Esparza), commanded their armies (e.g., Juan Seguín), and served in the republican government (Lorenzo De Zavala). Significantly, these names are not well known today even in Texas, thus affirming the racism inherent in Texan cultural identity.

There is one further way in which Goliad materially repositions the performance of the Texan. Unlike the identifiable façade of the Alamo and the monumental scale of San Jacinto, the Goliad site, with its somber mission La Bahía and small memorial, performs what is, ultimately, missing from all battle sites: the voices of the dead on all sides. While the Alamo Cenotaph serves as a tombstone, it is not, in actuality, a grave site. The ashes of the Texian army dead, burned on pyres after the battle, have long since dispersed. The Cenotaph marks the heroism of their sacrifice, not the futility of it. As one description states, "the theme of the monument is the Spirit of Sacrifice, represented on the main (south) face of the shaft by an idealistic figure rising twenty-three feet from the long sloping capstone emblematic of the tomb. This monolithic slab twenty feet long bears appropriate ornamental tracery."[31]

No marker exists there to acknowledge the thousands of Mexican army soldiers who perished in what Santa Anna later termed "a small affair."[32] At

San Jacinto, the emphasis is on the outcome—the capture of Santa Anna, Texas' independence, and nationhood—and not on the loss of life during the Runaway Scrape and during the battle that made these events possible.[33] Because no national narrative applicable to the performance of the Texan has come from it, the Goliad battle site represents the materiality of loss of life, the core of any war, with a force and permanence missing at its more famous sibling memorials. It is a memorial site that codifies and solidifies the absent voices in Texan cultural memory. What we learn from this instance is the ways in which even those sites whose stories seemingly contradict the heroism of Texan identity can be configured so as to reinforce the "correct" interpretation of the narrative. Goliad, the great, ignominious defeat, becomes the impetus for San Jacinto, the great victory.

MUSEUMS

Another major architectural repository for cultural memory is the museum, which allows for the preservation and construction of Texan national narrative through the structure of its building and exhibits. Although the museum as it is constructed today is a relatively recent invention, the practice of collecting, cataloguing, and displaying objects for study dates back to the library at Alexandria and traces its history through the curiosity cabinets of the Renaissance all the way to the Louvre and the British Museum.[34] Museums are no longer merely the purview of the elite; they serve to preserve and present information on a whole host of topics, from Dalí to Barbie dolls, fashion to football.

What has been slower to emerge than the museum is the understanding that all museum spaces are engaged in the telling of a certain type of story about the information they contain. The study of museums and the contexts that underlie their construction is called museology and is predicated on the notion that, as Peter Vergo writes, "the very act of collecting has a political or ideological or aesthetic dimension that cannot be overlooked."[35] Public or private, national or local, historical or cultural—museums use cultural artifacts to create an environment that tells a story, creating an architectural space of memory.

Museums abound in Texas that focus on Texas history (e.g., Washington-on-the-Brazos), culture (e.g., the Institute of Texan Cultures in San Antonio), and local sites of cultural memory (e.g., the Gonzales Memorial Museum). Each contributes, in its own way, to the creation and maintenance of a performance of Texan cultural identity and the Lone Star façade.

Washington-on-the-Brazos State Park contains two historical sites that have been turned into museums: the site of the signing of the Texas Declaration of Independence on March 2, 1836; and the home of Anson Jones, last president of the Republic of Texas. The Gonzales Memorial Museum contains artifacts relating to the "Come and Take It" battle and the Immortal Thirty-Two, the band of men from the town who answered Travis' call for help and died at the Alamo, as well as other bits of local culture and folklore.

The newest addition to the stable of museums of Texas history and Texan performance is "The Story of Texas," better known as the Bob Bullock Texas State History Museum. Located less than three blocks from the State Capitol in Austin and, according to its press kit, a "football's throw from the University of Texas campus,"[36] the Bullock museum was the pet project of the late Bob Bullock, a career politician best known as Texas comptroller of public accounts from 1975 to 1990. He also served two terms as lieutenant governor under Ann Richards and then George W. Bush, from 1991 to 1999.[37] The work on the museum officially began in 1997, when funding was appropriated by the legislature; when it opened on April 22, 2001 (as close to the anniversary of the Battle of San Jacinto as possible) the final price tag was approximately $80 million, from a combination of state tax dollars and private donations.[38]

In its traversing of Texas geography, the Bullock Museum calls to mind the vastness of the space that is Texas, even as its artifacts, performances, and displays call to mind specific architectural representations necessary to maintenance of its own primacy. The museum is a testament to the excesses that often characterize Texans: a thirty-five-foot-tall bronze star frames the building's granite-columned entrance. The exterior visuals are supplanted only by the huge floor mural in the grand foyer depicting Texas' history, culture, and economy (see Photos 2 and 3)

This opulence indicates to the visitor that Texas history is more than just dry old events; rather, it is grand, over the top, and bigger and better than the history of other states. Louisiana's state museum, for example, is a complex of buildings spread throughout the cities of New Orleans and Natchitoches. The rooms are laid out neatly and seem almost spartan in comparison to the amount of material stuffed into the exhibition rooms of the Bullock Museum. The latter's exhibits encompass three full stories. Many visitors cannot make it through in one trip (or without a stop at the snack bar)—especially if they throw in a trip to the Texas Spirit Theater or the IMAX theatre for a show.

The layout and contents of the museum's collection reinforce this excess, as well. Because of Bullock's political career and connections, the museum was able to secure special artifacts for "his" museum, including a circa 1940 AT-6 Texan airplane, a full-scale windmill, and the State Capitol dome's original Goddess of Liberty.[39] It also contains replicas of NASA space landers, oil derricks, a fifties-style movie theatre façade advertising the movie *Giant,* Indian huts, and the "Come and Take It" cannon to augment the authentic Spanish suits of armor, rifles, volunteer announcements for the Texian army, and photos of wildcatters, Confederate soldiers, and the space shuttle that adorn the museum's walls (see Photo 4).

While the collection itself seems eclectic, its arrangement reflects the subtle manipulation of focus found in the best museums today. These artifacts, and thousands of others, are arranged in a scene of controlled chaos within the three-story space so that they provide tantalizing glimpses of their offerings from the foyer below. The dominant image, however, is the Alamo façade, which is located in the center of the second floor, prominently enough to draw every entering eye—whether five years old or fifty—directly to it.

The Bullock Museum purports to tell "the story of Texas" from its first American Indian settlers until the present day. To do so, it uses a combination of traditional cultural artifacts on display along with more recent technological innovation.[40] The museum teems with objects, but a huge projection timeline linked to a series of touch screens allows users to access major events in Texas history in ever-greater detail and project them onto the rear wall for all to see. Movie clips from Pres. Franklin D. Roosevelt's speech at the Cotton Bowl to open the 1936 Centennial Exposition lay claim to the same architectural space as Juan Seguín's fictionalized video narrative of the fall of the Alamo (the viewing room is located inside the second-floor Alamo façade) and a projected display/narrative of Stephen F. Austin's imprisonment in Mexico City in 1834 that is based on his letters. The history constructed through the ethnographic objects moves up from the American Indians and Spanish conquistadores of the first floor to the Texas Revolution and Civil War on the second and NASA and scenes from *Giant* on the third. The museum's message is consistent: to help "neophyte" Texans "accelerate their patriot status" by walking through the "story of Texas."[41]

The Bullock Museum is also home to Austin's first IMAX theatre and the Texas Spirit Theater, whose offerings include both live, limited-run shows and the "The Star of Destiny," a projection-and-effects show produced by BRC Imagination Arts that tells the story of Texas from settlement to Revolution to the Galveston hurricane in 1900. It features a variety of visual, sound, and visceral effects to enhance its narrative, some of which are built right into the theatre seats (including the shock of a particularly nasty rattlesnake attack): "Historic events such as the Galveston Hurricane of 1900 come to life with sets, special lighting, and amazing sound effects. Seats shake as visitors witness a gusher exploding from an East Texas oil derrick and the takeoff of Saturn V as seen from Mission Control at the Lyndon B. Johnson Space Center in Houston. Other surprising effects, such as wind and smoke, help make The Star of Destiny a memorable learning experience for all ages."[42]

"The Star of Destiny" is a prime example of "extreme theatre" more common to rock concerts and professional wrestling. It is built around the (over)stimulation of the audience's senses. Learning occurs through experience—the feeling that "you are there." Because this is the experience, and the museum space constructs it as "authentic," the audience can feel satisfied that it has truly learned the history by "living" it in a vicarious, sound effect–enhanced fashion. Since "The Story of Texas" is Texan narrative on a grand scale, this kind of over-the-top sensory experience not only reinforces the grandeur of the narrative, it also subtly legitimates its authenticity.

The Texas Spirit Theater has also been used for short-run live performances. A 2002 temporary exhibit at the Bullock Museum which focused on the intersection between Davy Crockett the man, Crockett the myth, and the Davy Crockett phenomenon of the 1950's, featured as one of its offerings a live one-man show, *Davy Crockett in Texas,* in which the character of Crockett, on his way to Texas to seek new adventures, lays out his past exploits as "b'ar killer" and congressman and uses them to foreshadow his desire to go to Texas and his eventual demise at the Alamo.[43] In so doing, Crockett embodies those Lone Star values commemorated at the Alamo: bravery, honor, and a fighting spirit.

Another side effect of the new museology embodied in the Bullock Museum is the way that it blurs the boundaries between "cultural materials" and "art objects."[44] By placing pieces, often "products of other cultures," within the constructed aesthetic space of the museum, curators give them a museum aesthetic, turning them into "something that we can look at."[45] In the Bullock Museum, the merging of artifact, kitsch, and culture helps to further legitimate the museum's claim to contain the complete story of Texas. Placing well-known historical objects (and replicas, such as the "Come and Take It" battle cannon) next to "authentic" license plates and postcards gives the museum authority to influence the story of Texas. These contemporary reinforcements of Texan identity exemplify the marketing of Texas as a brand, a commodity that can be sold, hijacked, and manipulated to mean something other than the historical grounding which created it. (This branding effect will be discussed in greater detail in Chapter 5.) The "ethnographic objects" found in the museum, created through their placement within the architectural space of Texas' pedagogical national narrative, become part of the larger architectural "object" of the museum itself, whose entire function involves arranging and contextualizing its component parts into an eternal pedagogical national narrative, "The Story of Texas."[46]

The museum which bears Bullock's name is not, technically, "his"; it is an amalgamation created by professional museum planners, architects, fund-raisers, advertising and marketing firms, and all of the other people who go into creating the museum of today. Yet, by attaching his name to the museum and the story of Texas that it purports to contain, the creators of the Bob Bullock Texas State History Museum were able to legitimate their narrative before the doors even opened. As does the Alamo, this museum functions as both memorial and tourist attraction. However, the Bullock Museum does not attempt to present a sacred space, sanctified by the deaths of brave fighting Texians; rather, it is an architectural space that reflects the money, power, and political clout available to Bullock because of his background and career connections. As the grandest and most opulent museum in Texas (historical or otherwise), the Bullock Museum performs a national narrative that helps to legitimate "his" museum as the "real" story of Texas. It is an architectural marvel both inside and out, the power of its contents matched only by the beauty of its shell, like the monuments created for the Alamo and San Jacinto to mark those battle sites.

MARKERS

Some cultural artifacts, no matter how valuable, just cannot be placed within the confines of a museum or historical site. Buildings, roads, houses, and other important architectural landmarks are located throughout the towns and countryside of Texas and are still in use. However, Texan cultural memory ensures that even these sites fulfill a pedagogical function because they are, literally, marked as important historical sites with official Texas historical markers. These markers guarantee that, whatever function a place serves today, its previous role in Texas history and, by extension, its continued role in the maintenance of national narrative and the Lone Star façade, are never forgotten by the inhabitants of or tourists to the area.

As part of the 1936 Texas Centennial, the Centennial Commission began to mark important sites with specially designed plaques that would commemorate greater and lesser events in Texas' history. The ideas was to encourage tourists visiting for the Centennial to take driving tours of the state in order to better experience its natural beauty and historical importance. Maps were distributed to tourists which laid out different driving tours between San Antonio, Houston, and Dallas (the major cities of the Centennial).[47] In this way, citizens of and visitors to the state were provided with a literal geography of important Texas places and the memorable events that they contained.

From the nine hundred originally commissioned for the hundredth-anniversary celebration, Texas state historical markers now delineate over twelve thousand buildings, sites, and trails throughout the state.[48] There are historical markers located at all of the major battle sites of the Texas Revolution, as well as along the paths of famous historical events like the Runaway Scrape, the Mier Expedition, and the Chisholm Trail. Some towns contain more markers than people. In fact, it is difficult to travel very far in the state without running across one.

There are two types of markers. The first, subject markers, "are solely educational and reveal aspects of local history that are important to a community or region. These markers honor topics such as church congregations, schools, communities, businesses, events and individuals. A subject marker is placed at a site that has a historical association with the topic, but no restriction is placed on the use of the property or site. No legal designation is required for a subject marker."[49] Houses that date back to the Republic and other important historical buildings carry a special designation: the Recorded Texas Historic Landmark (RTHL). Recorded Texas Historic Landmarks "are properties judged to be historically and architecturally significant."[50] These sites must be preserved in as close to original condition as is feasible and be accessible, directly or indirectly, for public viewing. The Alamo's role as shrine to the fallen heroes is augmented by the marker that designates it as a Recorded Texas Historic Landmark. The double recognition reinforces the importance of the site; however, it also reduces said designation to a kind of redundant backup because of the already obvious importance of the site.

All markers, whether subject or RTHL, are simultaneously unobtrusive and significant. They must both blend in with the surrounding architecture or landscape so as not to disturb it and, at the same time, be visible enough to draw the attention of a visitor close enough to read the inscribed text. The markers contain a plaque that explains the historical and cultural significance of the site. The size of the plaques can range from small,

9 inches × 12 inches, to larger, monument-size ones. Their distinct shape—square with a round hump on the top, on which the state seal is engraved—calls to mind the Alamo façade (see Photo 5). These visible links with recognizable images of Texan cultural identity further reinforce the status conferred by the presence of a marker (and, conversely, the lack of status when a marker is not present). Likewise, all marked sites are linked into a kind of Texan road map, with the markers indicating important stops along the journey—an extended version of the original intent of the program when implemented in 1936.

This rhizomatic linking of sites creates a "plane of consistency" within the Texan landscape.[51] The markers form an ever-expanding single narrative from heterogeneous sites that are inextricably connected through their ubiquitous, yet historically grounded, presence to the idea of the Lone Star. Because the markers are designed to mark the landscape and not contain it, they cannot be "over-coded," in the words of Gilles Deleuze; they will bear whatever symbolic meaning is layered on them as part of the construction of Texan cultural identity. Each marker provides a visible link to its site and to the thousands of other markers across the state.[52]

Take, for example, Gonzales, one of the historically prominent counties of the Revolution. The town of Gonzales is swimming in historical markers: markers for battle sites, markers for old buildings, and markers of important sites throughout the county. There are markers which indicate where the actual battle was fought, markers that delineate the original layout of the town squares, markers that foreground historic homes within the community and their importance, and markers that memorialize the sacrifices of individuals during the Revolution. These markers remind the resident and visitor of what was there (or its original function). Most mark buildings or sites that the state has deemed worthy of preservation in some way, even if the state does not see itself as responsible for said preservation. Some of these buildings are designated as tourist attractions, such as the Eggleston House and the Old County Jail, and are maintained by the Gonzales Chamber of Commerce. The Old Gonzales Teachers' College is now a private home, but its marker sets it apart from the equally historic houses surrounding it as an integral part of the town's history. Other markers are located on the town's main squares describing their inception and importance to the town. Several churches, including the United Methodist and Episcopal churches, have subject markers that discuss the formation and history of their local branches. Larger monuments mark the "Come and Take It" battle site. A person walking (or driving) the city can use these markers to construct a map of the city's historical function overlaid on the town's contemporary existence. Gonzales, therefore, is constantly performing its own history for the benefit of those persons who are willing to enter into the show. Walking and driving through the city provides a continual performance of Texan cultural identity (see Photos 6 and 7).

The town of Gonzales, then, is a modern-day city of sixty-eight hundred overlaid with a geographical map of historical markers that creates, in effect, a city of the past within the city of today. The town itself is a marker: it marks the battle site and the beginning of the Runaway Scrape. Each of these markers lies within the town limits, except for the one at the battle site; there are more markers throughout the surrounding county marking cattle trails, important revolutionary sites such as the Braches House and the Sam Houston Oak, and other major historic places. All of these sites are linked by the historical markers and their conferred status. The "trail" created by these markers creates a geographic history of the space that performs the history of the sites and their relevance to Texan cultural identity.

Markers literally indicate their spaces as historically important, even if the land has been parceled out or changed in some way. They serve as reminders that the site of today's Wal-Mart, Jiffy Lube, or crosstown freeway was once the home of a former president of the Republic, part of the Chisholm Trail, or some other place of historical significance. The historical marker keeps the past alive and visible in the present, constantly invoking the pedagogical narrative which validates its claims. Yet, historical markers also mark the *absence* of what *was* there; they remind the reader that this space lacks the very thing that makes it significant. Even if the house, building, or other object being commemorated is still there, it is no longer what it was: the thing which gave it enough significance to be marked as a landmark. Houses like the Braches House (home of the Sam Houston Oak) and the old Gonzales College, the first women's college in the state of Texas, are now private houses that, occasionally, are opened for public tours. The Eggleston House, the oldest home in Gonzales County, rests in the center of a city park, not on its original grounds. The markers that hang on or in front of each of these spaces remind visitors and residents that they live in a space with a dual identity.

NATURE

Architectural spaces can be created by humans, as in the case of the Alamo and the Bob Bullock Museum, or natural with artificial markers, as in the case of the battlefield monuments at San Jacinto and Goliad. However, it is also possible to create a counter to these types of sites by engaging the natural setting within the geographic space of live theatrical performance. Paul Green's *Texas; A Symphonic Outdoor Drama of American Life* historicizes and commemorates Panhandle life around the turn of the century, at the close of the range wars. The plot revolves around the struggle for control of the space by farmers, who promise a rich crop, and cattlemen, who see themselves as the butcher shop for the nation. In the end, the fight to determine whether Texas will raise corn or cattle is moot: the state is so big that both are possible. The drama of *Texas!*, however, lies not in whether the characters will farm or graze, but in how they illustrate those practices which emphasize the grandeur, courage, and uniqueness of the Texas spirit in order to reinforce the pedagogical national narrative of Texan cultural identity.

This outdoor drama exemplifies pedagogical theatre practice, where theatrical representations of Texan-ness serve to codify, reinforce, and convey specific images of Texan cultural identity for audiences of Texans and non-Texans alike. Green's pedagogical theatre practice sets recognizable performance elements within a culturally specific architectural frame; the script contains "Native Ballads, Dances, Hymn Tunes, Folksongs and Worksongs, Especially Selected and Edited by the Author."[53] He combines this main story line with singing, dancing, and a celebration of Texas and its inhabitants reminiscent of the Centennial pageants of 1936.

What makes *Texas!* an architectural performance of Texan cultural memory is that it is performed each summer in the specially constructed Pioneer Amphitheater in Palo Duro Canyon State Park in Canyon, Texas. To go to *Texas!* is to enter into the natural "space" of the state. The road to the amphitheater takes one down into the heart of the canyon and its resident flora and fauna (cars often share the parking lot with a diamondback or two, which are wrangled into sacks by stagehands and released in less-trafficked areas). The back wall of the stage is a three hundred–foot cliff face, which serves as backdrop and delimiter of the stage space itself. The forestage area gradually merges backward into a section of natural landscape which slopes toward the wall of the canyon.

Green wrote the script for *Texas!* after viewing the impressive space and dictated much of its usage in his text. The cliff face is an integral part of the action. It is lit at various time throughout the play, including the spectacular thunderstorm and lightning strike which conclude Act I. The first act opens with the trumpet call of a Texas Ranger seated astride his horse on the cliff top, and the second act, which begins with the entrance of Comanche chief Quanah Parker, also focuses the action on top of the cliff. Here, the narrative does not control the organization of the space so much as the space controls the organization of the narrative. Scenes are chosen and arranged for maximum visual appeal and their ability to utilize the natural landscape as much as for their historical accuracy.

Texas! is not the only outdoor drama to utilize such backdrops. The stages for North Carolina's *The Lost Colony* (also written by Paul Green) and *Unto These Hills* also have been inserted into the natural spaces where the events which the texts present supposedly occurred: the Smokey Mountains and the Outer Banks. However, the subject matter of these two dramas—the disappearance of the Roanoke Island colony and its most famous inhabitant, Virginia Dare, and the "Trail of Tears" march by the Cherokee Nation from North Georgia to Oklahoma—focuses on loss, removal, and disappearance. *Texas!,* on the other hand, centers around the settling and taming of a space to make it a home; therefore, it plays directly into Texan cultural identity and the construction of the Lone Star façade. It is the space in which Texas' national narrative is, literally, performed, and the performative critique of that narrative comes out of the use of the space itself.

The grandeur of the canyon backdrop is a localized representation of a larger Texan geography. This mise-en-scène is but a fraction of the state's eternal natural beauty, as evidenced by Calvin's speech in Act I: "You can look around you here and you can read the record of a lot of the earth's age—in these walls—a record of death and life that has happened here, Elsie, hundreds of millions of years of it. And here you and I stand in this great gully of eternity—thinking about it—and it doesn't know we are here—it doesn't know." [54]

The cliff face and the lands behind the stage serve a tactical function by allowing the play to interact with the Texas landscape throughout the performance and also allow the "Texans" in the play as well as the audience to position themselves within the eternity of the state by ordering the wild, natural space of the canyon into the place of performance—the town of Henrianna, Texas, and, more generally, the State of Texas itself.

The characters also reflect this understanding of the Texan as a unique identity. In his opening monologue, Uncle Henry—the narrator—organizes the drama's physical space of representation into the place of Texan performance by locating his character within the pedagogical Texan cultural narrative: "I'm a Virginian by inheritance, a Kentuckian by birth, and a Texan by choice and education and the grace of God. Amen." [55] Like Crockett, he cannot claim native Texan birth but can lay claim to the geographic space he owns and, through it, the selfsame behaviors of the Lone Star which make him a unique phenomenon. Through this, he is able to become a part of the architectural memory of Texas' national narration, as true a Texan as ever rode the prairie. Throughout the play, Uncle Henry guides the action—and the audience's understanding of it—in much the same way as pageant characters like the Muse of History and the Spirit of Progress (allegorical characters used to signify the importance of history and progress to the construction of Texas' historical narrative and cultural identity) highlighted formative events in Texas history for the benefit of school and community audiences during the Centennial celebrations.

However, Uncle Henry's sense of his Texan performance is grounded in cultural memory, not in actual events; he is not the generalized personification of an allegorical concept or metaphor. He is cut from the same cloth as the characters around him, not to mention some of the audience members. This representation makes his performance of national narrative particularly powerful. The rest of the cast, while representing a cross section of musical theatre characters and limited cultural diversity, reinforce Uncle Henry's initial Texan discourse in their own words and actions, regardless of their status as farmers or cattlemen. The Texan motto of "Friendship" binds even those who are bitter enemies, such as farmers and cattlemen.

Like Palo Duro Canyon, *Texas!* carves itself into the cultural space of Texan representation by encapsulating and ordering the state's history according to a series of "proper" Texas virtues: courage; perseverance; forthrightness; love of the land (whatever its use); belief in fair play; and respect for others, despite ideological differences. These virtues set a Texan apart from the average person: one is not merely another citizen of Texas; one becomes, through hard work and initiative, an individual, a Lone Star.

Yet even *Texas!* has started to recognize that natural beauty alone cannot sustain the narrative contained within its canyon stage. The theatrical nature of its representation contains an implicit critique of the Texan cultural identity. The new director, Lynn Hart, initiated changes in the script in 2002 to make it more historically "accurate."[56] Quanah Parker will no longer introduce his father, Nocona, in a pivotal party scene; the old chief was long dead when Parker made peace with the Panhandle settlers. Now, he introduces three of his seven wives, breaking apart the heretofore stereotypical musical theatre depiction of male-female relationships and inserting a transgressive, if imperialistically depicted, gender dynamic into this Texan landscape. Likewise, the character of Uncle Henry has been changed drastically, mostly in response to criticism from the local cattle ranchers he purports to represent. He no longer directly opposes the building of the railroad, only the government's interference with his land, a sentiment more in keeping with those of the ranchers who, in reality, were instrumental in bringing the railroad through the Texas Panhandle.

By casting the story of *Texas!* in historical rather than straight theatrical terms, Hart and her writers domesticate the performative engagement present within the characters and render them more pedagogically accurate. It is becoming apparent, at least to Hart, that the natural reality of the performance space must be reflected in the stage reality of Henrianna, Texas, and its Texan inhabitants; any confusion caused by inappropriate or outdated representations must be updated to reflect modern pedagogical ideals and eliminate possibilities for performative engagement. In fact, the depiction of Paul Green's *Texas!* has given way to Hart's vision; Palo Duro Canyon is now host to *The Best of Texas,* a new musical extravaganza that, in the words of its press, "enhance[s] the struggles, strengths, and celebrations of the early settlers. You [the viewer] may leave emotional, proud or humbled, but you will certainly leave with a deeper understanding of why Texans are proud to be called Texans."[57] Be it Green's vision or Hart's, the central function of Palo Duro's amphitheatre is still to reinforce and transmit Texan cultural identity to audience members from across the state and around the world.

Texas! is a prime example of the idea that "spectacle and text, image and word have always been dialectically related, not least in theatre itself, and this unity has been the site of an intense struggle for meaning . . . it is in 'theatre' that word and image come together in highest tension and perhaps find uneasy resolution."[58] The tension between the wilderness and the archive of Texan cultural memory that is performed there makes *Texas* more than a typical summer musical offering or even a historical outdoor drama; it provides a continually shifting space for cultural critique and performative engagement.

CONCLUSION

The architectural spaces of Texan cultural memory operate to legitimate a pedagogical national narrative grounded in heroic discourses of sacrifice, bravery, and freedom, as well as the larger-than-life grandeur and spectacle that is often associated with the Lone Star State. Indoor, outdoor, old, new—the marking of the space creates an area in which cultural memory can grow and flourish, regardless of whether any traces of the actual event that is being remembered remain in the space. Kirk Savage notes that "the world around a monument is never fixed. The movement of life causes monuments to be created, but then it changes how they are seen and understood. The history of monuments themselves is no more closed than the history they commemorate."[59] This lack of permanence can be literal, as in the case of the Alamo, which has been found to be suffering from termite damage.[60]

However, the shifts can also occur in meaning and signification as different groups attempt to mark the space with their own histories. Institutions like museums or historical associations may preserve architectural spaces of cultural memory by setting them aside as shrines or state parks, or may create spaces like museums to preserve ethnographic objects. In so doing, however, they also alter these same spaces and objects so that they tell a story that visitors recognize as authentic.

Yet, these architectural spaces also function as tourist attractions, designed to give both residents and nonresidents a specific type of cultural experience: the telling of the story of Texas, as the slogan of the Bob Bullock Museum directly implies. There are gift shops at all of the aforementioned sites, including Goliad, selling everything from miniature Texas flags to coonskin caps to Texas history coloring books. Buying a piece of such Texas memorabilia gives the visitor a sense of participation in the history it represents.

Texan cultural identity draws on its own set of hallowed places to ground its national narrative in a concrete geographic space. The battle sites, museums, and performance spaces located within the state help to reinforce Texas' national narrative by providing a space for literal and figurative pedagogy. Yet, these sites, despite their tight construction and desire to represent the real story of Texas, also provide opportunities for performative engagement with these narratives and their historical biases. Within the context of Texan cultural identity, the idea of "history" and, more specifically, history in performance, occupies a place all its own. That is the subject of the next chapter (see Photo 8).

THREE

TEACHING "TEXAN"

The Pedagogical Function of the Texas Revolution

Like most passionate nations, Texas has its own private history based on, but not limited by, facts.

JOHN STEINBECK

In December 1994, Texas state senator Carlos Truan of Corpus Christi attempted to retrieve the flag captured by the Mexican army at the Alamo in 1836 by offering to swap three Mexican army flags captured after the Battle of San Jacinto.[1] To the dismay of the DRT and many Alamo history buffs, the exchange could not take place because the Mexican government had apparently mislaid the Alamo flag.[2] Approximately three months later, a brief note in the *Chronicle of Higher Education* discussed a recent archaeological dig on Alamo Plaza which had recovered Indian relics and raised speculation about the presence of a burial ground within the original Alamo compound. The DRT, however, refused to allow excavation within the Alamo shrine.[3]

These incidents serve to remind us that "Texan" is a term with many claimants. This split between identification as a Texan or a non-Texan can be traced to the Texas Revolution, the 1835–1836 battle against Santa Anna's centralist government.[4] The events of the Revolution set the framework, delineating the field of Texan cultural memory today.

The contemporary re-presentation of revolutionary events reflects a Texan *pedagogy*, a didactic matrix that presents Texas history in performance. I use the term "pedagogy" to make explicit the didactic function of these performances. Unabashedly, these texts purport to "teach" Texas history and, through their lessons, to help define Texan cultural identity.[5] This pedagogy is then marketed for overt tourist consumption and covert indoctrination as the attitude toward the events and their major players.

Historical plays serve as a form of ritual sacrifice presented as if for all Texans, but, in fact, they operate within the Anglo/Mexican binary. René

Girard writes that, because ritualistic action is "primitive" (his word), it is "hospitable to all ideological interpretations and dependent upon none. It has only one axiom: the contagious nature of the violence encountered by the warrior in battle—and only one prescription: the proper performance of ritual purification. Its sole purpose is to present the resurgence of violence and its spread throughout the community."[6]

Since the majority of Texan historical plays in some way reference the greatest perceived sacrifice of the Revolution—the Battle of the Alamo—without actually showing the battle onstage, they function much like Greek tragedies in their ability to purify and purge events of violence. The irony of this purgative function is that it affects only the historical events themselves and has done little to mitigate the social and political injustices perpetrated on the Hispanic community in the decades following the Texas Revolution and the resulting disparity in status between the two ethnicities. As this chapter will show, representations of Mexicans and Tejanos (or their absence) in these plays have contributed to the marginalization and stereotyping of "the Mexican" in performance.

From the historical pageants and plays of the early twentieth century to later popular films, outdoor dramas, and battle reenactments, the creation and maintenance of the Texan centers around often-exaggerated representations of the "heroes" and "villains" of the Revolution, whose actions are linked to larger discourses of race and ethnicity. The performances retell these stories in a variety of ways, drawing on disputed events in order to perform, for many people, what it means to be Texan.[7] The Texas history pageants of the early twentieth century founded the idea of Texas as a performance narrative and used it to educate schoolchildren and future citizens (see Photo 9).[8]

When the popularity of pageantry began to fade after World War II, historical dramas (many of them performed outdoors) emerged and directed the didactic narrative of Texas toward a larger, more tourist-oriented population. Most of these pieces remained static, however, becoming over time more like museum pieces than living history. As a result, most historical dramas lasted only a few years (summers) before closing or giving over to a newer interpretation of the story.

There have been numerous films centering on the events of the Texas Revolution, particularly the Battle of the Alamo, dating back to the very beginnings of cinema.[9] They have certainly reached a wider, more international audience than their live counterparts, yet the films reflect the historical attitudes of their time periods as much as the historical events they represent.

Battle reenactments are the current popular trend; they blend the historical "accuracy" of weapons and costumes with the prevailing viewpoint of the times to present a didactic historical narrative.[10] These performances combine the didactic re-presentation of the Texan for the tourist with the education mandate of the pageants; indeed, reenactments draw their audiences from both school-aged children and visitors to the state.[11] In the case of the reenactments, however, descendants of the "real" heroes of the Revolution often participate either as soldiers or as spectators and are honored as part of the event. The presence of the descendants within the same space as the constructed performance helps to legitimate the performance as a pedagogical narrative designed to support Texan cultural memory.

In each of these venues, Texan cultural memory is constructed as a pedagogical narrative, a stylized, didactic representation of a heroic sacrifice for freedom. Yet it is also a memorial to the desire of some Texans to create an eternal space which represents past events and contested occurrences as unilaterally real and continually present. In *Destination Culture,* Barbara Kirshenblatt-Gimblett states that "a key to heritage productions is their virtuality, whether in the presence or absence of actualities."[12] Some historians claim that "it does not matter" whether any of the events which constitute the narrative of the Revolution "really happened."[13] Walter Lord, for example, claims that whether an event occurred (or did not) is, in the end, no impediment to believing that it *did* occur.[14] To the viewing and touring audiences who "see" historical plays, films, and reenactments every year, whether in a theatre or at a battle site, the events depicted did take place. It is precisely their performance within specially constructed historical contexts that gives these events their power. Regardless of whether they actually occurred between October 2, 1835, and April 21, 1836, these images, gleaned from stories and reminiscences, constitute the Revolution's status as a pedagogy and contribute to the production of its virtual heritage. If historical authenticity is the goal of these performances, then whether or not they depict actual events is a crucial aspect of their representations. For the audience to have concrete knowledge that what it is watching is not real would undermine the pedagogical potential of these dramas.

The image of a small but dedicated band of heroes fighting against an enormous and potentially unbeatable opponent, an image that began to emerge in the first accounts of the battle and the Revolution that has been maintained through pageants and films, is present even today in revolutionary pedagogy. The Daughters of the Republic of Texas maintain the Alamo shrine and grounds without charging admission to visitors by relying on donations and proceeds from the gift shop, all the while staving off attempts by the legislature and LULAC to gain control of the property. Many members of the Latino community in San Antonio condemn depictions of Tejanos in the Revolution as "subservient, of loose morals, less-involved and less heroic than their non-Hispanic counterparts" and demand revisions.[15] Others maintain that those Tejanos who did fight on the Texian side were not heroes but traitors to their people and, therefore, attempts to revise the Revolution into a more multicultural experience is yet another form of Anglo "whitewashing" of Texas history. Missing entirely from the narrative are the American Indians, who inhabited the land prior to the arrival of Spanish, Mexican, or American settlers but who have been reduced to shadows or endnotes in Texan historical pedagogy.

Each of these groups sees the performance of the Texan as a personal monument to their ancestors, a remembrance of their presence, one which reaffirms their exploitation, or heroism, or any of the other cultural narratives which have perpetuated Texan historical memory to this day.

PAGEANTRY AND HISTORICAL DRAMAS

In addition to architectural constructions like the Alamo Cenotaph and the San Jacinto Monument, and the placement of historical markers to commemorate sites of revolutionary battles, the Celebration Committee of the 1936 Texas Centennial also endorsed the creation and performance of historical pageants to educate the people about Texas history and culture.[16] Many pageants scripted the events of the Revolution and also included dramatizations of famous Texas legends and of stories based on important subjects within the State of Texas, such as drought relief and education reform.

The performance of pageants in connection with cultural celebrations was not a new phenomenon; in fact, the first decades of the twentieth century saw a tremendous resurgence in the pageant tradition throughout the United States under the guidance of professional theatre practitioners like George Pierce Baker, Percy MacKaye, and Paul Green (whose outdoor musical *Texas!* is discussed in Chapter 2). As a reflection of early-twentieth-century Progressive Era politics, the pageantry movement of pre–World War I America created a space in which citizens could, according to David Glassberg, practice "creating the illusion of the public appearing to speak for itself, in the process defining the terms under which particular local interests appeared as the public interest."[17] Pageants commemorated local histories and heroes while providing a way to move the people toward a bright new future by encouraging the assimilation of immigrant populations into the larger American culture.[18]

Post–World War I pageantry, on the other hand, mythologized the "past" as a series of static events related to, but not necessarily the direct cause of, present circumstances.[19] Before the war, pageantry was used as a performative force for community building among disparate cultural groups and as a vehicle for social change through direct participation in represented events. Now, it became the purview of education professionals seeking to dramatize a particular view of history, a pedagogy, for the benefit of students and their proud parents. The writers and dramatists were able to create a new set of educational practices by adapting pageantry to promote a specific version of Texan cultural identity.

In 1921, a pageant entitled *Texas under Six Flags: An Historical and Symbolic Pageant, Depicting in a Symbolical Way, in Story, Song, Dance and Tableaux, the History of the Lone Star State* contributed the founding of the first "Anglo-Saxon colony" by Stephen F. Austin to the Texan narrative. The pageant is divided into six episodes, one for each flag that flew over Texas, and consists of scenes which convey the events which occurred under that particular banner. Most of the story in this pageant is told through pantomime. Allegorical characters, such as "Liberty," "Immortality," "John Bull," "Mexico," and "Miss Texas, the fair republic of the South," appear frequently. Unusual in this pageant is an episode under the Confederate flag, in which slaves watch mournfully as their owner leads a Texan Confederate army regiment off to war.[20] This scene is located not at the end where, according to the historical chronology, it should appear, but immediately prior to Episode Six, which depicts Texas' entrance into the United States in 1845. Relocating the Confederate Texas segment means that the pageant's last two scenes concern the entrance of Texas into the Union in 1845 and its current status as (at that time) the largest state. This historical liberty also prevents the events referenced in the Confederacy sequence (slavery, the Civil War, Reconstruction) to detract from Texas' ultimate (and, by implication, appropriate) destiny of entering the Union. In this way, the pageant performs its didactic function: it locates the Texan as a separate, unique part of the larger American cultural landscape.

The practices by which the events of the Texas Revolution would become stabilized into a historical pedagogy are visible even in this pre-Centennial pageant. By far the longest episode of the pageant is the third—the events which occurred under the Mexican flag. Unlike the allegorical portrayals later in the pageant of Texas as a republic, its entrance into the Union, or depictions of life under the French, Spanish, and Confederate flags in general, historical characters are carefully inserted throughout the Mexican episode. In addition to Stephen F. Austin—the "Father of Texas"—the pageant features Texian army scout Deaf Smith, Sam Houston, and Santa Anna. In the final episode, "Texas Crowns Her Heroes," the allegorical figure of Texas, "attended by Immortality and Justice," crowns each of her heroes with a laurel wreath as Immortality reads off their contributions to the revolutionary cause. In addition to the usual figures of Houston, Crockett, Bowie, Travis, Ben Milam, and James Bonham, the author also includes Lorenzo de Zavala ("Friend of Texas," the first vice president of the Republic) and Johanna Troutman ("Maker of the First Texas Flag").[21]

The attention to such diverse historical figures in just one scene prevents an alternative to the Anglo, male-oriented pageant. Such a moment of rupture shows how pedagogy can be used not only to reinforce but also to subvert the dominant discourse emphasizing the events of the Revolution as the central event in the creation of Texan cultural identity. Such in-depth detail helps draw a distinction between the importance of the other flags and the cultures they represent in the development of Texan historical memory and the events which led to the Lone Star flag of the Republic of Texas.

This pageant also highlights the ambivalent early relationship between Texas and the United States. In Episode Four, the young Republic of Texas pleads unsuccessfully for help from Uncle Sam to rebuff Mexico, and in Episode Six (dramatically choreographed as a "roll call" of the states), Texas, played by a young girl, is first spurned by Uncle Sam then rescued by him from the attentions of Mexico and John Bull (the British counterpart to Uncle Sam) and added to the list of states.[22] This representation casts Texas as a damsel in distress, first spurned by the heroic United States in the person of Uncle Sam, then rescued and protected by him, just as Texas was defended by her own brave heroes in Episode Three.

The feminization of Texas history through this allegorical character is unique among Texan pageants and casts the representation of Texan identity into an uncomfortable role, away from the traditional representations of Texans as amalgamations of Crockett, Bowie, Travis, and Houston. Such a performance also subverts the supposedly amiable relationship between Texas and the United States by providing a reminder of the state's inability to function as a separate nation and its eventual annexation.

Architectural sites also play a major part in the construction of revolutionary pedagogy. The siege and fall of the Alamo are major events in Texas history, and representing what occurred there in the most "authentically" didactic fashion is key to the maintenance of Texan cultural memory. Documentation of exactly what happened during that fateful two-week period in 1836 has been particularly difficult, due to the thorough nature with which Santa Anna's attacking troops carried out his decree of no quarter. The lack of survivors, particularly those who could write down their own accounts and read those of others, has only added to the confusion. Neither Alamo survivor Susanna Dickinson, the wife of Texian army lieutenant Almeron Dickinson, nor Moses Rose, the infamous man who didn't cross the line in the sand, could read or write. Rose's version of the final days, the source of the story about Travis' line in the sand, was recorded third-hand by W. P. Zuber in 1871, based on an account given by Rose to Zuber's parents.[23] Published accounts by Tejanos who were present in San Antonio during the battle were translated into English decades following the event, and these stories were often treated with skepticism, especially where they did not support Texian heroism.[24]

"Official" Mexican records of the battle are always suspect. In his report to the Mexican secretary of war, Santa Anna inflated the number of troops in the Alamo garrison from 187 to over 600 and downplayed his own losses in order to make the victory seem more impressive to the folks back home, whose depleted resources had paid for the campaign. Santa Anna, the self-styled "Napoleon of the West," who imitated his idol in governmental structure, command bravado, and dress, wanted to transform the Alamo battle into a "small affair" instead of a bloody, needless assault which cost the lives of one-third of his troops (it has been estimated that eight Mexican soldiers perished for every Alamo defender).[25]

Texian reports are only slightly more reliable. Estimates of the number of troops held by Santa Anna prior to the assault have ranged from fifteen hundred to six thousand. The accounts of the battle and the subsequent treatment of the dead given by Susanna Dickinson to Sam Houston at Gonzales only increased the panic and rage felt toward Mexicans in general, and Santa Anna in particular, as the Texas army and its entourage of refugees retreated toward Louisiana. Following the end of the war, the publication of letters written by those who perished and of accounts by survivors immediately sanctified the Texian defenders and vilified the Mexican attackers, turning the entire event into a racial binary that polarizes the area to this day. "Remembering the Alamo" meant remembering that Mexicans were butchers, the enemy, but (ultimately) losers.

The few historical documents from the Alamo battle which have been preserved have been integrated into revolutionary pedagogy to foster Texan historical memory and promulgate the narration of Texas as a nation. The most famous piece, Col. William Barret Travis' letter of February 24, 1836, is housed in the Texas State Historical Archives.[26] Entitled "To the people of Texas and All Americans in the World," the letter contains phrases such as "I shall never surrender or retreat," "I call on you in the name of liberty, of patriotism, and of everything dear to the American character to come to our aid," and "Victory or Death." This letter is one of the cornerstones of the Alamo narrative, casting Travis and his band as the last best hope for victory against a tyrannical opponent. Travis' call to "Americans" reinforces the defense of democracy as central to the Alamo story, but it also implies a racial binary. By asking only Americans for aid, Travis implied that the United States represented freedom.

The Alamo-as-event figured prominently in most pageants in the early part of the twentieth century; its heroes were commemorated in both song and story. Travis' letter was a favorite recitation piece for schoolchildren and politicians during the years leading up to the Centennial Celebration. Various pageants and historical plays from the Centennial era, such as *Westward the Course of Empire: The History of Texas from Exploration to Annexation* (1924), *The Messenger of Defeat* (1936), and *Texas, Land of the Strong* (1936), with lines like these all gave significant attention to the bravery and courage of the Texas fighting spirit in the face of certain defeat:

> TRAVIS: Say that we died with our faces to the enemy. A hundred and eighty-two of us. Say we were proud to give our last breath for Texas. It will probably be over in an hour . . . Don't surrender, boys!
> CROCKETT: Not while old Betsy will fire a shot![27]

Despite its prominence within the narrative, however, many pageants refrained from actually portraying the Alamo battle onstage. *Texas under Six Flags* represents the fall of the Alamo through the eyes of its most famous survivor, Susanna Dickinson, by having her tell her tale after her escape.[28] Bessie Roselle's play *The Messenger of Defeat* deals entirely with the fall of the Alamo, but the three scenes mentioned in the title take place before and after the battle, not during it.

The limitations of pageantry itself were a consideration. Because the pageants were performed by and intended for young children, most pageant authors steered away from the depiction of carnage, death, or actual battle in their texts. Many authors felt that it was inappropriate for schoolchildren even to portray (or represent) an event of such monumental importance on stage, because the inauthenticity of using children in the performance would somehow lessen the brilliance of the Alamo-as-event. In the preface to her pageant, *Following the Lone Star: A Pageant of Texas* (1924), Rebecca

Washington Lee states that "only such incidents have been chosen as are practicable for children to portray; that is why such hallowed scenes as the Alamo have not been attempted."[29] Many of the sequences were mimed and contained little, if any, dialogue. This gave the images on stage particular didactic power, and that power needed to be controlled so that it did not undermine the representation of the Texan that it was trying to convey. The deletion of the battle scenes, by keeping everything visual and larger-than-life, also preempted any challenges to the accuracy of the representations by adult members of the audience. As with ancient Greek tragedy, hallowed sites of violence are not shown on stage; they are removed from visual representation in order to sanctify revolutionary events as beyond critique, as a narrative that needs no explanation because it cannot be adequately represented.

As Richard Flores states in his study of the Alamo-as-event, "the case of the Alamo demonstrates how events from the past serve to advance various plots in the present by endowing them with a sense of historicality and genuineness."[30] This simulated appearance, then, works to "advance a plot of social and racial difference with a myth of origin."[31] Because Texan cultural identity uses the Alamo as the seminal event in its pedagogical narrative, it depends on the establishment of an Anglo-Mexican binary. Whether represented literally (as in battle scenes) or figuratively (as, e.g., through the recitation of Travis' letter or the presence of Susanna Dickinson), the Alamo remains central to the creation, maintenance, and transmission of Texas history. The ability to control how the event is portrayed becomes important in the creation of ethnic binaries that can influence other aspects of Texan cultural memory.

Even though the Alamo-as-event is absent, however, other events depicted in pageants reference it. The most popular by far is the Battle of San Jacinto and its aftermath. The battle cries of San Jacinto—"Remember the Alamo! Remember Goliad!"—link these events with a larger historical narrative: the formation of the Republic of Texas through the sacrifices of its heroes. The final battle of the Revolution, in which Sam Houston routed Santa Anna's army in under eighteen minutes by attacking during siesta, balanced the defeat at the Alamo by delivering Santa Anna directly into the hands of the Texian army. Representations of San Jacinto in historical pageantry usually focus on the historic meeting between president-turned-prisoner-of-war Santa Anna and Texian army commander Sam Houston following the battle.

The meeting between Santa Anna and Houston in pageants is based not on documents from the Revolution but on aesthetic renderings of the event held in almost as high esteem as the event itself. The tableau of San Jacinto found in *Texas under Six Flags,* for example, was taken from "the well-known picture which hangs in the corridor of the State Capital," and stage directions instruct players to follow its composition and actions "closely":

> Houston's . . . leg bandaged from knee to ankle . . . blanket spread under a large tree . . . surgeon (*prepares*) to dress the wound . . . Mexican prisoners nearby . . . man dressed in garb of a common Mexican soldier . . . recognized by other Mexicans . . . "El Presidente, El Presidente!" . . . patriots start towards their oppressor, knives raised . . . Houston prevents this by the raise of his hand . . . Deaf Smith puts his hand to his ears as if trying to hear . . . Santa Anna . . . draws himself up to his full height (*congratulating Houston on capturing the Napoleon of the West and*) . . . expecting Houston to recognize his greatness . . . Houston refused to be overawed and with a wave of his hand orders him treated like the other prisoners.[32]

Centennial Celebration pageants also include this tableau. Episode 7 of the pageant *Indian Paintbrush* contains almost the same pantomime.[33] In *We Are Texas,* after the character of History sums up the Alamo and Goliad in one line—"The Texans lost at the Alamo and Goliad, but finally Santa Anna was defeated at San Jacinto"—the same tableau appears once again.[34] In most cases, there was no dialogue; the tableau itself was seen to be a didactic representation of the event.

The significance of these twinned representations is vast—a performance of "history" based on a representation in a work of art, not a historical account. Such accounts affirm that Santa Anna indeed met with Houston, but though the event is historical, its authenticity in performance cannot be trusted to history. Instead, the authenticity of the representation is verified by another, already accepted, depiction of the event. The tableau draws on William Henry Huddle's *The Surrender of Santa Anna* (1886). This painting was commissioned by the post-Reconstruction Texas government to hang in the new State Capitol, along with paintings of famous Texas leaders and other historic events, to help inscribe Texan historical memory on the halls of the legislature itself (see Photo 10).[35]

Huddle's work is one of three painted during the post–Civil War explosion of revolutionary nostalgia concerning the Battle of San Jacinto, due in part to the growing popularity of the Alamo as the focal point of Texas' revolutionary history.[36] The emphasis in the picture is on the two central figures: the standing Santa Anna and the reclining, wounded Houston.

Despite his lower position in the composition, Houston is the focus of the painting. His victory is clearly evident in his manner—he is about to speak as he gestures with his hand—and in the reactions in the faces around him, listening and ready. Santa Anna is silenced, his capture reduced to an imitation in an aesthetic reproduction of the historical event.

Most pageants focus on a confrontation between two leaders who became the embodiment of revolutionary pedagogy, a visible representation of its Texan versus non-Texan (read: Mexican) binary. This binarization of the "good" Texan versus the "bad" non-Texan formed the groundwork for racial tensions between Anglos and Hispanics in the years after the Revolution while simultaneously eliminating any other races (blacks, American Indians) from the picture. Remembrances of the event begat the artistic representation of the event on canvas. This representation was then recreated live and in person as a historical tableau. In an interesting bit of circular logic, this tableau, and its reliance on the painting, then served to legitimate the painting as an authentic historical document. This authentication ensured that the historical representation of the Texan would eventually pass through the painting's framework as a reference.

This painting currently hangs in a public building toured by thousands of people each year; its location in the State Capitol further reinforces it as an authentic representation of a historical event. This extended chain of significations reinforces the importance of maintaining both the event and its representation of the Texan in exactly that format.[37] As with the legends of Davy Crockett's death and Travis' line in the sand, historical accuracy often has little bearing on revolutionary pedagogy. What is important is the impact of the image on its audience and its ability to reinforce Texan cultural memory in its participants.

The Alamo-as-event was used to reorganize preceding events so that they linked more directly to the Alamo's status. A direct cause-effect relationship between it and other material events did not exist. In *Texas under Six Flags,* Susanna Dickinson's arrival from the Alamo precedes a scene which commemorates the signing of the Texas Declaration of Independence, even though the Declaration signing actually occurred on March 2, four days before the fall of the Alamo on March 6. The scene utilizes sections from William Barret Travis' letter as a catalyst for the signing and a promise of the future glory of the state: "I shall never surrender or retreat . . . Victory or death."[38]

While visual representation provides one vehicle for pedagogical performances, another, equally effective, one is the words of its heroes. Instead of portraying the site itself, the dead heroes of the Alamo—Travis, Bowie, and Crockett—were often called, in early-twentieth-century pageants, to speak for "her." Once again, masculine bodies and masculine language reinscribe the space of Texas as a feminine one that must be defended and protected from invaders. *The March of the Immortals* is "a pageant of Texas heroes,"[39] in which "the Muse of History" (a blonde with a wreath in her hair in a long blue robe and sandals, who writes on a long scroll) teaches a class of schoolchildren about those "noble valiant [men of Texas] who rise above the ordinary and must be called famous."[40] Her list not only includes regulars like Houston and Austin but also immortalizes Confederate general Albert Sidney Johnston, Capt. R. M. Coleman of the Texas Rangers, and Mirabeau B. Lamar, the second president of the Republic and the "Father of Education" in Texas. As she reads his accomplishments, each man (and they are all men) crosses the stage and takes his place on an elevated platform. Travis, Crockett, and Bowie represent the Alamo. The Muse says that, "when Travis drew that fateful line at the Alamo, he also drew a line between liberty and oppression which all Texans follow."[41] Once again, the essences of past heroism and future bravery intersect along Travis' line in the sand, the line which separated the cowards from the heroes and the Texians from everyone else.

The role of the cowardly (Mexican) Other, the counterpoint to the heroic character of the revolutionary Texan, is most often performed by Santa Anna. No other named Mexican or Tejano characters appear in the historical pageants. Depictions of Santa Anna were common in Texas history pageants, especially around the Centennial. They are all exaggerated and highly unflattering, reflecting both the Mexican dictator's reputation for brutality and his egocentric personality as the Napoleon of the West.[42] Santa Anna's presence helps foreground why the Revolution (supposedly) occurred: to secure the independence of Texas (rather than to restore the Mexican Constitution of 1824). Santa Anna and, by extension, Mexico are the enemy in the pageants, and a visual representation of this relationship is necessary to reinforce the didactic message. Unlike the relatively humble Texians, Santa Anna boasts of his achievements as a military commander:

> Santa Anna enters with a group of Mexican soldiers. Mexican flag raised. Soldiers stand at attention while Santa Anna speaks to them:
>
> Our good work is going on,
> We have the Texans on the run.
> I am sure that you all know

Of our victory at the Alamo
Not one Texan was left alive.
At Goliad, only a few survive
We'll follow Houston and his men
One more battle we must win.[43]

Through his referral to the deaths at the Alamo and Goliad as "good work," Santa Anna shows that he is the enemy of the Texan traits of freedom and liberty.

Santa Anna's most graphic embodiment as a Mexican stereotype occurs in the pageant *Did You Call Me?* (1936). A student, working in the late hours of the morning on a paper about the history of Texas before the Republic, is visited by the characters about whom he has written. Explorers Cortés and LaSalle; Stephen F. Austin; Alamo defenders Travis, Crockett, Bowie, and Bonham; Goliad commander James Fannin—each adds a piece to the structure of the events. Santa Anna enters and defends his actions at the Alamo, but it is the defense of a coward, hiding behind the actions of others and expressed in a stagy dialect often given to Indian characters: "Me no Alamo. Me no Goliad. General Cos, he at Goliad."[44] He gloats over the deaths of Fannin and the others, gradually gaining the upper hand in the narrative, until he is silenced by the arrival of Sam Houston, who visualizes the Mexican general's defeat and surrender: "The Alamo, Goliad are avenged. Here is a nation born. A lone star shining above, and transcending the greed, the treachery, and every hardship that men and women endured for liberty. From the blood of San Jacinto may every generation with problems of state, take heart and keep green the memory of those who died for Texas freedom."[45] Houston puts "El Presidente" in his place by invoking actions that characterize Texan heroism and re-presents them as part of revolutionary pedagogy.

Centennial-era pageants that focused on Texas history served a function similar to that of pageants performed in other states: to create a clear, simple message about a given event that literally brought it to life. Rather than engage in questions of historical accuracy, however, pageantry kept its representations on the surface of historical events, promoting allegorical figures and stereotypes over character depth and detail. Superficial characterizations allowed the pageants to be embodied by their typical performers—schoolchildren—who then transmitted this revolutionary pedagogy to the parents, neighbors, and members of the community who turned out to watch the children's enactments. The performances created a template to lay over the Revolution that transformed conflicting and disparate stories into the unified, heroic space of Texan historical memory that celebrated one hundred years of Texan culture in 1936.

While pageants were an effective way of communicating Texan cultural memory within the framework of celebrations like the Centennial, historical dramas were a way to educate tourists and native Texans about Texas during the summer. History plays appeared as part of the Centennial Celebration, although in lesser numbers than did pageants, which they surpassed in the decades that followed. As with Paul Green's *Texas!* many historical dramas were performed in outdoor venues. Whereas pageants tended to focus on the grand scope of Texas history and the representation of allegorical characters, historical dramas focused on an event. That did not necessarily mean that the representations were more accurate (the basic ideas, or ideals, of Texas historical memory were rarely fractured, particularly in the early dramas). Historical plays, however, did provide the opportunity for representing an aspect of revolutionary pedagogy different from the pageants. More character development (based mostly in fiction) and historical accuracy in the presentation of events were attempted in the dramas than in pageantry, which was primarily visual and used pantomime. Yet, certain events remained sacred—if not in their absence, then in their continued re-presentation (the line in the sand, for example). The ethnic gulf was always in view, if not reinforced outright by the words and actions of the characters. American immigrants, Anglo Texans, Mexicans, Tejanos, free and enslaved blacks, and Indians all milled together in dramatic structures (if not deeper points of view) that both upheld and commented on the nature of revolutionary pedagogy and the Texas historical memory that it reinforced.[46] These historical dramas also reinforce the inscription of the Texan as white and male, and rarely do their texts deviate from this simulated norm.

One redeeming Mexican character, also a woman, to break the centrality of white men to revolutionary historical pedagogy is the Angel of Goliad, Francita Alavez.[47] The "traveling companion" of a Mexican army officer, Alavez is credited with saving from execution several of the men under Fannin's command following the Battle of Coleto. She is the subject of a Centennial Celebration one-act play entitled *The Angel of Goliad,* set in the "early morning, Sunday, March 27, 1836 [the day of the executions]" (see Photo 11).[48]

The first half of the play consists of an ideological debate (the general points of which are still part of the annual Goliad Massacre reenactment at Presidio La Bahía) between two Mexican army officers concerning the struggle between a soldier's duty to his orders and his personal honor.[49] Colonel Guerrier is the conscience of the massacre, "handsome and distinguished."[50] Guerrier recognizes that the executions will only fan the Texans' hatred of Santa Anna. Captain Álvarez [Alavez], the *señora*'s husband, asserts that, once "they have had a taste of Santa Anna's vengeance, . . . they will not want another soon."[51] Álvarez is clearly the bad guy in this scenario; he believes that "the fools brought it on themselves."[52] Despite his misgivings, Guerrier carries out the orders; the Mexican soldiers are given no way to justify their actions or redeem themselves.

The second half of the play offers what little redemption there is for Mexican characters in the form of "Senora Alvarez," Duenna, and Álvarez's orderly, Pedro. The *señora* removes as many Texian soldiers as possible from the chapel, under the pretext of needing skilled labor, and then gives the men horses (secured by Pedro) and money for their escape. The only rescued man seen on stage is John Edwards, "a carpenter."[53]

As with the "hallowed scenes" of the Alamo battle, the massacre itself is represented offstage: "Just then, the sound of shooting is heard in the distance, mingled with hoarse cries, and more shots."[54] As Edwards escapes, he promises to "pray for her always" (a gesture which reinforces her unique position within revolutionary pedagogy), then,

> SENORA ALVAREZ: (*Sinks wearily into chair before fire, wrings her hands and moans softly to herself as occasional shots are heard in the distance. Looks up suddenly at the woman [Duenna] opposite her and asks in a wild, frenzied voice*) What is the use of it all—this madness of war? Will men ever stop killing each other?
> THE DUENA [*sic*]: Q[u]ien sabe? or (Who knows?)[55]

The *Angel of Goliad* indicts Mexican barbarity and slavish devotion to duty over honor, but Señora Álvarez is venerated for her attempts to save the soldiers and, in so doing, serves as a model for appropriate womanly behavior: nurse, messenger, camp follower. Since these roles lie outside of the performance of Texas heroism on the battlefield, the central story in Texas revolutionary narrative—women's contribution to early Texas history—is never central to their presence in historical dramas. Acceptable as handmaids to the white, male Texas identity, women serve precisely this function in Ramsey Yelvington's *A Cloud of Witnesses: The Drama of the Alamo* (produced 1958; published 1959), a popular outdoor drama written for and performed at the Mission San José Outdoor Theater in the late 1950's and early 1960's. Yelvington drew heavily from the Greek theatre and medieval morality play traditions in his construction of an epic tale that remembers the Alamo. There is a chorus of women, "the widows of Gonzales," who provide "poetic insight into the minds and hearts of these pioneer women of Texas (they are the "cloud of witnesses" of the title).[56] As in the pageants, the voice of Texas is feminized and stands as a spectator, while the brave heroes of the Alamo fight to rescue her from the clutches of Santa Anna.

According to the original director of *A Cloud of Witnesses,* Paul Baker, the play "was a highly incisive picture of the real men of the Alamo . . . here was history, and Texas history at that, denuded of the usual cheap, sentimental, and over-glorified approach, honed down to the bare skeleton of the real living essence of what the men of the Alamo fought for."[57]

A Cloud of Witnesses attempts to bring to life the complexity of emotions that exist outside of pageantry's celebration of the ultimate victory of Texas over Mexico. Yelvington's script, though full of moving lyrical passages and beautifully staged in the courtyard of the Mission San José de Béxar, reinforces revolutionary pedagogy, albeit with greater dramaturgical skill than in pageant sequences that focus on the Alamo.

The character of Moses Rose, for example, is devil's advocate, literally, Satan in disguise, questioning the resolve of the men in the Alamo and undermining their belief that they are dying for a noble cause. Although the historical Rose is said to have left the Alamo, the character Rose is discredited by the "witnesses" as a completely mythical figure in the midst of the historical ones on stage, a myth because no real Texian would have abandoned the fight for freedom. Also, Bowie charges that Travis maligned the men under Bowie's command, many of whom were Tejanos, claiming that they were "born corrupt."

Travis does not deny this charge; in fact, he reiterates it, claiming that he "spoke of birth; irrefutable birth, destined birth. They were born Mexican . . . these were not born on edge to be free!"[58] Here, Yelvington has Travis speak aloud the implications of his February 24, 1836, letter and its appeal to "everything dear to the American character" in asking for reinforcements.

By the end of the drama, the historical performance of the Texans is set even more firmly than at the beginning. By denying Rose's existence (i.e., refuting Satan in the character of Rose) and denigrating the Tejano soldiers at the Alamo—not as traitors but as people fundamentally incapable of understanding the "freedom" for which the (Anglo) Texans fought—Yelvington has created a narrative structure in ironic contrast to the skeletal outline of the Alamo chapel, which serves as the production's setting and through which, in Baker's view, the audience was supposed to see a "powerful poetic and honest expression of Texas history" (see Photo 12).[59]

Twenty years beyond Yelvington's play, the state of historical drama had changed little. First produced in 1977 and revived for the Texas Sesquicentennial Celebration in 1986, Paul Green's *The Lone Star: A Symphonic Drama of the Texas Struggle for Independence* is more in the vein of a historical drama than is his outdoor drama *Texas!* (discussed in Chap. 1). While *Texas!* capitalizes on the strength of its geographical backdrop, *The Lone Star* creates an epic historical narrative surrounding the events of the Texas Revolution and "the struggle . . . to establish Galveston as a life-line seaport guaranteeing her strength and stability for the future."[60] (Galveston's centrality to the script disappears after the opening sequences, which depict the landing of Spanish conquistadores and the French pirate Jean Laffite.)

Green's script overwhelmingly reinforces the performance of Texas found in earlier historical dramas. The Texans are brave, heroic, full of fighting spirit, and primarily Anglo. Although the Tejano vice president of the Republic, Lorenzo de Zavala, is seen on stage, he has no dialogue. Congressional delegate Antonio Navarro gets two lines when he moves that the body adjourn and reinforce the Alamo, an idea immediately dismissed by Houston.

This didactic negation-through-representation of the Tejano contribution to the Revolution continues in Act 2, when a chorus of women (once again named "the widows of Gonzales") makes its way onto the stage to confront Houston about the deaths of their husbands at the Alamo. The fifth woman to speak says, "I am Victoria Esparza. My husband Gregorio and five of his Mexican comrades died there for Texas."[61] The characters of Zavala, Navarro, and Esparza are the only attempts to represent historical Tejano figures in the play.

These are not, however, the only Hispanic characters in Green's drama. In a nod to the traditions of historical pageantry, Santa Anna is given his customary burst of bravado in the scene prior to the Battle of San Jacinto and his postcapture face-to-face meeting with Houston, which Green gives a humorous twist:

> HOUSTON: Great God in heaven, it's Santa Anna himself. (*shouting*) We've captured Santa Anna! (*He hobbles forward with help and wraps the prisoner in his arms.*) Am I glad to see you![62]

Though unconcerned with the representation of real Tejano figures from Texas history, *The Lone Star* does offer a fictional (and stereotypical) alternative: the Flores family. Throughout the play, its members are referred to as

"Mexican," although they are residents of San Felipe both prior to and during the conflict. In fact, the only nonhistorical character in the play to die is Juan Flores, a Mexican shopkeeper who speaks broken English. Nonetheless, his beautiful daughter, Barbara, who has only "a touch of accent,"[63] ends up paired with loyal soldier and friend of General Houston, Andy Merritt.

Despite attempts to portray Tejanos as sympathetic to the Revolution, Green's drama ultimately reinscribes the racial/ethnic stereotype of the Mexican as loyal to Santa Anna over the Texas cause. One piece of dialogue depicts Barbara Flores as a Mexican loyalist in the face of Texan freedom fighters:

> MERRITT: Everybody says trouble's coming. Old Santa Anna, blind as a bat, is trying to make slaves out of us and—
> BARBARA: Stop it! . . . He is our presidente—your presidente. We have no right to criticize, to insult—Good night! (*She starts to go.*)[64]

The first act ends with the announcement that the Alamo has fallen, an event which brings latent racial tensions into full view. The Flores family becomes the target of animosity from the (Anglo) Texans:

> *(Rebecca Cummings screams and beats about her with her fists. Suddenly she points her finger at the Flores family.)*
> REBECCA: There! The Mexicans—traitors! (*She spits out the infectious word.*)
> VOICES: (*in quick agreement*) Traitors! Traitors! (*Some of the people, led by Rebecca, make a rush toward Juan and his family. For a moment it looks as if they will be beaten up. But Merritt, Deaf Smith, Murph, and others push the people back.*)[65]

Less than two lines later, after the Flores family has fled the stage, Houston swears "to avenge the dead [at the Alamo] in Mexican blood" as *some of the women shriek out their cries* (emphasis mine).

With the ethnic binary firmly established, Juan Flores—the representative of "old" Mexico—dies, leaving Barbara free to marry Andy Merritt and become part of the victorious, whitewashed Republic of Texas. The didactic image of Texas as a haven for distinctively Anglo notions of freedom and heroism remains a constant, despite the apparent staining of this purity by the intermarriage of Barbara and Andy. However, Barbara's earlier assertion of her Texas identity has liberated her from the apparent bonds of

Mexican oppression, just as Houston's victory at San Jacinto liberated the Texian rebels.

Characters who challenge the primacy of the Anglo-Mexican binary, however, receive less support, particularly when their roles subvert the heroism of the traditional narrative. Take, for example, the case of the "Yellow Rose of Texas." Historically, she is known as Emily Morgan or Emily West. According to *San Antonio Light* columnist Mike Tolson, "the legend of Emily Morgan is simple enough." She was a mulatto slave of Col. James Morgan who, whether out of Texian patriotism or survival instinct, is said to have "entertained" or "occupied" Santa Anna in his tent on that fateful afternoon of April 21, 1836, thereby allowing Texian general Sam Houston to mount his surprise attack on the Mexican army camp on the San Jacinto plain. She is also believed to have been the inspiration for the famous song, "The Yellow Rose of Texas."[66]

After the battle, Emily faded into obscurity. It was not until the long-delayed publication in 1956 of *William Bollaert's Texas,* the diary of a British traveler through the Republic of Texas from 1842 to 1844, that her supposed connection to the Battle of San Jacinto became known. Bollaert refers to her as a "Mulatto Girl (Emily) belonging to Colonel Morgan."[67] It is the only mention of her role in the Revolution found in any documents from around the time.

Emily's inclusion in dramatized revolutionary history is cloudy at best; she appears only briefly in Paul Green's *The Lone Star* and is never mentioned in any earlier pageants or plays. Most of the trouble surrounding Emily came in 1985 (the year of the Texas Sesquicentennial), when the old Medical Arts Building in San Antonio was converted by the Dallas-based (but California-operated) Vantage Corporation into the Emily Morgan Hotel. Vantage had applied for a federal Urban Development Action Grant (UDAG) to aid in the renovation of the building. Since the building was located across the street from the Alamo and its upper floors overlooked the Alamo grounds, members of the Bexar County Historical Commission mounted a very public campaign to have the name changed on the grounds that the naming of the building for Emily Morgan was "inappropriate" in light of her alleged role in the Revolution. Some citizens were less subtle in their disapproval; in the words of commission member Thelma Cade Perdue, "they're saying 'this is the prostitute hotel, San Antonio, come on all you prostitutes.'" Other commission members seized on the fact that there was "little or no basis in fact of her [Morgan's] existence or her participation" in the Revolution and claimed that "this matter should not be confused with Texas 'patriotism.' It is strictly a matter of correct history or deliberate distortion."[68] The Bexar County Historical Commission was even kind enough to send Robert Pincus of Vantage a list of "authentic Texas heroes" whose names would be more suitable—all of them male, and none of them black.[69]

By the end of the dispute, during which both the Bexar County Historical Commission and the Texas Historical Commission tried to get the U.S. Department of Housing and Urban Development to rescind the UDAG due to the building's name, more information was published surrounding the legend and mystery of Emily Morgan than in the preceding 150 years. It started a flurry of investigation into exactly who she was and what exactly her role was in the Revolution. Unfortunately for Tolson and his constituency, it proved to be more complex than a mere slave waylaying Santa Anna. Even the name was wrong; Emily Morgan, originally named after her supposed owner, Capt. James Morgan, was in fact Emily West, a free woman of color believed to be a relation of Emily de Zavala. Morgan/West was head of Morgan's plantation household in the absence of his invalid wife (who was back east) but was not a slave. Various historians, including Stephen Hardin and Margaret Swett Henson, have not only cast doubts on her background, but have also asserted that her "dalliance," if any, with Santa Anna, was more the result of being a young, attractive prisoner of war (she had been captured at Morgan's plantation five days earlier) than of any plan of Sam Houston's or even patriotism on her part.[70] In addition, James E. Crisp has asserted that the song "The Yellow Rose of Texas" does not refer to Morgan/West at all but to a member of another household living in New Haven, Texas, at the time.[71]

The combination of gender, sexuality, and racial issues within Texas historical memory makes Morgan/West a much more complex character than her unilaterally male counterparts. Her supposed role is equal to that of other spies who supported the Revolution, but her implied sexual dalliance with Santa Anna reduces her to a gender stereotype which belies any serious connection to the performance of the Texan, which must be kept pure, one-dimensional, and family-friendly for the benefit of tourists. The possibility of the continued performance of this identity as the name of a hotel overlooking the Alamo, itself a performative site of the most holy of sacrifices in Texas history, was too subversive for the overly white, male discourse of Texan cultural identity.[72]

Nonetheless, the legend of the Yellow Rose of Texas remains a powerful force in Texas cultural memory. Along with William Barret Travis' slave

Joe, she is the only African American widely acknowledged to have played a role in the Texas Revolution.[73] Because she was a free woman of color, she has been embraced by the African American community in Texas as a true hero of the Revolution and a symbol of the black contribution to the fight for Texas' independence.[74]

Yet, the position of Morgan/West and other African Americans in Texas after the Revolution, whether slave or free, became as precarious as in other parts of what would become the Confederate States of America when the proslavery factions in the Republic began to enact legislation to drive them from the territory.[75] One of the reasons that Morgan/West's contribution to the war effort remains a part of the revolutionary narrative is because she was able to obtain a passport to leave the Republic and return to New York, an "exceptional" accomplishment.[76] It could only have happened, one historical novel speculates, as payoff for her pact with Sam Houston to help defeat the Mexican army and win the war.[77]

Morgan/West is also the only woman in the Texas Revolution connected with a victory by the Texian army (Dickinson was at the Alamo with her husband; Alavez was at Goliad). If the legend is true, Morgan/West's intervention was crucial in helping the bedraggled Texian forces under Sam Houston, who had been on the run from Santa Anna's army for over a month, achieve victory and capture El Presidente himself. Yet the nature of her contribution foregrounds female sexuality even as it objectifies her identity (she must be a "prostitute," "mulatto," or "slave" so that she is not conflated with the "purity" of the representations of Dickinson and Alavez). She becomes the latest incarnation of Terence's Thais, the prostitute with the heart of gold, a necessary evil in a tumultuous world, a role that would later be emulated by *The Best Little Whorehouse in Texas'* leading lady, Miss Mona. Yet the sexualization of Morgan/West is more in line with the traditional sexualization of the ethnic Other, which characterizes what María Lugones calls "ethnocentric racism,"[78] distancing her heroism, however central to the success of the actual Revolution, from less-proactive female representations of Texan cultural identity.

Although on the surface Emily Morgan/West's performance in the construction of Texan identity may appear to be a binary of female "virtue" against "vice," it must be remembered that, in real life, none of the historical Texas women remembered within the revolutionary narrative could claim Perdue's moral high ground. Susanna Dickinson's later life included five marriages and a stint in a Galveston bordello, and her daughter, Angelina, "the Babe of the Alamo," worked as a prostitute. Francita Alavez was not, in fact, the legal wife of Telesforo Alavez, but Dickinson, the wife of a Texian army lieutenant, had a legitimized presence at the Alamo and, therefore, a position of importance as the bearer of tragic news. Some writers assert that Francita Alavez may not have even known her colonel was married and so considered herself his legal wife.[79] In any case, Alavez did not "sacrifice" her body as Morgan/West reportedly did; instead, she used her relatively invisible position within the Mexican army camp to spirit several members of Col. James Fannin's captured forces away before the executions. Dickinson's white privilege allowed her later life, and that of her daughter, to be elided from her role in the pedagogical narrative, thereby maintaining the Anglo supremacy of Texan cultural identity when Dickinson appears in pageants, plays, and films.

Other aspects of Texas' revolutionary history have been obscured by pageants and other historical dramas. Contrast the treatment of Crazy Horse in "Brawl #6, At That Time of Whiskey," in Ruth Margraff's *Centaur Battle of San Jacinto,* with the representation of American Indians in the 1936 history pageant *Texas Was Mine.* In the former, the other Texans unite so that they can gang up on Crazy Horse and get him drunk. Crockett is angry that Crazy Horse came to the bar, because "you peepin tom us every night. BUT HERE IS THE PLACE OF MAN AND WHISKEY AND A PLACE TO SIT AND NO BARBARIANS!"[80] The Yellow Rose tries to help Crazy Horse, but Stephen F. Austin restrains her. Later, Crazy Horse gives her the "potion" that she needs to make all men lust for her forever as The Yellow Rose of Texas—blood from his "ancient wound."[81]

In *Texas Was Mine,* young schoolchildren learn about the "Chinese puzzle" of Texas history from the personified Six Flags over Texas. Each flag—France, Spain, Mexico, the Republic of Texas, the Union, and the Confederacy—speaks of the wonderful things gained from the land when it flew over Texas. The last character to speak, however, is an Indian, "gorgeous in Indian suit, feather headdress, bow and arrow":

> I am the Red Man. Before the Pale Face set foot on American soil, Texas was mine. I had no flag, nor any government such as he knew. Around my council fires, great chieftains made laws for the good of people, and the Great Spirit spoke to me the wind and the water. Texas with her wild life; her buffalo, her deer her birds, was a hunter's dream. I loved the Pale Face, whose words were magic, but scalped him and burned his wigwam, when he took all those things from me. I saw great nations rise and pass away, till the Great Eagle came from the North with the flag of many stars. His words are good medicine. The Red Man is his brother now.[82]

Whereas the Indian of the pageant represents a clear stereotype, both visually and in his conciliatory attitude toward the "Pale Face," Crazy Horse depicts the Janus-faced nature of racial discourse within revolutionary pedagogy. Like the African Americans who fought for a freedom that was later taken from them, Crazy Horse acknowledges the loss, as a result of the Texan victory at San Jacinto, of a culture that existed prior to his birth. Within Texas' historical memory, the very nature of Texas created by the Revolution is re-visioned from freedom to bondage, liberation to oppression. The Red Man's point of view may sit best within revolutionary pedagogy, but it is Crazy Horse's experiences and memories that are the more historically accurate. The two plays are separated by several decades, but they both function as part of the re-presentation of Texan cultural identity—one to reinforce the traditional white, male perspective, the other to problematize such a characterization by foregrounding a racial character previously omitted from Texas historical plays and pageants.

Within the space of historical drama, it has been possible for subversive engagement with revolutionary pedagogy to occur. *The Angel of Goliad,* despite its historical inaccuracies, presents a far more complex picture of the Mexican soldier than does any depiction of Santa Anna in the pageants. Margraff's deconstruction not only of the archetypal characters but also of the heroic mythology that surrounds them recasts the roles of Anglos, Tejanos, and Mexicans alike into a more complex field of performative interactions than allowed by revolutionary pedagogy. Margraff sees her drama as "an inquiry of the space between a stage combat blow, its acoustics, and its point of contact. Possibly a point of suture/complicity for all those who dwell or pass through its geography in such shapes as Texas and who come into contact with any relic conjuring its residual 'vibratto.'"[83]

The impact of historical dramas in modifying the didactic messages of revolutionary pedagogy has been slight. *The Angel of Goliad,* ultimately, tells a fictional tale about a fictional character, the wife of Captain Álvarez (Alavez). While still compelling, Álvarez' own true story becomes subsumed within that of the Goliad Massacre. Both Travis' derogatory, if not outright racist, speech in *Cloud of Witnesses* and the white- (or brown-) washing of Tejanos as Mexican enemies in Paul Green's *Lone Star* make the accuracy of most historical dramas more a reflection of revolutionary pedagogy than of the true complexity of the historical events they claim to depict. These portrayals downplay the sacrifices of all while they play up racial stereotypes and animosity. The power of Texas' historical memory is strong, but what it remembers is deliberate. What it represents on stage is a tribute to its heroes and a prison to its perceived foes.

FILMS

The role once occupied by pageants and historical dramas, particularly in the first half of the twentieth century, has been usurped by Hollywood (and its satellites). The cinema has contributed greatly to the creation and maintenance of Texas' historical memory by allowing for films that craft a narrative that reflects both the events represented and the time period in which the film was produced. Over the years, the Alamo story has been represented a dozen times on the big screen and even more times on television. The first film about the battle, *The Immortal Alamo,* was released in 1911, before the earliest pageants on the subject began to appear. The most recent incarnation, Disney's new live-action *The Alamo,* opened across the country in the spring of 2004.[84]

Perhaps the most famous of these films is John Wayne's *The Alamo* (1960), a cinematic monstrosity that merges the historical setting with fictional characters and events, ideological conjecture, and a heroic, if inaccurate, battle sequence complete with the destruction of the famous Alamo chapel by a dying Crockett, who tosses a torch into the powder kegs stored there. The film, which Wayne directed and in which he stars as Davy Crockett,[85] was filmed on location at Happy Shahan's Alamo Village, a constructed set located two and half hours west of San Antonio and a little over half an hour from the border towns of Del Rio/Ciudad Acuña and Eagle Pass/Piedras Negras in southwest Texas. Located in the midst of Shahan's 22,000-acre cattle ranch, the replicas of the Alamo compound and its nearby companion small town rise out of the landscape, providing a much more satisfying image of historical "authenticity" than the real Alamo's setting in urban San Antonio. Some Texas guidebooks even suggest visiting Brackettville, not San Antonio, for a "purer" Alamo experience.[86] The Alamo shrine may be the archaeological repository of Texas' cultural memory, then, but revolutionary pedagogy favors a site that provides a sense of "authenticity" (see Photo 13).

Attempts to make the Texas Revolution less of a monument to American colonialism or to victory over Mexico seek to make the Alamo "perform" for all cultures, often by inverting and contesting the story as it has been previously written. The story of Juan Seguín (who was in the Alamo until sent out as a courier by Travis) was told in a 1982 film made for the PBS series *American Playhouse* by director Jesús Treviño. The film is the first to represent Tejanos within the revolutionary narrative and to consider not only their contributions to the Revolution but also their mixed feelings about their participation. In one scene, set inside the Alamo, two

Tejano soldiers debate the situation. One says, "We're on the wrong side." The other responds, "There is more to brotherhood than blood."[87] The two men reach no conclusions about the "right" thing to do; they fight and die with the rest of the soldiers when Santa Anna attacks.

Treviño's film, shot at Alamo Village, caused a controversy among Chicano scholars at the time (advisor Rudolfo Acuña resigned in protest). *Seguín* also featured Edward James Olmos as Santa Anna in, according to one critic, "the most despicable, snarling, vicious portrayal since Walter Long's drug-crazed Santa Anna in *Martyrs of the Alamo.*"[88] The focus on Tejano characters in a complex historical moment and blended with a stereotypical representation of Santa Anna captures the legacy of omitting non-Anglo characters from Texas revolutionary pedagogy: now they are welcome to appear as defenders of the Alamo, but Mexicans are still the enemy.

The representation of Tejanos (Mexican Texans) who sided with the Texians and their role in the Revolution has long been fraught with tension.[89] This is due, in large part, to Santa Anna, who, as the self-styled Napoleon of the West, treated all of Mexico in general and the uprising in Texas in particular as an opportunity to showcase his military brilliance. Texas was not the only province to mutiny after Santa Anna abolished the federalist Constitution of 1824; indeed, he spent much of 1835–1836 crushing rebellions in other Mexican provinces. Although historical representations depict the American Texians as the instigators of revolutionary thought, members of Santa Anna's own government—including Sen. José Mexía, Coahuila y Tejas governor Agustín Viesca, Mexican plenipotentiary to France and first vice president of the Texas Republic Lorenzo de Zavala, and Texian army captain Juan Seguín—fanned the flames of resistance in Texas after Santa Anna declared himself dictator in 1832.[90]

Despite these and other contributions to the defeat of tyranny, Tejanos living in the Republic of Texas after the Revolution were dispossessed of their property, harassed, and forced to flee or, in some cases, killed.[91] Many of them used their political knowledge, gained from having fought for Mexico's freedom from Spanish rule in 1808, to set up the federal government and to help elect Tejanos to positions in city and republican governments. And they did not hesitate to petition (unsuccessfully) the newly formed Republic for redress of wrongs committed against them by Anglo-Texans and newly arrived American immigrants.[92]

Historians have more recently asserted that the presence of Tejanos in the Alamo and at San Jacinto indicates that the Revolution was not a racial or an ethnic conflict but a struggle against tyranny by all freedom-loving people. They point out that these fighters were entitled to land grants just like every other defender of the Alamo.[93] Others insist, however, that the presence of Tejanos on the Texian side is not an indication of equity between or unity among the native-born and the immigrants but, rather, of greed. Lorenzo de Zavala and Juan Seguín, for example, are seen as betraying their own government and culture in order to reap the economic benefits of closer ties with the United States, making them, in the words of Rudolfo Acuña, "a bunch of *cabrones* who sold out their own people."[94]

The stakes involved in representing Hispanics and the Alamo-as-event on film have resulted in the most extreme struggles over the representation of Texas and the Alamo. In 1967, the crew of the comedy *Viva Max!* came to San Antonio to film in front of the mission. (The interiors were to be shot in Rome, but the film's producer, Mark Carliner, decided to stage Max's procession to the Alamo in the streets of San Antonio and his showdown with American authorities in Alamo Plaza, with the Alamo itself positioned in the background.) While *Viva Max!* did what *Price of Freedom* did not—film at the actual Alamo site—it was the contents of the film and not the location that caused controversy.

Unlike the majority of Alamo films, *Viva Max!* is not a veneration of legendary events or mythic heroes. Peter Ustinov plays Max, the modern-day military leader of Mexico who decides to retake the Alamo to prove his military prowess. The film, like the book on which it is based, inverts many of the long-standing revolutionary tales like the line in the sand and plays them to comic effect. It also ridicules contemporary individuals, among them Pres. Lyndon B. Johnson, Texas governor John Connally, and a fictitious organization of outspoken "little old ladies in tennis shoes" called the Daughters of the Texas Revolution.[95]

The linking of present performances with the traditional representations of Texas heroism ruptures the historical distance fostered by pageants, dramas, and even earlier film versions of the Alamo battle. *Viva Max!* forces the Alamo, and the Texan performance that it supports, into a twentieth-century context that exposes how little about the image of Texas had changed in the intervening 130 years.

Although DRT members on site originally voiced no objections to the crew's presence (provided they stayed off the grass), on learning of the film's plot, the then-president, Mrs. William Scarborough, informed Carliner that his crew could not come anywhere near the shrine or include shots of the chapel in any of its scenes. Carliner, however, had already won permission to film on Alamo Plaza (over which the DRT has no jurisdiction) from the San Antonio City Council. (The council saw the advantages of having a film company inject over a million dollars into the local economy.) Mrs. Scarborough tried, and failed, to get a court injunction to stop the filming. When it became obvious that there was not a thing the DRT could do to prevent Carliner from including the chapel face in his film, they closed the Alamo to tourists during the film company's residency and draped the chapel doors in black. Scarborough couched her actions in the DRT's rhetoric of protecting the Alamo from desecration by outsiders who were misusing its image. She directly attacked the film's departure from earlier didactic representations of Alamo events, saying, "Why can't they make a nice movie like John Wayne?"[96]

Despite Wayne's obvious liberties with the historical events, his vision of the Alamo-as-event and its participants was more in line with the images of Texans and outsiders that were central to the maintenance of revolutionary pedagogy; therefore, Scarborough preferred his version, however inaccurate, to a satire which called the purity of the Alamo-as-event in Texas' cultural memory into question.

Ustinov, who plays the title character, Gen. Maximilian Rodrigues de Santos, was particularly mystified about all the controversy, saying, "Surely Texas is now a part of the United States. Otherwise they should be in permanent mourning over the U.S. occupation of the Republic."[97] In a way, Ustinov's sarcasm unmasks a provocative truth. *Viva Max!* was a performative moment which created a rupture in the performance of the Texan. By inverting the story of the Alamo, transporting it into contemporary society, and placing it in proximity to the Alamo itself, the film threatens the didactic power of the Alamo to perform within Texas' cultural memory. It reduces Texas performance to a series of stereotypical behaviors just as laughable as those of the enemy and, in fact, more so, since the Mexican general, Max, is the hero of the film.

Ultimately, *Viva Max!* does little to redeem the image of Hispanics and, by extension, Tejanos like Gregorio Esparza, who gave their lives in the Revolution. Max is an amalgamation of the comic "Pedro" figure—"usually pronounced as 'Paydro,' he is the fat, stupid but basically harmless peon"—and the Mexican bandit stereotype, "Pancho," whose attempted coup is unsuccessful.[98] To add insult to injury, Max is played by a European actor with a bad accent and stereotypical Latin American dictator mannerisms. He eventually inspires the loyalty of his men and the respect of his enemies, but it is winning the love of the young, blonde, blue-eyed Baylor University student who works in the Alamo gift shop that makes Max feel that his quest has been worthwhile.

The *Viva Max!* controversy did not affect the film's release or reception.

Contemporary viewers agree that the film has not aged well, but Ustinov's performance is brilliant, if overstated, and it remains "a family film with a sense of American history and some delicious ironies."[99]

Another engagement between Texas' cultural memory and those forces which have demanded new representations of the Alamo occurred in 1987. It concerned the newly built San Antonio Rivercenter IMAX Theatre and its feature attraction, *Alamo . . . The Price of Freedom.* The forty-eight-minute "documentary" was the brainchild of George McAllister, a Texas businessman and former college instructor who wanted to tell the "real" story of the Alamo. The film was designed specifically for the new Rivercenter IMAX Theatre (the lobby of which overlooks Alamo Plaza) and was intended to run until at least the turn of the century for the viewing benefit of tourists. At the outset, the Rivercenter IMAX Web site claimed that "the IMAX experience is so real you will feel you are at the center of history's unforgettable 13-day siege."[100] After its release, *Alamo . . . The Price of Freedom* was recognized by the National Cowboy Hall of Fame for its role in preserving the history of the West, a validation of its content and approach by persons involved in similar work.[101]

The initial script for *Alamo . . . The Price of Freedom* was meticulously researched. McAllister and the film's director, Kieth Merrill, made a serious attempt to create an "authentic" Alamo narrative. They took the bulk of the film's dialogue from historical accounts of the battle, hired battle reenactors to play the troops, renovated the compound at Alamo Village to reflect the latest theories about the structure and appearance of the mission in 1836 (although the chapel windows were left in place), and staged the battle in the predawn darkness. The film not only emphasizes the slaughter on both sides (the ending of the battle includes a pull-back shot which shows the compound littered with Mexican and Texan dead), it also includes the story of the Esparza brothers, one of whom died in the Alamo and the other of whom, a Mexican soldier, received permission from Santa Anna to bury him. The presentation, however, reinforces traditional revolutionary representations. The focus is still on the heroism of Travis, Bowie, Crockett, and the other Alamo defenders, and the prominent myths (the line in the sand, Moses Rose, Crockett going down swinging) are all present. Once again, Santa Anna is depicted as an egomaniacal, bloodthirsty dictator who refers to his soldiers as no more important than chickens and characterizes the battle and his losses as a "small affair."

Since it is difficult for earlier films to compete with a sixty-five-foot screen and fourteen thousand watts of stereo-surround sound, viewers of *Alamo . . . The Price of Freedom* are meant to feel not only that they have been in the heat of the battle but that the film battle and the narrative surrounding it are an accurate portrait of the events leading up to March 6, 1836. The film and its technological format convey a (literally) larger-than-life heroism which erases the changes made to the story, masks conflicts, subverts ideals, and erases any information that might negatively affect the protagonists' legendary status.

Prominent members of the Latino community, in particular, San Antonio city councilman Walter Martínez, were concerned about the portrayal of Tejanos and Mexicans in the film, especially in such a high-profile, tourist-oriented production.[102] An initial reading of the script did little to assuage their fears. The screening of the film to an invited audience caused a firestorm of controversy.[103] The Esparza brothers subplot was whittled down to one line in a scene with Santa Anna. Particularly grisly and disconcerting is a scene in which the body of Jim Bowie is hoisted aloft on bayonets by Mexican soldiers (shown in silhouette). In the end, the controversy surrounded the use of an "undocumented" flag as the one flying over the Alamo when it fell, undermining the supposed accuracy of the depiction which had been heralded by the writer/producer.[104] These events precipitated a press war in San Antonio and a series of public protests which lasted until the official opening of the film and the theatre on March 6, 1988.[105]

The fact that an IMAX film excited such controversy demonstrates the importance of performance to the maintenance of Texan identity and the didactic power of such performances over audiences. The attempt (however unsuccessful) to recast the role of the Alamo in Texan cultural memory into one more friendly to the Hispanic community indicates that the Alamo is not a dead space, even on film. Its story and presence remain a source of competition and contention in Anglo-Hispanic relations in Texas today, more than 150 years after the events it wants us to remember.

BATTLE REENACTMENTS

Battle reenactments provide the opportunity for a very compelling interactive form of performance. They are inherently performative precisely because they strive to present the look and feel of the battle and not to represent the battle events (including the deaths of one or more participants). The Musketeer Battle Club, based in Calgary, Alberta, for example, is "a social club for *17th century* enthusiasts who want to study or reenact these times in a fun way" (emphasis theirs). It is devoted to the study and performance not only of seventeenth-century battlefield technique but also of "costuming, music, food, and anything reflecting that era."[106] The club handbook states that "it is important that everyone participating in these battles wear as historically accurate clothing and arms & armour as possible, to enable everyone participating, to have a real feeling of going back in time." This distinction also heightens the reenactment's didactic potential. Since such great care has been taken in the costuming and firearms, audience members assume that equal care was taken making the decisions about what aspects of the story to represent. This desire for authenticity, however simulated it may be, is what gives the battle reenactment its power: through its desire to re-create the event as precisely as possible (short of actual fatalities), it becomes the event.

Civil War reenacting is the most famous type in this country. As many as fourteen thousand battle reenactors and their entourages of sutlers, medics, and camp followers can appear at the most popular Civil War events,[107] and a growing number of reenactors are being drawn to twentieth-century battles from World War I, World War II, and Vietnam. Twentieth-century portrayals, in the minds of some, raise questions of appropriateness, because the "safe historical distance" between historical event and current representation "collapses."[108] Even Civil War battles have the potential to reopen old wounds through their presentation of the Confederacy as a country struggling alone to resist Union tyranny. In many ways, Civil War reenactments function to create and maintain a "Confederate" identity, just as Texas revolutionary battle reenactments work to promulgate Texan cultural identity.

The role of the battle reenactor in the creation and maintenance of Texan cultural memory is that of spectator/participant. In order to convey the most accurate performance possible, the participant studies documents, visuals, and other remains of the time and place to gain a sense of the context of the event. Then he (usually, the soldiers are male; women play camp followers and nurses) begins to construct his own view of the events that he can perform for the benefit of spectators and fellow reenactors. Texan battle reenactor Gene Fogerty states that "re-enacting is about learning history by living it. It's about experiencing the hardships and the challenges as well as the victories of those who came before us, about paying tribute to men and women who made our country what it is, and very much about learning history in a more accurate way than reading books."[109]

In reenactments of Texas revolutionary battles, "amateur" history supplants "scholarship"; performance becomes the pedagogy. This is achieved not through visual memorialization, as in pageants, or theatrical characterization, as in historical drama, or spectacular visual effects, as in the cinema, but through the transformation of contemporary individuals into historical Texians and, subsequently, the Texans of today.

The most prominent battle reenactments in the United States focus on Civil War battles: Gettysburg, Vicksburg, and even Louisiana's Port Hudson. Reenactments and commemorations are also a large part of the Texas Revolution's pedagogical performance and occur yearly at battle sites and other locations, for example, the Alamo shrine in downtown San Antonio and at Happy Shahan's Alamo Village, the set for John Wayne's movie.[110] Reenactments may be small-scale affairs featuring local residents or large, semiprofessional shows staged by members of the many reenactment clubs throughout the state.

Sometimes the reenactments are part of larger festivals or celebrations. Since 1975, the town of Gonzales has commemorated its role as the "Lexington of Texas" (it was the site of the first shot fired in the Texas Revolution) with a three-day celebration entitled "Come and Take It" (the motto from the town's battle flag). Highlights of the event include a parade, tours of historic homes, a chicken-flying contest, and a reenactment of the battle (participants often include residents of the town).[111]

The annual reenactment of the Battle of Coleto and the Goliad Massacre at Goliad's Presidio La Bahía, begun in 1985, is a two-day affair that features three battle sequences; a candlelight tour of the mission featuring vignettes, lectures, and videotapes about the historical significance of the site; and a conjectural restaging of the execution. According to Presidio La Bahía director Newton Warzecha, the primary function of the entire event is to serve as a "teaching tool" (see Photo 14).[112]

The reenactment includes not only the battle sequences but also living history displays of period weapons, cooking styles, and military drill; the screening of films about La Bahía; and lectures by noted authors about the history of the area and major historical figures like Col. James Fannin. These extras give the visitor a sense of immediacy about historic events that is lacking in cinematic venues, even big-budget extravaganzas like *Alamo . . . The Price of Freedom.* They also help to prime the audience for its role as spectator in the reenactment: cheering when the Mexican army retreats; gasping at the sound of a cannon shot; or applauding as the armies leave the field (see Photo 15).

While there are battle reenactors who strive for complete accuracy and immersion in character—they attempt to become the character they represent in thought, word, and deed—the Goliad reenactors are more flexible. They use the modern restrooms available within the presidio and are more interested in conversation with one another than in maintaining a constant character façade. They freely converse with the visitors about everything, from what they eat to their real jobs. In this way, they present an approachable history, one that is neither removed by cinematic distance nor demarcated by the space of pageantry or historical drama.

Battle reenactors typically play more than one role, depending on the venue, and many find themselves on both sides of the field during the same event. At Goliad, Ricardo Villerreal, a longtime reenactor, plays both the Mexican officer who demands that the Texians be executed as Santa Anna ordered and Carlos de la Garza, a Tejano rancher who saves his Texian friend Nicholas Fagin (and several others) from execution.[113] (Villerreal plays Juan Seguín at Alamo reenactments.) Another reenactor, who plays the Mexican battlefield commander at Goliad, joked to me that he would be sure to "die" during the battle at San Jacinto either because the Texan reenactors treat the POWs badly or because the woolen Mexican uniform was too hot for late April in Baytown.

This ability to choose their roles in the events gives reenactors a performative perspective and allows them to craft an individual sense of revolutionary pedagogy that is comfortable for them. Unaddressed are questions of ethnicity—most of the Mexican army officers are played by Anglos—and the resulting animosity caused by the massacre of Fannin and his men following their capture (see Photo 16).

These events continue to have an impact on the relations within the space today. At the reenactment of the Goliad Massacre I watched, two men articulated diametrically opposing views of the importance of battle reenactments to remembering and learning from the events of the Revolution. They were roughly the same age and of roughly the same ancestry (European Mexican). One was a battle reenactor from San Antonio playing a Mexican at Goliad but scheduled to play a Texan at San Jacinto the next month. The other was a lifelong resident of Goliad who lives three blocks from Presidio La Bahía. One thought that the battle reenactments were a fun way to connect with his dual heritage and help other people, especially children, learn about history. He played both sides of the Revolution: at some events, he was a Texian soldier; at others, a Mexican officer. The Goliad resident saw the reenactments as damaging to what remains of the history—he and other Latino residents of Goliad who found the term "massacre" offensive. This resident, who did not participate in the reenactments, wanted the directors of La Bahía and the battle reenactors to leave the ghosts of the presidio in peace and focus more attention on the current socioeconomic problems of the area. He said that, with each successive reenactment, the real story of what happened at La Bahía became more fragmented and diffused, lost in the cheers of spectators and smoke from blank cannon and rifle shots.

These two men, unknown to one another but related through shared historical events, see the re-presentation of Texan historical memory from two diametrically opposing viewpoints, viewpoints which reflect the tensions in revolutionary pedagogy. To not represent the Revolution, they think, risks its eventually fading into obscurity, but with each representation, events become less about history and more about performance. As Don DeLillo observes in *White Noise,* using as an example the "most photographed barn in America," successive representations merely prevent the viewers (and, to some extent, participants) from actually seeing a site.[114] Such elision in battle reenacting also blocks the viewers' ability to reflect on a reenactment's subsequent impact on the performance of the Texan in contemporary society. If, as Gene Fogerty asserts, "re-enactors also know the value of teaching history as it really was, so that the memories of those who shaped today do not become blurred or forgotten and that the truth might be known,"[115] the choices made by reenactors as to their roles and performed actions not only determine the structure of the events that they portray but also foreground how, and even when Texan historical memory returns to the site of the revolutionary event.

Revolutionary pedagogy determines the nature of the regional performance at a grassroots level, reinforcing the larger, grander cinematic and theatrical pedagogies that have come down over time. As a 1998 editorial in the *Austin American-Statesman* observes, "It feels good, after all, to be a Texan—to be a part of something big and grandiose and part of a sweep of history that began with the first Indians to set foot on this part of the world."[116] Yet this "big, grandiose something" has, at its heart, a very particular mission: the creation, maintenance, and dissemination of Texan cultural identity as a very specific set of racial and gender practices, practices that privilege traditional white, male viewpoints. The conflicts surrounding their performance show how Texan cultural memory reinforces traditional oppositions of race, ethnicity, and gender as a part of its contribution to the performance of regionality.

CONCLUSION

Texan historical memory makes no distinction between facts and legends, at least when defining the Revolution as a heroic space of Texan sacrifice and victory over the Mexican menace. Myth *is* history and is commemorated as such, as, for example, with the plaque at the Alamo shrine that marks the spot of Travis' line in the sand in front of the chapel and another nearby that indicates where, "legend states," David Crockett fell. The numerous "historical" fictions which take as their central characters Moses Rose, Emily Morgan/West, and Francita Alavez further cloud the construction of revolutionary pedagogy. Even contemporary Texas historians and filmmakers acknowledge that the stories surrounding the Alamo are often more powerful, and more easily remembered, than the facts of the siege and the battle, and therefore can contribute more easily to the maintenance of the Alamo as a pedagogical object of national narration.

Yet the entire mission of Kevin Young, Stephen Hardin, and many of the historians who study the Revolution has been to re-present that story by contesting its most famous elements.[117] Did Travis draw the line in the sand? Was Moses Rose ever inside the Alamo? Was Davy Crockett cut down in the heat of battle while swinging Old Betsy, or did he survive only to be executed minutes later on Santa Anna's order? Did Emily Morgan/West, the Yellow Rose of Texas, really "distract" Santa Anna in his tent?

In the present moment of the pageant, past and future scripts combine through pageant performance. *Texas under Six Flags,* for example, contains a parenthetical notation that the March 2 signing scene is "optional."[118] Who needs a scene about a piece of paper to solidify one's history when a grand national narrative can perform the same function? The Revolution-as-event has been transformed into a revolutionary pedagogy for Texan cultural memory. Through performance, Texans and outsiders are constantly reminded of the conflicts inherent in their cultural identities. These performances also provide a context for contemporary debates surrounding the maintenance and communication of Texas history to future generations.

As the historical facet of Texan cultural memory fulfills its pedagogical function, it clearly delineates between the heroes and the villains within revolutionary narrative. The casting of Mexicans and Indians as others and crises surrounding the accurate representation of revolutionary events continually foreground those events' heterogeneous nature. It is the ability of Texan historical memory to forge these disparate strands of revolutionary narrative into an unbroken fabric of heroism versus tyranny on which Texan cultural memory depends.[119] The historical accuracy of this narrative is related less to the actual events it claims to represent than to the "spirit" of those events and leads to the re-visioning, misrepresentation, and re-presentation of multiple and, often, conflicting narratives as different groups vie for control of the histories of the Texas Revolution.

PHOTO I

The Alamo, San Antonio, Texas, 1997. Photograph by the author.

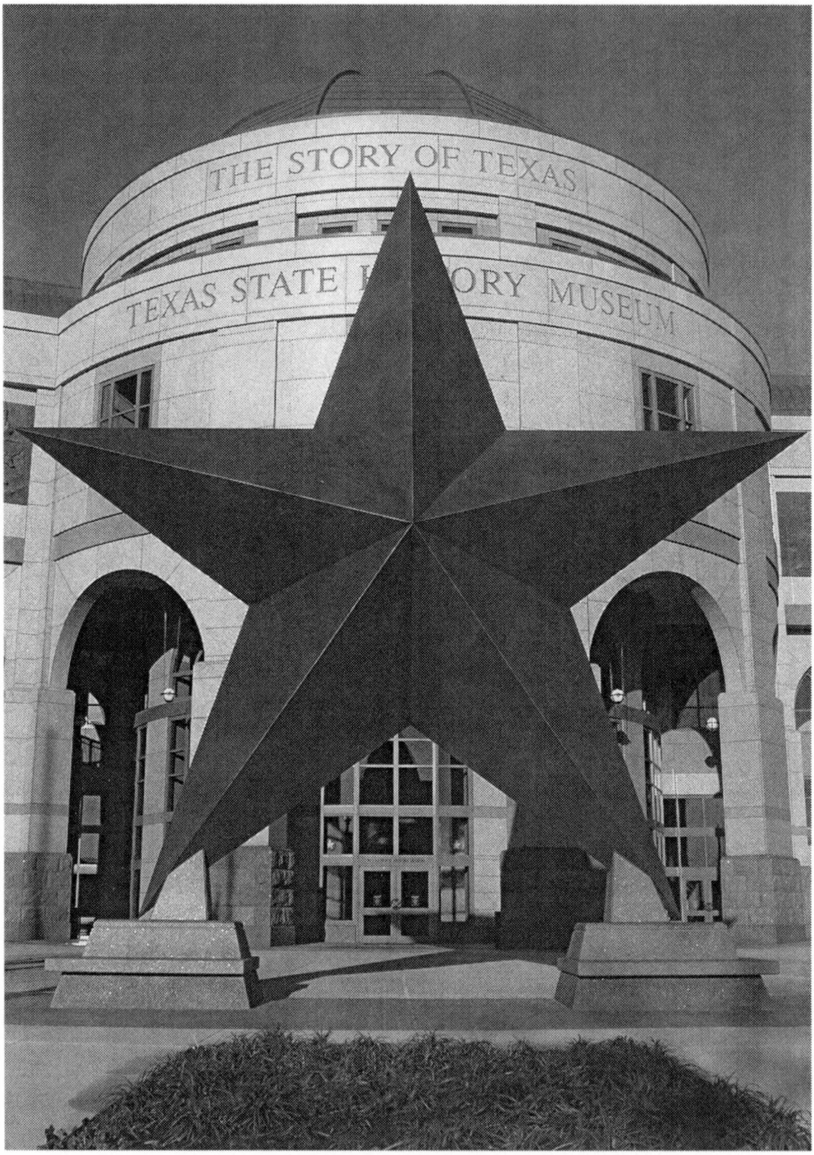

PHOTO 2
Entrance to the Bob Bullock Texas State History Museum, Austin, 2002.
Used with permission.

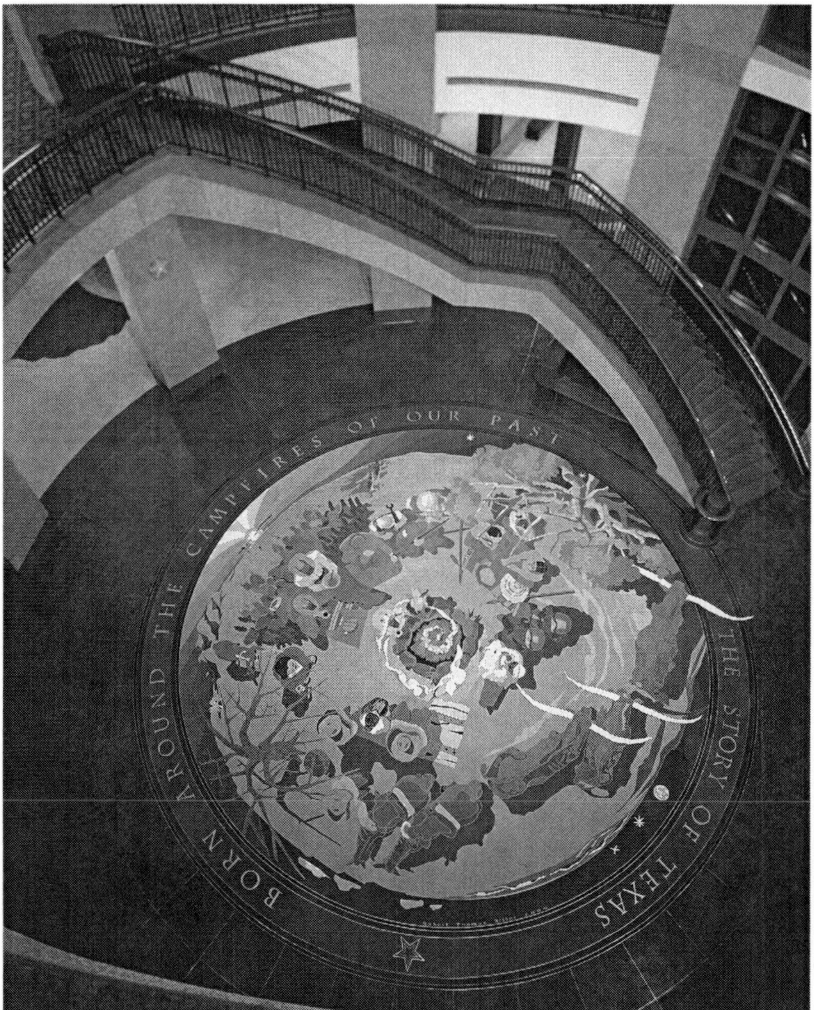

PHOTO 3

Rotunda, Bob Bullock Texas State History Museum, 2002.

© Robert Ritter. Used with permission.

PHOTO 4
Exhibit Hall, Bob Bullock Texas State History Museum, 2002.
Used with permission.

PHOTO 5

Historical marker, Shiner Opera House, Texas, 2005. Photograph by the author.

PHOTO 6

Historical markers, the Battle of Gonzales, Texas, 2005. Photograph by the author.

PHOTO 7

The Eggleston House with historical marker, Gonzales, Texas, 2005. Photograph by the author.

PHOTO 8

Dawn at the Alamo. *Courtesy of the State Preservation Board, Austin, Texas, CHA 1989.81. Photograph by Perry Huston, August 3, 1994, postconservation.*

PHOTO 9

Reenactment of the execution of the wounded Texians, 20th Annual Goliad Massacre–Fort Defiance Living History Program, 2005. Photograph by the author.

PHOTO 10
The Surrender of Santa Anna, *William Henry Huddle, 1886.*
Courtesy of the State Preservation Board, Austin, Texas, CHA *1989.46.*
Photographer unknown, pre-1991, preconservation.

PHOTO 11

Angel of Goliad memorial, Fannin Battleground State Historic Site, Goliad, Texas, 2005. Photograph by the author.

PHOTO 12

Cast photo, A Cloud of Witnesses, *1958. © Getty Images.*

PHOTO 13

The Alamo chapel façade, Alamo Village, Brackettville, Texas, 1997.
Photograph by the author.

PHOTO 14

Reenactor Dennis Reidesel as Texian soldier Isaac Hamilton in "Isaac Hamilton—A Prisoner," first-person living history performance, 20th Annual Goliad Massacre–Fort Defiance Living History Program, 2005. Photograph by the author.

PHOTO 15

Texian army reenactors in their campground, 20th Annual Goliad Massacre–Fort Defiance Living History Program, 2005. Photograph by the author.

PHOTO 16

Reenactment of the execution of Col. James Fannin, 20th Annual Goliad Massacre–Fort Defiance Living History Program, 2005. Photograph by the author.

PHOTO 17

Jaston Williams (left) as Vera Carp, and Joe Sears as Aunt Pearl Burras. Photograph by Bill Records. © Greater Tuna Corporation, 1999.

PHOTO 18

Jaston Williams (left) as Charlene Bumiller, and Joe Sears as Bertha Bumiller. Photograph by Bill Records. © Greater Tuna Corporation, 1999.

PHOTO 19
David Crockett, *John Gadsby Chapman. Harry Ransom Humanities Research Center, The University of Texas at Austin.*

FOUR

"WHAT'S THE MATTER WITH YOU PEOPLE?"

The Performance of Authentic Behavior in Small-Town Texan Plays

If you can find someplace you like better than Tuna . . . MOVE!

GREATER TUNA

In 1932, writer and Texas native Nelson Algren wrote about the life and travels of the vagrant rail rider, whose ability to stay out of small-town jails depended on his knowledge of the behavior of the towns' inhabitants.[1] Through traveling, the rider learned which towns and trains were friendly: "I should go to Mobile, to Tucson, to Orange [Texas]—anywhere I should choose to go. I could get my right arm tattooed in New Orleans . . . I'd ship out from Houston or perhaps from Port Arthur, I'd get to know all the tough spots as well as the easy ones. I'd always know just where to go next, I'd always be larking and joking with people."[2]

Algren's characterization of the Texas regional landscape as a (hostile) field of relations through which the traveler must move in order to survive directly mirrors the performance of Texan cultural identity as a learned behavior, a body of information that keeps the traveler safe and ensures an entertaining, or at least interesting, journey.

While the better-known locations of Texan performance occur within the confines of specifically demarcated architectural and historical spaces, the entire idea of Texas' geography is itself a large part of the construction of Texan cultural identity. A web of small towns weaves through the disparate landscape, like the trains in Algren's stories, tying together such historical and contemporary cities as San Antonio, Austin, Dallas, and Houston. These cities draw on a map of small-town behaviors often categorized as typically Texan performances.

Images of small-town Texas have been immortalized in mainstream media by such diverse visionaries as Larry McMurtry (*Lonesome Dove*), James Michener (*Texas*), Tobe Hooper (*The Texas Chainsaw Massacre*), and Buzz Bissinger (*Friday Night Lights*). Mainstream and corporate media performances focus on primarily white male actors and characters.[3] Most tourists experience small Texas towns only through such images and may even expect residents to behave in the quaint, backward, or bizarre fashions that they have read about in books or seen in films. Confined to either urban centers or specially crafted tourist areas, tourists' wanderings often convey the same otherworldly strangeness as the Alamo and other designated pedagogical destinations.

Television's renditions of small-town Texas life address a wide range of behavioral topics—from Mike Judge's animated comedy *King of the Hill* (1997–) to headline-inspired movies (*The Texas Cadet Murder* [1997] and the *Positively True Adventures of the Alleged Texas Cheerleader-murdering Mom* [1993]) to cinematic dramatizations of such Texan obsessions as college and high school football (*Necessary Roughness* [1991] and the film version of *Friday Night Lights* [2004]). Such representational practices indicate the ways in which film and television have perpetuated Texas as a place of otherness within the United States.

It is unusual for dramatizations of small-town Texas life to draw overtly on revolutionary pedagogy, the practice through which citizens and tourists are inculcated with appropriate attitudes toward Texas' revolutionary history and that history's impact on Texan cultural identity. Instead, dramatizations use the inhabitants of Texas towns to create the common, everyday persons whose values and virtues reflect the sense of place and history unique to Texan cultural identity, even as these inhabitants search for meaning in their own lives. Plays that create small-town Texas life on the stage (e.g., the towns of Bradleyville [from Preston Jones' *Texas Trilogy*], Tuna [from the *Tuna* plays by Joe Sears, Jaston Williams, and Ed Howard], and Harrison [from Horton Foote's *Orphan's Home Cycle*]) present the contemporary small town as home to racism, religious fervor, and corruption in everyday life and reinforce a view of Texan cultural identity as white and male dominated. These matrices of character type resonate with viewers and remind them of their own regional identities.

One can "walk" through imaginary Texan towns as one might walk through any city, large or small, and distinguish between larger, generic narratives (such as revolutionary pedagogy) and the smaller, yet more universal, behavioral narratives found in each town. In "Walking the City," Michel de Certeau says that only the "big things" are visible when one looks at the city from the top down. Walking the city, on the other hand, allows the tourist to take in the sights from eye level, to temporarily merge with the city and become a part of the site he or she is touring yet remain distinct from the natives. The experience of walking through the city as a process through which fields of relationships not visible from above becomes apparent. These fields of relationships form what Certeau terms "spaces" and "places," where spaces mean images of a field, and places, the practical fields themselves. In Certeau's view, "places are fragmentary and inward turning histories, pasts that others are not allowed to read, accumulated times that can be unfolded but like stories held in reserve, [remain] in an enigmatic state."[4] Although a place implies stability, this stability masks divergent and often contradictory messages and their relationship to larger historical and cultural narratives. In the case of Texan cultural identity, small towns appear to be stable entities but, on closer examination, are in fact continuously shifting fields of behaviors that keep identity fluid.

Certeau's concepts offer a unique insight into Texan cultural identity, because "walking the city" provides a way to localize larger discourses, such as those analyzed in Chapters 2 and 3, in representations of the small town and to identify within them points of reference to the previously developed notions of Texan cultural identity. Small-town plays and celebrations of small towns "open up clearings"; they "allow a certain play within a system of defined places." Small towns expose a discourse constructed from a "system of defined places,"[5] just as local authorities, in Certeau's view, create "a crack in the system that saturates places with signification and . . . reduces them to this signification that it is 'impossible to breathe in them.'"[6] In small-town celebrations, and the fictive Texas towns of Tuna, Bradleyville, and Harrison, the historical Texan is subverted and reorganized into a story of the "real," "average" Texan, a Texan at a further remove from the originary myth of the Revolution but clearly the inheritor of it.

CELEBRATING THE SMALL TOWN: THE TEXAS CENTENNIAL CELEBRATION, PART I

In 1936, Texas turned one hundred years old, and from January 1 to December 31, 1936, the state revisited all of the major occurrences in its history as part of the Texas Centennial Celebration. The purpose of this twelve-month statewide party, according to one historian, was twofold. It served both "to honor the heroes who helped establish Texas and to exhibit to the world the achievements of one hundred years of independence . . . In this period Texans openly professed a deep sense of pride in their heritage, while at the same time . . . they harbored an inferiority complex when compared to the older, settled regions of the nation."[7]

Regional and local elements remained central to the overall celebration.

While nothing of the exposition would remain in Dallas after 1936 but the Cotton Bowl, the performance of Texas history would continue indefinitely. In 1935, the Centennial Commission officially designated the town of Gonzales "the Lexington of Texas" for firing the first shots at the Mexican army, and a monument was erected in the town.[8] That same year, the town held its first "Come and Take It" celebration during the first weekend in October to commemorate the battle.

Other towns across Texas planned festivals which celebrated either a historic event (such as the observance of the fall of Fort Parker at Groesbeck-Mexia [May 19]), offered a particular delicacy for which the region was known (such as Yoakum's Tom Tom Festival [June 5–6]), or commemorated a long-standing tradition (such as Odessa's Jack Rabbit Rodeo and Roping [September 17–19]).[9] These celebrations were incorporated into the overall Centennial structure, appeared in the Centennial calendar, and were advertised through the Centennial Commission's weekly newsletter, the *Texas Centennial Review,* which sustained, at its height, an average issue readership of nearly fifteen thousand.[10] After the celebration ended, these small-town festivals continued, most to this day, serving as both a remnant of the original statewide celebration and a reminder of the importance of small towns in the construction of the state's image.

The "mapping" of Texas began as part of a plan to market the state to newly developing automobile tourism. Using the historical markers discussed previously, the Centennial Commission made it possible for people to virtually walk (or, more accurately, drive) the paths of famous and not-so-famous events. Festivals provided the small towns with an opportunity to showcase their unique features to visitors and to build a sense of contemporary identity not necessarily grounded in revolutionary pedagogy.[11] These festivals constructed an image of small Texas towns that was grounded in particular attributes found in the individual towns and unique to their own space of representation. They allowed visitors a glimpse beneath the heroic grandeur of the revolutionary narrative at battle sites and attractions, and the commercialization of Texas' resources at the Centennial Exposition turned the real Texas into a witness for authentic behavior in small-town life.

The Centennial Commission foregrounded the celebration of small-town life in the State of Texas to help develop the image of the Texan and represent it in terms other than those characters of the Revolution. These towns located themselves as the local authorities, the true repositories of stability in Texan cultural identity. The Centennial's desire to stabilize small-town Texas discourse served the opposite effect: it created a permanent landscape of instability, a constantly changing field of relations that must continually be renegotiated, as each town claimed its own centrality and importance to Texan cultural identity.

The importance of Texas' small towns did not wane once the Centennial passed. In fact, as Texas grew and small towns became not-so-small towns in population, small-town behaviors became even more necessary to keep the small-town space stable. Small-town life started popping up on-screen in films such as *The Last Picture Show* (1971) and *Paris, Texas* (1984) and on television in miniseries such as *Lonesome Dove* (1989). The comedic elements of small-town life, however, have proven more enduring, nowhere more so than in Texas' most famous small town of the moment, Arlen, home of the Hill family.

THE TELEVISED SMALL TOWN: ARLEN, TEXAS

Mike Judge's successful animated comedy *King of the Hill* (1997–) is the story of the Hill family and its circle of friends, neighbors, and relatives living in the town of Arlen (loosely based on a small-town version of Austin). Hank, a former high school football star, proudly sells propane and propane accessories, while wife, Peggy, is a substitute Spanish teacher. Their only child, Bobby (who by Hank's own admission is "just not right"), provides the couple with opportunities for concern and distraction as he gets involved in all of the things that run counter to Hank's notions of "manliness": modeling (season 2), home economics (season 6), witchcraft (season 7), and peer counseling (season 8). Rounding out the main cast are Hank's niece by marriage, Luanne; his friends Dale (the conspiracy theorist), the unintelligible Boomhauer (who, according to Molly Ivins, longtime reporter and writer about Texas, is "the first real Texan I ever saw on TV"),[12] and Bill, who is still trying to recover from the departure (and frequent reappearance, especially when he dates former Texas governor Ann Richards) of his wife, Lenore. Hank's next-door neighbors are the Kahn family from Laos. Khan Sr. frequently locks horns with Hank over lawn care and the best way to cook hamburgers; however, Bobby and Khan Jr. (who is female) are best friends. Semirecurring cast members include Hank's boss, Mr. Strickland, a mini-J. R. Ewing throwback; Hank's father, Grandpa Cotton (who had his shins blown off in "The Big One"); John Redcorn, a Native American who is the real father of Dale's son (and Bobby's friend), Joseph.

In many ways, Hank embodies what many would call the typical male Texan in his behavior. Hank does not cook, except for hamburgers on the propane grill; he loves mowing the lawn with his riding lawn mower, watching the Dallas Cowboys, fishing, camping, and working on cars. Some popular reviewers have compared Hank's compelling character with earlier icons of cultural identity: "Like Archie Bunker before him, Hank Hill is challenged by the culture clashes of modern American life. But where Archie wore blinders, Hank stumbles toward enlightenment as he deals with new Laotian neighbors; supports wife Peggy's foray into pro Boggle tournaments; doggedly resists the charms of Peggy's airhead niece, Luan[n]e; and does his fatherly best with his sharp-but-schlubby teenage boy ('Bobby, if you weren't my son, I'd hug you')."[13]

Hank may do his "fatherly best," but he is concerned that he pass authentic Texan behaviors on to his only son, just as his father, Cotton, tried to pass them on to him (as the episodes reveal, however, these were not the same types of behaviors; Cotton celebrated Hank's high school graduation by taking Hank and his friends to a brothel). Hank spends much of his time trying to make Bobby a "man" by teaching him to fish and shoot (Bobby is a better shot), getting him to play football and baseball (he plays soccer and ends up on the wrestling team), taking auto shop as an elective (he becomes a peer counselor). As a result, his efforts to stabilize typical male behavior in the Texan is only further undercut, as Bobby gravitates toward activities that seem, in Hank's eyes, to be less manly than those of which he approves.

Despite the traditional point of view displayed by Hank in certain areas, the show deals with and shows him and his family reacting to situations with behaviors that might not be considered typically Texan. Peggy's anger at her father-in-law for teaching Bobby sexist behavior marks her as a latent feminist, despite her assertions to the contrary: "I am not a feminist, Hank. I am Peggy Hill, citizen of the Republic of Texas. I work hard, I sweat hard, and I love hard and I gotta look pretty while I'm doing it. So, I comb my hair, I reapply lipstick 30 times a day, I do your dishes, I wash your clothes and I clean the house. Not because I have to, Hank, but because of a mutual unspoken agreement that I have never brought up because I am too much of a lady."[14]

Peggy is not the only member of the Hill family whose behavior destabilizes the authenticity of small-town Texan behavior. Bobby's modeling career positions him as a latent metrosexual (or at least a parody of one), and his fondness for "nonmanly" activities such as gardening and counseling further reinforces his departure from the norms of manly Texan (and childhood) behaviors.

Even Hank illustrates such tendencies against the stereotypical behaviors of his friends and other townspeople. In one episode, he forgoes watching the Cowboys in the Super Bowl to watch Luanne's local show, "Manger Babies."[15] Another time, he supports Bobby's work on the school's organic garden, despite its pitting Hank against his beloved football team (of which he was the star in his day).[16] Hank is, in the end, less stereotypical than the other residents of Arlen are.

The supporting characters highlight the fact that the Hill family is "progressive" in its behavior while still standing by its traditional Texan identity traits. In Arlen, then, there has been some progress; while the focus of *King of the Hill* is still on the central white male character, there is an acknowledgment of diversity and complexity on the part of its characters.

The map of Arlen created by the behaviors of its main characters problematizes the seemingly stereotypical characters who populate the town. Actions taken by Hank, Peggy, and Bobby stand out against the more stereotypical reactions of their friends and neighbors, as when Bobby and Kahn Jr. resolve the potential gender conflict over who will win a school wrestling team tryout match between the two of them by choreographing a "professional" match like those in the video games they play.[17] Likewise, Hank Hill always seems to make the nontraditional decision, even if he arrives at it for the traditional reasons. Usually his decisions spring from guilt or other emotions that force him to change his mind. The fact that he arrives at the right choice, however, legitimates his less-than-intelligent way of getting there and, in fact, upholds his ignorance as the "appropriate" behavior for a plain-speaking Texas man. When supposedly more enlightened, "liberal" characters appear on the show (e.g., Anthony Page, the latte-swilling social worker;[18] Emily, the guitar teacher with "dreadlocks, a tattoo and combat boots";[19] or Mona, the environmental activist),[20] they are shown to be more narrow-minded in their expectations of how Hank will behave than the supposedly "redneck" Hank is in his expectations of their behavior.

King of the Hill plays with issues of gender, race, and sexuality about which Texans supposedly hold backward views—Title IX, gays—while poking fun at the so-called liberals (social workers, witches, etc.) who populate the town. The Hills find novel solutions to the most pressing personal and social issues while retaining their supposedly guileless, narrow-minded Texan point of view. The map created by *King of the Hill,* then, is one that permits Texans to behave in an unsophisticated manner within a field of relationships that includes the ability for them to make progressive choices about social and cultural issues that apply to their own families. None of these behaviors directly draw on Texas history or revolutionary pedagogy, Peggy's assertion that she is "a citizen of the Republic of Texas" aside,[21] and only one episode of the show prior to 2006 deals directly with Texas history.[22] Instead, the show uses the historical backdrop created by revolutionary pedagogy to put forth the point of view of the small-town inhabitant, the modern-day Texan, with all his traditional, and not-so-traditional, ideas. This interplay keeps the map created by the interrelationships of these characters perpetually unstable, as new ideas come in contact (and conflict) with old. As one reviewer has said, "Hank Hill has managed to remain 'King' among his friends, even when, at times, he is plainly wrong, and his traditional values and conventional thinking prove inadequate to current situations."[23]

King of the Hill is important to the understanding of Texan cultural identity. It is a contemporary television show that reaches millions of viewers each week, with both new episodes and repeats. It has an advantage over similar comedies, such as *The King of Queens,* which purport to represent a distinct regional identity, in that the Hill family is animated, not "real." The show has been around since 1997, but Hank, Peggy, Bobby, and the other characters have not aged much at all.[24] This lack of chronological growth on the part of the characters means that the show does not have to focus solely on adolescent development and the other issues that many situation comedies must take up. Since nobody on the show grows old (or, in the case of the children, grows up), *King of the Hill* has the freedom to explore issues that more traditional situation comedies might pass on, due to age limitations on the cast.[25]

Yet, despite this inherent freedom, *King of the Hill* is a reification of the historical Texan in contemporary terms. Hank's sense of pride in his Texan ideas is part of his performance of regionality and helps reinforce the viewers' ideas of what life in a real small Texas town is like. The characters are stable signifiers of traditional Texan values. The show depicts liberals as flawed or fools and valorizes the attitudes of the "king," which are traditional revolutionary ones: independence, suffering, the prevailing spirit of victory.

TEXAS HUMOR GOES NATIONAL: PRESTON JONES' *BRADLEYVILLE/TEXAS TRILOGY*

In 1975, the Kennedy Center for the Performing Arts sponsored a Bicentennial Humanities Program (seminar 26 May 1976) to celebrate and promote the study of American literature and culture during the country's two-hundredth birthday. One of its offerings was a trilogy of plays by Preston Jones, a Texas playwright who worked with the Dallas Theater Center. These plays—*The Last Meeting of the Knights of the White Magnolia, Lu Ann Hampton Laverty Oberlander,* and *The Oldest Living Graduate*—form the "Bradleyville Trilogy," an overview of life in a fictitious town in West Texas. When the plays returned to the Kennedy Center for a run from April 29 to June 7, 1976,[26] they became known as the *Texas Trilogy.* The three plays are set in the fictional town of Bradleyville, Texas (population 6,000), which Jones describes as "a small, dead West Texas town in the middle of a big, dead West Texas prairie between Abilene and San Angelo. The new highway has bypassed it and now the world is trying to."[27]

The plays feature a diverse cross section of the town's population, including the town scion and his scheming family, members of the local answer to the KKK, and one of the town's longtime residents: a twice-married hairdresser with a teenage daughter, a drunkard elder brother, and an invalid mother. Characters move in and out of all these plays, which provides the loose web of relations on which Jones hangs his examination of small-town Texas life.

Jones' Bradleyville resembles many of the small towns linked by the Centennial marker project that were later bypassed by the interstate system. The town is a vehicle through which Jones maps Texan behaviors in all their complexity, beginning with the way that he structures the interconnection between the scripts themselves.

The three plays do not form a linear temporal sequence: *Lu Ann Hampton Laverty Oberlander* ranges from 1953 to 1973; *The Oldest Living Graduate* is set in 1962; and *The Last Meeting of the Knights of the White Magnolia* takes place between Acts 1 and 2 of *Graduate.* This fluidity of time makes traditional outlining of the events nearly impossible; one must fully engage with these three plays at eye level in order to master the landscape. The order in which the plays are performed also has a profound impact on the look of the terrain and is crucial to the process of destabilizing the town's narrative. Colonel Kincaid appears in *Magnolia,* for example, where he seems to be a doddering, senile, wheelchair-bound man. In *Graduate,* however, he displays strength of will and character when he refuses to attend a celebration planned in his honor as the oldest living graduate of the Mirabeau B. Lamar Military Academy: "To hell with it! Git your ass out of here and take your by-God oldest living graduate outfit with you. Ah don't want it, don't want no part of it. Not worth it. Not worth a bumble-dickin' goddamned thing! It ain't no honor to be the oldest livin' anything. Oldest livin' graduate, oldest livin' Indian, oldest living' armadillo, oldest livin' nuthin', cause that means that you're all alone! Stand around lookin' at the next-oldest livin' whippersnapper and wonder where the hell ever'body went."[28]

Similarly, Claudine Hampton, who plays Colonel Kincaid's nurse in *Graduate,* ends up an invalid from a stroke by the end of *Lu Ann.* If *Lu Ann* opens before *Graduate* (which was the case both at the Kennedy Center and on Broadway), the audience's perceptions of time are destabilized, because it has already "seen" her fate, disrupting the traditional narrative form.

Another way in which Jones deceives Texan cultural identity is by having no actual heroes in his plays. Unlike historical pageants or dramas of Texas history, there are no Bowies, Crocketts, or Spirits of Progress to champion the causes of freedom and growth. The characters in Jones' plays are everyday people (some more likeable than others) who are just trying to make a living in a forgotten town while dreaming of starting a better life or gaining some sense of accomplishment, however fleeting. They succumb to the same stereotypical behaviors that have long been associated with, but are not limited to, "Texans": racism, sexism, militarism, and so on. Their solutions, however, unlike those of Hank Hill and his family, belie an understanding of exactly how the system works and what it means to buy into those ideas. For example, while it is true that Bradleyville has seen the last meeting of the Knights of the White Magnolia, the racist spirit is still alive there. Former Knight of the White Magnolia Red Grover explains: "You don't put down the sons-of-bitchin' freedom riders and minority bastards with all this crap any more. You got to look for the loopholes, pal. Let 'em squawk about lunchrooms and schools all they want. In mah place ah simply reserve the right to refuse service to anybody. You look for the loopholes."[29] Grover's bar, featured in Act 2 of *Lu Ann,* does indeed contain a sign bearing these words. Nobody walks in to challenge the sign, indicating that racial lines are clearly and concretely drawn in this town.

Jones complicates racial roles when he adds a black character to the narrative. Ramsey-Eyes, the old black man who works as the caretaker of the Cattleman's Hotel (the building in which the Knights of the White Magnolia meet), has been entrusted with keeping safe the sacred ritual book needed for initiations, even though the Knights themselves are a white-supremacist organization:

> L. D.: But why Ramsey-Eyes? Why not one of the brothers?
> COLONEL: Because for one thing he is an old and faithful employee, and for another thing ah wouldn't trust any of you bumble-dicks with the rule book if it were writ on the side of an elephant![30]

Ramsey-Eyes' desire to keep the book appears to stem from his own sense of superiority over the Knights themselves, and their dependence on him to clean up the mess they make. The play ends with Ramsey-Eyes alone on stage, cleaning up the debacle of the group's aborted initiation of a new member:

> (*He closes the door and snaps the cross light switch a couple of times. When it doesn't work, he moves to the cross and raps the wall next to it with the broom handle. The cross lights up. He chuckles and moves back to the door, turning off the overhead lights. A piece of paper [from the initiation book] catches his eye. He picks it up and moves to the light of the cross to read.*) "Ah am da moon. By night ah cast beams down upon you, lightin' your way along your journey toward the truth." (*He chuckles.*) "Ah am de moon." Oh, Lawdy. "Ah am de moon." (*He chuckles again.*)[31]

While the Knights are defensively antagonistic about the organization and its importance in (then) contemporary Bradleyville, Ramsey-Eyes, the person who should be the most offended by what the Knights represent, sees them as one big joke. Here, Jones' depiction of a racial minority shows that the character has a stronger sense of self-identity than the supposedly superior Knights.

Jones' Knights of the White Magnolia find their female counterparts in another small-town Texas play, Del Shores' 1995 *Daughters of the Lone Star State,* who reluctantly attempt to induct a poor Hispanic girl into their lily-white society in order to keep the organization alive. Whereas Shores relies on a near-farcical mania to sustain his narrative, Jones' picture is one of slow development of character relationships and situations. No character appears in all three plays, but all characters who do appear in more than one play do so to provide a more complex view of their nature and their desires.

How successful is Jones' representation of Texan behavior? The somber atmosphere that overshadows the trilogy gives a hint of his ultimate message, but even it is destabilized by the large amount of humor Jones uses to keep his audience from feeling his characters' pain too keenly. For example, Lu Ann refuses to marry her high school sweetheart because she thinks his last name—Wortman—is "just plain silly." Much of the racial prejudice of *The Last Meeting of the Knights of the White Magnolia* is defused with broad humor, ending with the disintegration of the group in all different directions after its newest pledge flees in terror during one of the Colonel's flashback episodes. This use of humor, which will recur even more frequently in the *Tuna* plays, keeps the audience aware of the bustling, continuously shifting field of interrelationships that constitute Texan cultural identity.

Jones' scripts emphasize the interrelationships among the characters, but many critics saw the performances as authentic representations of Texan cultural memory. This point of view was furthered by production publicity. In 1976, the *Washington Post* published a "map" of Bradleyville showing the locations of all the buildings and homes mentioned in the text,[32] a transparent attempt to authenticate Jones' fictive town as "real Texan." This spirit of authenticity pervaded the reviews of the play, as well, which were generally positive.[33]

When the trilogy opened on Broadway in late September 1976, the New York critics had a different response. Despite its success at the Kennedy Center and good advance word of mouth, Broadway was not ready for plays which showcased regional behaviors. It did not help that the advance press compared Jones' work to that of Tennessee Williams and Eugene O'Neill.[34] The major critics at the *New York Times* and the *New York Daily News* panned the trilogy, causing ticket sales to drop off sharply. Clive Barnes was especially insulting, stating in his review that Jones was "making his Broadway debut as a playwright and, as far as one can tell, his debut anywhere," despite the trilogy's two successful runs at Washington's Kennedy Center after its premiere at the Dallas Theater Center. In Barnes' view, the problem was that the plays did not seem to resolve any aspects of the lives they depicted: "His plays are not boring—not at all. You watch them with interest, and any of these evening's [*sic*] can be recommended as an unusual and thruthful [*sic*] evening in the theatre. But each play is oddly inconclusive. What is Mr. Jones trying to tell us? That life in small towns in Texas is hell? That we might have guessed. But beyond this caring and careful despair, there seems to be no statement, no purpose. It is as though a dramatist had prepared notes for a drama, and then just put them on stage."[35]

Barnes and his colleague Walter Kerr, as well as Martin Gottfried of the *New York Post,* all saw the plays as backward, unsuited for Broadway.[36] Many of the outlying papers, however, particularly the neighborhood ones, praised the production.[37] This disparity may be due to neighborhood critics, who saw their own environment reflected in Jones' scripts, and metropolitan critics, who did not. So viewed, Broadway sources may not measure a play's effectiveness as a reflection of American life. On the other hand, Texan regional culture may have lacked the performative power of foundational myths like those of the Texas Revolution.

The closing of all three plays after only sixty performances touched off a debate about the role of Broadway in determining what qualifies as American theatre.[38] The Dallas Theater Center insisted that regional theatres also contributed to the growth and development of new plays and playwrights and that Broadway success did not automatically equal greatness. The power of reviewers like Clive Barnes was compounded by the fact that the regional bias of Broadway at that time was not openly acknowledged.[39]

The myth of the Texan, twice removed from its initial setting and replayed as an attempt at a national myth on Broadway, foregrounded the gap between representations of regionality on the local and national scales and, ultimately, contributed to a misreading of Jones' trilogy within Broadway's performative context. It also opened the door for a better understanding of the connections between regional theatres and the professional New York theatre scene by causing critics to question the status quo.

Bradleyville's fictional location in Texas may be stable—West Texas between Abilene and San Angelo—but its placement within Texan cultural memory is not so apparent. Nothing that occurs in Bradleyville references Texas' revolutionary history directly, but the reflections of behaviors are apparent. The Colonel, purported to be a war hero in the tradition of Houston and the like, is in fact a broken man who never recovered from combat. His behavior in the plays and his constant reliving of the horrors of war destabilize the revolutionary pedagogy on which his character is based. Likewise, the town of Bradleyville is itself a poor reflection of Texan cultural memory: it is a dying town full of dying people who have none of the supposed Texan spirit imbued in all residents of the state by its glorious history. Yet, the town does serve as a valuable stopping point on the rail line of Texan cultural identity. Some towns may be more hospitable than others, but each defines the relationship between the grandeur of revolutionary pedagogy and the mundane nature of everyday small-town life.

PARODY OF THE TEXAS SMALL TOWN: THE *TUNA* TRILOGY

The Tuna Trilogy, by Joe Sears, Jaston Williams, and Ed Howard, provides an overview of life in Tuna, Texas, the third-smallest town in the state. The first play, *Greater Tuna* (1982), introduces us to an assortment of local residents. The characters run the gamut of oddballs: the local busybody and leader of the antiobscenity crusade; an assortment of "good ole boys" in various jobs; the lone animal-rights activist; and a firearms enthusiast with a UFO-sighting husband. The play ostensibly centers around the Bumiller family: Bertha, the long-suffering wife of a philandering husband; Charlene, the fat girl who wanted to be cheerleader; Jody, the sensitive animal lover; and Stanley, the black sheep of the family.[40] The characters twang their way through such events as the death of a prominent local judge (found in a 1950's-style bathing suit, courtesy of Stanley); UFO landings; poetry contests; the accidental poisoning of a prized hunting dog; and the meeting of the local decency group, the Smut Snatchers (who take issue with using the word "snatch" in their name but decide that it would be too expensive to change the stationery right now). Much of the dialogue and many of the circumstances contained in the script are clichés, and the fictional inhabitants of Tuna, Texas, run the gamut of southern stereotypes: white trash, Baptist, racist, bigoted UFO-spotting rednecks who would do comedian Jeff Foxworthy proud (see Photos 17 and 18).

Unlike other plays about Texas, *Greater Tuna* was created through improvisation by Joe Sears and Jaston Williams, who play all twenty residents, male or female, through changes of costume, mannerisms, and voice.[41] This performance style would seem to run counter to the myth of the Texan as virulently masculine, as found in the characters of *King of the Hill* or *A Texas Trilogy.* The same actor who plays Charlene Bumiller (Williams) also plays Vera Carp (the Smut Snatcher) and Petey Fisk of the Greater Tuna Humane Society. As a result, these characters are linked in the minds of the audience, even though the characters themselves represent drastically different perspectives on life. This initial and continuing mode of presentation adds layers to the map of the city as one travels farther and farther into the field of relations between characters created by the fast changes and cross-dressing of the two performers.[42]

Tuna's underlying assumptions in both text and performance send disturbing messages not only about how these men view Texas but also about how willing audiences across the country are to endorse that viewpoint through their continued patronage of its performances. The plays also raise questions regarding not only the promulgation of a Texas identity but, more specifically, the manner in which this popular text represents rural Texas women as old, physically repellent, and genderless, in effect, erasing women from the stage and from the state, even as they attempt to gain more political and economic power. *Greater Tuna* functions as a postmodern nostalgic pastiche—a lighthearted imitation based on a simulated understanding—of a fictitious small town. Tuna, Texas, becomes the working out of a rigidly defined set of small-town behaviors, and it does so without once referencing any historical or cultural events which are specifically Texan in nature. This destabilizes its position as a point on the map of the small Texas town, even though many of the same elements are present in Tuna that were present in Bradleyville: frustrated women, cynical men, disheartened children, all of whom have little to look forward to. In the words of Joe Sears, "Our characters are just everyday, run-of-the-mill people who shop at Wal-Mart. Jaston and I were raised properly, we don't make fun of people."[43]

The *Tuna* plays' reception outside of Texas was mixed initially, as critics attempted to concretize the characters as authentic representations of life in small-town Texas. When *Greater Tuna* premiered at New York's Circle in the Square on October 21, 1982, *New York Times* theatre critic Mel Gussow stated that the show "only proves that some people will laugh at anything." Not only was the humor "tattle-tale gray," the "social commentary" of the piece was limited to "Tuna's banning of *Roots,* 'because [in the words of one Tuna resident] it only shows one side of the slavery issue." All in all, the show was "so corny that, in comparison, Cousin Minnie Pearl look[ed] like Lena Horne."[44] *Village Voice* reviewer Michael Feingold called the show "an act of comic revenge . . . which should really be performed all over Texas and the Southwest before audiences that could recognize themselves." To produce the play in New York seemed to him more like "a distant act of condescension toward an alien culture that has closed itself off from reality," and he advocated "sending missionaries to rescue [Tuna's] children from fundamentalism and illiteracy" instead of simply laughing at them onstage.[45] The reaction of the New York critics implies that they incorrectly saw the parody and broad humor in *Greater Tuna* as an accurate reflection of Texan behaviors.

Gussow might have wanted to move away from Tuna, and Feingold wished to bring it into the twentieth century, but, by and large, audiences flocked to Tuna in droves, accepting and enjoying it just as it was. *Greater Tuna* ran for a year at Circle in the Square, playing to mostly sold-out houses throughout the week.

In 1989, *A Tuna Christmas* introduced new characters to the Tuna scene and enjoyed a successful 1994 holiday run on Broadway with its original cast, a first for any Austin-based show.[46] In 1993, Sears and Williams used the *Tuna* characters in a series of commercials for a Houston-based grocery store chain, a clear example of how Texan cultural identity can be transformed into a consumable brand.[47] Also, 1994 was the year in which HBO brought the characters from the original script to televised life in a made-for-cable version which expanded the Tuna population (all speaking characters were still played exclusively by Sears and Williams). *Red, White and Tuna,* the third play in the *Tuna Trilogy,* played to expectant audiences at the Kennedy Center in 1999 after its world premiere in Austin the previous year. There was a longtime venue for the play, the Tuna Little Theatre, at the Wyndham Anatole Hotel in Dallas, that offered eight performances of *Tuna* each week in its three hundred–seat amphitheatre. The success and firm references to Texan culture have stabilized the *Tuna* narrative into one that reaffirms the Texan-ness of its characters, despite their broad appeal to others outside the state and the lack of any historical referents in the text.

Greater Tuna initiates outsiders into the practices of the state, although its Phinas Blye, who has run for Tuna City Council fourteen times without success, attributes his failure to his outsider status: "I'm short, and I was born in Indiana, and people just naturally seem to hate me."[48]

The portrayal of less-inconsequential forms of otherness, such as race, further distances the *Tuna* plays from reality. As in the *Texas Trilogy,* the *Tuna* plays skirt the issue of race relations by presenting views on race held by the townspeople. It is the job of the people of Tuna, says Elmer Watkins, who announces the weekly meetings of Klan 249 on Tuna's radio station, OKKK, to make "this world a better place for the right kind of people. Amen."[49] Similar sentiments are expressed by Vera Carp regarding bilingual education. In the Tuna school system, Spanish class consists of learning five basic phrases, which is "all the Spanish any red-blooded American oughta feel obligated to learn."[50]

The absence of nonwhites, particularly Latinos, from these plays is even more egregious. The one Hispanic character mentioned in the original play, the Judge's maid, Juanita, did not exist until the HBO film in 1994, and there are no African Americans in the trilogy. Their absence makes race an issue,[51] just as the use of men to play the women's roles makes gender an issue.

If Texan cultural identity remains white, signifying that Tuna is a "typical" Texas small town in the traditional reading of the Texan, the avant-garde nature of the plays' performance style complicates that signal, since there can be no fixed Texan behaviors in a town where everyone is, essentially, the same two people. The residents of Tuna organize their own dramatic space through the representation and parody of various small-town stereotypes. Those stereotypes are packaged, in turn, as national representatives of the small-town Texan, and the local-become-global Texan cultural identity circulates on the map created by these towns. Unlike Bradleyville, Tuna does not take itself too seriously; yet its characters, especially the long-suffering Bertha, strive in their local environment for something uniquely bigger.

WIDOWS AND ORPHANS IN SEARCH OF A TEXAS HOME: THE PLAYS OF HORTON FOOTE

Not all representations of small-town Texas use humor or farce to foreground their constructions of Texan behavior. Horton Foote's *The Trip to Bountiful* and his nine-play *Orphan's Home Cycle* map aspects of Harrison, Texas, as a decaying, turn-of-the-twentieth century small-town façade more appealing in memory than it ever was in actuality. Harrison is based on Foote's hometown of Wharton, Texas, a small town located in the south-central Gulf region of the state,[52] and Foote makes no attempt to hide that his plays are semiautobiographical and based on his father's family. So site specific is his identification with his locale in the state that he prefers to be called "a native of Wharton, Texas" instead of a "native Texan."[53]

Critics of Foote's work apologize for his use of "real" Wharton as the stand-in for fictional Harrison. As a result, "Foote has been considered a Texas writer, an east Texas writer, a Gulf Coast writer, and (more accurately) a coastal southeast Texas writer."[54] His ability to map these spaces, however, stems from his capacity to position Harrison as a local authority from which behaviors can be re-created that accurately represent the complexities of each of these designations. Foote's best-known play, *The Trip to Bountiful,* for example, depicts a scene of lost family, lost friends, and the town's lost glory days. Carrie Watts, sneaking away from her son and overbearing daughter-in-law for a last visit to "Bountiful," her childhood home in Harrison, is overcome with the knowledge that her home is now abandoned and dilapidated and that she has hung onto memories here as much as she has done in Houston. Her acceptance of the loss of Bountiful and, with it, her sense of self in the world, opens her up to the possibility of living more peacefully with her relatives. Her behaviors and attitudes toward them (the new repository of her family memories rather than a hindrance to them) have radically changed.

Although the film version of *Bountiful* (which won Geraldine Page an Oscar) and Foote's screenplay for *Tender Mercies* (which won him an Oscar) are better-known pieces of his work, it is in the nine-play *Orphan's Home Cycle* that Foote realizes the most complex map of Harrison and its environs.[55] The protagonist of the cycle, Horace Robedeaux, is the offspring of a marriage between two of the town's most prominent families, the Thorntons and the Robedeauxs, but his childhood is far from idyllic. The opening play, *Roots in a Parched Ground,* shows Horace's father, Paul Horace Robedeaux, dying from the effects of alcoholism and his mother moving to Houston in search of a better life—without her son. Horace struggles to grow up and find a family for himself, and the story travels back and forth between Houston and Harrison, making stops along the way.

As the cycle unfolds, Horace grows to manhood, marries, and has a family and business of his own.[56] He attempts to make peace with his family and seeks to understand the socioeconomic changes coming to Harrison and, by extension, the State of Texas as a whole. As economic progress ends plantation-style labor, the growing of rice, cotton, and sugarcane changes in early-twentieth-century Texas. Horace's positioning by Foote as an Everyman-cum-Job figure, searching to right the wrongs done to him as a boy by his family, parallels the personal, dramatic, and historical texts which run through the cycle. As does Lu Ann Hampton Laverty Oberlander, Horace dreams of a home with "growing things, fruitful things, fig trees, pecan trees, pear trees, peach trees."[57] His desire for this home stems, in part, from the resentment he feels toward his "real" family and, in particular, his mother, for depriving him of a home life following the death of his father by marrying again. Yet Horace's behavior, his slowly learned ability to plan ahead and look toward the bigger picture (learned the hard way through being double-crossed and abandoned several times) makes his behavior unique among that of the other characters throughout the cycle (with the possible exception of Elizabeth Vaughn, whom he marries).

In *Convicts,* the antebellum master/slave relationship seems alive and well as the white plantation owner, Mr. Soll, uses black convicts to work his fields and sells wares in his store to poor black families who populate the county ("there's only two white families between [the plantation] and Harrison," remarks one character).[58] Soll, the plantation owner, relates, "It was my daddy's idea to get convicts. We tried after slavery to have tenants out here. We had three hundred at one time living on the place, but we had a series of bad crop years and we all nearly starved."[59] Convicts were cheap labor; the state paid landowners to keep them, and the convicts' "wages" went toward paying off their fines and to support them.[60] The play centers not around the work that the convicts do, however, but around the numerous shootings and murders of convicts by each other or by overseers. The convicts do not help the plantation; their unmarked graves populate the land set aside for farming sugarcane, and their numbers seem to multiply no matter how many die. As Mr. Soll, the plantation manager, puts it, "The more you kill, the more there are."[61]

The black characters portrayed in Foote's *Convicts* (as in all the plays in the cycle) have depth; they display a savvy world-awareness much like that of Nelson Algren's rail-riding vagrants. Yet the convicts are trapped in their own cycle of violence, in Horace's view, for no apparent reason:

HORACE: How come you kilt him?

CONVICT: Because he was always bothering me.

HORACE: How was he bothering you?

CONVICT: Just like I say I told him to stop and he wouldn't. I told him if he didn't stop I was going to kill him first chance I got. I reckon he knew I meant what I said now.[62]

While events in *Roots in a Parched Ground* and *Lily Dale* haunt Horace in his adult years, the events portrayed in *Convicts* appear peripheral to his overall development, much as do those of *The Widow Claire*. The widow of the title exists to document Horace's transformation from boy to man. Though Horace has seen the death of his father and endures what he sees as his own hardships as an overworked, underpaid shop boy, he does not comprehend the plight of the convict with whom he speaks (who is referred to in the dramatis personae only as "Convict").

Critics have not understood the role of Foote's work in creating and maintaining Texan cultural identity any better than they have the work of the other writers discussed in this chapter.[63] Like Jones' work, Foote's plays have also been labeled "sentimental and nostalgic by critics . . . His characters have been described as ordinary and uninteresting, and his plots have been called flat."[64] Critics on the whole have seen very little of value in the depiction of small Texas towns on stage, despite the fact that many of the behaviors attributed to Texans are supposed to come from those towns.

The cycle, however, is not simply an exercise in fictionalized genealogy for the stage. Foote claims, "I'm a social writer in the sense that I want to record, but not in the sense of trying to change people's minds."[65] What Foote records is less his family tree than the shift in socioeconomic status that many old Texas families faced in the early twentieth century.[66] Rather, his characters mark a transition point in how Texans behaved toward money, family, and the "traditional values" articulated by the 1910–1930 generation (and by the Colonel in Jones' trilogy). The Texas Centennial Celebration of 1936 marked the completion of this transition in the small-town landscape. Foote's critics commend his avoidance of "cliche, formula, and melodrama" but find him guilty of an "anti-theatre" that "invites repetition and encourages boredom."[67]

His plays, then, evoke the pageants and norms of pedagogy brought up in other mass-culture performances of Texan cultural identity. Foote's dramas, however, create a firm point of reference on the map of small Texas towns. Though not specifically linked to Texan historical myth, Horace's spirit of perseverance, self-sacrifice, and eventual triumph over the forces which threaten to overwhelm him reflects the historical struggles of great Texas heroes such as Crockett, Bowie, and Travis. Horace also links to the aforementioned characters in the *Texas* and *Tuna* trilogies. He is not a historical figure but the representation of an average (albeit historical) small-town resident trying to find himself in the grand geography of his home state and make his mark on the landscape. He finds himself, and his home, inside himself and within his home territory.

CONCLUSION

Each of the plays considered in this chapter takes us on a journey through a different city, in a different time, in order to construct a matrix of complex behaviors that signifies something uniquely Texan. As Paul Auster states, "what we are really doing when we walk through the city is thinking, and thinking in such a way that our thoughts compose a journey, and this journey is no more or less than the steps we have taken, so that, in the end, we might safely say that we have been on a journey, and even if we do not leave our room, it has been a journey, and we might safely say that we have been somewhere, even if we don't know where it is."[68]

A culture is not automatically built in a small town, despite its spatio-cultural map. As Terry Eagleton states, "people who belong to the same place, profession or generations do not, thereby, form a culture; they do so only when they begin to share speech-habits, folk lore, ways of proceeding, frames of value, a collective self-image."[69] Small-town behavior creates a space in which the white male Texan still manages to do the right thing. What is most interesting is that none of these authors play on Texas history or revolutionary pedagogy directly (although their ideals permeate the plays).

Marsha Norman observes that the "power of Southern writers' work" lies in the fact that southerners "share the notion that you cannot escape your family. You can't escape where you were born, who you were born to and what you've inherited . . . our writing is absolutely linked to this problem of how do you change when the perceptions of the people around you don't change? . . . How do you move at all with all these people hanging on to you?"[70]

Texas playwrights also shift these burdens: Foote's family hangs onto Horace, Jones' characters are brought down by their families, and Tuna's families are the source of frustration and amusement. The families of small-town Texas plays create a form of Texan cultural identity that is more personal than the configurations of pageants and museums. The writers of these plays base their characters on people—real or imagined—that they have known, yet, they do not attempt to probe the depths of authenticity present in architectural and historical sites of Texan performance. They do not need to, because the legitimacy has already been authenticated. Therefore, the maps stand as drawn—space has become place.

Yet the environments represented by Bradleyville, Tuna, and Harrison offer different potential behaviors. The goal is not to represent people but behaviors in such a way that audience members can distance themselves from undesirable behaviors and see themselves in desirable ones. Tuna is a place where audiences, Texan and non-Texan, can interact with stereotypical Texan behaviors. In Bradleyville, on the other hand, life is pathos. Jones' characters seem trapped, and this feeling of claustrophobic Texan cultural identity gives them more depth and complexity. Jones' Texans are searching for something: a sense of place in the universe, or at least in their own communities. Jones himself recognizes that the very inability of the characters to function within one set of behaviors proves to be their salvation in the end. Thus, the lack of Texan behavior, not to mention the idea that these two characters are better prepared for life than are their parents and other townspeople, foregrounds the gaps, rifts, and shifts in characters' respective towns and their ability to navigate them.

In Harrison, on the other hand, life is progress—of a sort. There, Horton Foote's nostalgic Texas past and the "common man" Horace Robedeaux construct a place where the search for meaning can occur.

The towns are repositories for what Francis Barker calls "the incoherence . . . between the powerfully nostalgic drive toward restitution and the deployments of actuality where recovery is impossible."[71] Nostalgia also traps the characters, making it impossible for them to recapture the past behaviors they seek. There is no Revolution for them—only the mundane life of the small town. Yet there is revolution in the identities forged through behavioral change, behaviors that allow the perception of Texan cultural identity as something larger than the events of the Revolution rewritten into small-town lives.

The tension between the unique and the common, the small and the large, reflects the two-faced nature of Texan cultural identity.[72] Texan behavior either moves at a frenetic pace (so nobody can see you) or crawls along at a snail's pace (so that others get tired of staring and look away). The behaviors in Bradleyville, Tuna, and Harrison claim no specific link to Texas. What they accomplish is to bring revolutionary discourse—itself a form of bird's-eye mapping of Texan cultural identity—down to earth, creating a haptic space full of everyday people who resemble those outside the Lone Star State.

The map created by the dramatic depiction of small-town Texas interweaves with the architectural sites and historical commemorations that mark larger, more "heroic" Texan attributes and contrasts those ideals with the supposedly authentic behavior of average residents. This matrix both legitimates the claims of authenticity made by the big events and allows for co-optation of those ideals by everyday citizens. It is the map which makes the towns, yet, the reading of each town is related to its shifting positionality on the map of Texan behaviors.

The historical, cultural, and commonplace practices of Texan life illustrated in performative sites throughout the state produce a heterogeneous discourse of the Texan-as-subject. Texan cultural identity creates a shifting matrix which allows for various points of engagement, depending on one's knowledge of Texas history and culture as organized by local authorities. The better one knows the rules, the easier it is to move through the state. The space of Texas represented by these three Texas playwrights is open to all for viewing and residence; the place of Texas, however, is a closed, tightly organized field which precludes acceptance of those not designated as Texans. This seeming authenticity comes from outside as well as from within, since those who are not native impose their perceptions of real Texan behavior onto residents of the state.

The various mapping procedures of Texan behavior construct stability, provide additional layers to Texan cultural identity, and keep the boundaries separating Texans from the outside world intact. A poem by Tuna resident Charlene Bumiller parodies these ideas:

> My Tuna, oh my Tuna, the only place I know, I've often thought of leaving you, but don't know where I'd go. For Paris has no bar-be-que, and Rome just can't compare to a lovely Texas sunset when the dust is in the air . . . But Tuna, oh my Tuna, please stay just the way you are, 'cause I just think the world outside of Tuna is bizarre.[73]

Clearly, however, conflicting messages about the nature of Texan cultural identity, its regionality, and the need to establish a specific set of Texan behaviors underlie the seemingly stable surface. The small-town Texas plays discussed in this chapter suggest that what makes the citizens of Texas unique is that their behaviors rest on a complex map of local interactions prefaced by a larger understanding of Texan cultural identity. This identity helps to separate Texans from non-Texans by presenting the actions of characters on stage as distinctly and uniquely Texan in nature. Tuna, Texas, may have much in common with Tuna, Ohio, but productions of *Greater Tuna* will still draw on perceived Texan behaviors and visual cues in performance to ensure that there is some critical distance between the Texans on stage and the Ohioans in the audience.[74]

If the historical heroes of Texas pageants and plays are larger-than-life figures, the heroes of contemporary Texan plays are the life-size inhabitants of Texas towns like Bradleyville, Tuna, and Harrison. The everyday Texan lives on stage through the practice of everyday life, which become "real" in the language and actions drawn from the real and transferred to the characters who populate the small towns of Texan plays. In literature, small Texas towns contain vibrantly complex characters who resonate with many native Texan writers: "If I can hear the characters speaking and they sound like people I've known, then you're what I think of when I think of Texas Writers."[75] Texan cultural identity becomes one way of identifying other Texans who fit into the same mold of behaviors. Towns like Tuna, Bradleyville, and Harrison function as dramatic sites of parody and/or praise for the behavioral practices of the "average Texan." It is these qualities, and how each town interprets and represents those qualities on stage, that make these plays "Texan."

In their attempts to inscribe their tactics on others within the space, these theatrical performances become part of a discourse of Texan-ness which creates its own need but promises a stability and order that it cannot deliver. Gianni Vattimo asserts that the desire for stability this and other regional discourses promise is created by "local rationalities" through which participants believe they are asserting their individuality and authenticity.[76] These practices also have a disorienting effect, since within the act of affirmation, participants must acknowledge that, without a specifically constructed, ordered discourse to create the "place" they inhabit, there would be no difference between us and them, between Texans and everyone else. The plays discussed in this chapter have transformed the Texan on stage from a mere reflection of historical icons to a complex interweaving of behaviors, attitudes, and beliefs, a construction farther and farther removed from originary models of the Texan at the same time those models are brought closer and closer to a world audience.

Drama plays a very particular role in the construction of Texan cultural identity. It takes the grandiose heroes of revolutionary pedagogy and transforms their unique traits into the average Texan. This ability to shift identity is important, for it makes the small Texas town a synecdoche for Texan cultural identity.

Each playwright discussed in this chapter adds a different layer to the picture. Jones' characters represent the soft, white—very white—underbelly of the Lone Star in performance. Heroics are replaced with pathetic attempts to hold onto the old ways. The *Tuna* plays parody Texas small-town life by casting various stereotypical characters into a frame of virtuosity, allowing the audience to laugh without feeling affronted or ridiculed. Horton Foote's plays create a history for the small Texas town, indicating how it has shifted and changed over time while the overarching revolutionary history has remained stable, white, and male.

In the next chapter, we examine the Texan's legacy to the world, from the most famous small Texas town of the moment, Crawford, home of the most famous contemporary Texan, Pres. George W. Bush, to international sites of power and commerce. As Texan cultural identity moves into the global sphere, it becomes more a brand, a commodity to be marketed and sold. This shift, however, is neither new nor accidental, but part of a long-developing construction of "Texan" as surrogate for "American" and the world.

FIVE

SELLING TEXAS

The Political Branding of Texan Cultural Identity

Texas could get along without the United States, but the United States cannot, except with great hazard, exist without Texas.

SAM HOUSTON

The State of Texas has a number of images that it uses to market itself to a consuming public, and Texans guard the sanctity of those icons jealously.[1] The Texas Department of Transportation has launched a campaign to prevent "illegal" usage of the "Don't Mess with Texas" slogan, even though the trademark has been owned by a South Carolina man, Richard Tucker, since 1993, when he filed an application to use the phrase in his western-clothing business.[2] The importance of such brands to Texan cultural identity is grounded in the need to ensure their authenticity and uniqueness with regard to architecture, history, and behavior. Characters as diverse as David Crockett and George W. Bush have helped to shape the Lone Star brand into the complex matrix of real and simulated images that it is today.

The Texan "brand" is both a process and an image. The branding process is the means by which the idea of the Lone Star—the mainstream white, male Texan—is created as a commodity. The brand itself, then, is the image that is marketed to and consumed by the public. This chapter will briefly discuss the branding process, then show how the brand has been marketed, appropriated, and transformed by successive attempts to control it.

The supposedly quaint, historically motivated Texan behaviors represented in the small-town plays discussed in Chapter 4 take on a new significance when shifted into another arena: politics. Here, the map of small-town behaviors is thrust into the national and world arenas. In this context, Texan cultural identity is solidified into a type of brand, or label, that is then imprinted on those who claim to represent Texan values or perspectives, regardless of actual ideological position.[3] This brand comes about not in spite of the political ideology of the state but because of it. According to

Terry Eagleton, "the nation-state does not unqualifiedly celebrate the idea of culture. On the contrary, any particular national or ethnic culture comes into its own only through the unifying principle of the state, not under its own steam. Cultures are intrinsically incomplete and need the supplement of the state to become truly themselves."[4]

If this is indeed the case, then we must explore Texan cultural identity's use in national and international political performances to fully understand it.[5] In this context, we can see how Texas created itself to become the brand seen today on stage and screen. The brand has entered the public arena, intersecting with everything from television shows to movies to actual political figures, as well as plays. This chapter will deal with the authenticity of Texan cultural identity and the marketing of the Texan as a brand with economic and political power.

In the political arena, representations of Texan cultural identity strive for the same types of authenticity as their historical and small-town counterparts. Central to this identity is the idea that Texas justice is somehow more real than that of other states. Political figures are more directly engaged in the arena of law and order. The same state has produced U.S. presidents as ideologically diverse as Lyndon Baines Johnson and George W. Bush, both of whom initiated preemptive wars in foreign countries to root out "evildoers."[6] Television representations of Texas justice run toward Chuck Norris' *Walker, Texas Ranger* and Judge Larry Joe Doherty from the court drama *Texas Justice*,[7] where straight talk (or martial arts) is the order of the day. One need not be a television law enforcer to mete out Texas justice: a Texas woman's punishment for neglecting two horses was thirty days in jail and a restricted diet of bread and water for the first three days so that she would know how the horses felt.[8]

Writers also invoke Texas politicians when they want to stress the severity of a situation, as does *New York Times* writer James Bennet in a 2003 article on Israeli prime minister Ariel Sharon's criticism of West Bank settlements. Bennet compares Texas' association with the United States to the settlements' association with Israel: "For settlers, it was almost as though President Bush had described Texas as American-occupied territory."[9] This kind of description reinforces the notion that a Texan response to a situation is somehow different from that of an average American. When thrust into the political sphere, this linking forms a political façade based on the small-town behaviors, revolutionary pedagogy, and architectural landscapes that support Texan cultural identity. The same strange behaviors found in a fictional Tuna or Bradleyville become labels, not simply a culture's mode of presentation. The vision of the Texan put forth in the political arena capitalizes on the state's history, how it is perceived by outsiders, and the larger-than-life monuments that populate the state to create a powerful presence: the Lone Star.

The Lone Star is not only a form of branding—Lone Star beer is "the national beer of Texas"[10]—but also a performative brand created out of Texan cultural identity into an image easily marketed across the country and around the world. Lone Star beer uses the designation to legitimate its place within the pantheon of American regional beers;[11] politicians such as George W. Bush use the Lone Star brand to establish and legitimate their political actions. The brand is designed to preserve the image of the Texan as a being superior to those around him. The image is predominantly male and overwhelmingly Anglo; women, Hispanics, American Indians, or African Americans need not apply.[12] The most obvious depiction of the Lone Star is that of the inhabitant of the small Texas town who represents the virtues and vices of Texan cultural identity—strong, loyal, brave, but a bit behind the rest of the country. The Lone Star is not a historical figure; rather, it is a performative process by which the idea of the Texan is marketed or represented to those who consider themselves to be outside of Texan cultural identity.

The notion of branding is borne out in the "bigger is better" mentality that clings to all things Texan, cultural and political. Bigger is better in Texas—home of the largest bass drum (owned by the University of Texas at Austin Longhorn Band), the world's largest pecan (Seguin), and a seventy-foot working fly fishing rod (Port Isabel).[13] In 2004, the British cable television channel Trio aired two specials foregrounding the idea of bigness: *Texas: America Supersized,* a "sampling [of] everything from high school football to rodeo, gun nuts and Border Patrol,"[14] was one of them. Larry Hagman, *Dallas'* J. R. Ewing, narrates a special entitled *Fat City,* a look at several of the more obese residents of Houston, dubbed "the fattest place on earth."[15] These images, flattering and not, testify to the centrality of bigness in the creation of the Texan brand. Claims made or reinforced by insiders—persons whose status as native Texan or whose Texan persona grants them legitimacy—reinforce a very specific interpretation of Texan cultural identity. Hagman fulfills both of these categories: he was born in Fort Worth and played one of television's most beloved villains, J. R. Ewing, on the long-lived Texas oil drama *Dallas* (1978–1991).[16]

The Lone Star brand brings together the "bigger" mentality and the behavioral and historical spaces that characterize those whom it represents. Under the image of the Lone Star, Texans are small-town folks even if they have lived their entire lives in Dallas or Houston. The image legitimates the matrix of architecture, history, and behavior that creates Texan cultural identity both on stage and off. In Preston Jones' *A Texas Trilogy,* Col. J. C. Kincaid is a Texas hero of epic proportions, whether he is the leader of the last chapter of the Knights of the White Magnolia or the oldest living graduate of the Mirabeau B. Lamar Military Academy. He embodies the same qualities as his revolutionary predecessors, Sam Houston and William Barret Travis, and as his theatrical counterpart, Calvin Armstrong, the erstwhile cowboy in the outdoor drama *Texas!* The colonel has his faults, but they are part of what makes him a unique individual, a Lone Star. The brand itself, seemingly static, is, however, a shifting field of relationships that belies the supposed solidity of the grounding which supports it.

THE POLITICS OF NATIONHOOD: THE REPUBLIC OF TEXAS, 1836–1845

The politics of the Texas Revolution were themselves more complex than is often portrayed in films. The Revolution's inception was chaotic: Texas began as a part of Mexico (the province of Coahuila y Tejas) and was held by the Spanish until the Mexican revolt of 1824. Conflicts were rampant during the Revolution itself. The Provisional Government of the Republic of Texas, deeply divided between those who supported U.S. president Andrew Jackson and those who wanted nothing to do with him, clashed over the assignment of Sam Houston as commander-in-chief of the Texian army.[17] Some scholars assert that Texas existed as an independent republic for nine years because then-president Jackson refused to annex the territory following Santa Anna's capitulation at San Jacinto,[18] a reticence particularly galling to former general Sam Houston, the first president of the Republic and an old friend of Jackson's. The need for a buffer zone with Mexico led to Texas' annexation in 1845.[19] While annexation did not give Texas the right to secede from the Union, Texas did retain ownership of its public lands, harbors, ports, and armaments and the right to divide itself into as many as four states of roughly equal size if it chose to do so, thereby adding four proslavery states to the Union.[20] Slavery had been a major issue during the Revolution and Republic years because Mexico did not recognize slavery, and many free blacks were uneasy about the number of proslavery whites settling in Texas.[21]

Even this brief history makes clear the complex politics surrounding the Revolution and the Republic of Texas. Inconsistencies in the telling of that history have begun to appear in representations of revolutionary events. In

Disney's retelling of the Alamo story in 2004, director John Lee Hancock attempted to problematize the relationship between mythic Alamo figures and their "real-life" counterparts. The character of David Crockett (played by Billy Bob Thornton) experiences a moment of indecision. Captured and facing execution, he is invited by Santa Anna to beg for his life. Crockett, who earlier in the movie informed Jim Bowie that "David Crockett" would go over the wall and get out while he could, but "old Davy" would stay until the end, must decide which of his historical selves to play—the blustering frontiersman or the more circumspect politician—in the last moments of his life. In the end, the character remains true to his constructed history by demanding Santa Anna's surrender then defiantly stating, "I'm a screamer"—a signature line from Davy Crockett stories and Colonel Nimrod Wildfire, the stage character loosely based on them—before being executed.[22]

The inclusion of this moment in the latest installment in the pantheon of Alamo films is itself notable and signals a change in film representations of the event. For the first time, a major figure in the Alamo is portrayed as having doubts about the viability of the legend of which he is a part.[23] Director Hancock has been quoted as saying that he has "always been attracted to flawed characters." This sentiment was apparently the rationale for including Crockett's moment, the depiction of Travis' fractured relationship with his wife and son, and Bowie's flashbacks to memories of his dead wife. Indeed, Hancock's *Alamo* actually seeks not to be "ahistorical spectacle . . . [or fully] Hollywood contrivances" such as the romantic subplot found in Wayne's movie.[24] A *Smithsonian Magazine* article by Bronson Tate ("a pseudonym for a writer based in Texas") claims that Hancock's version is the most historically accurate rendition.[25] (Tate casts Mexico's desire to hold onto Texas after winning independence from Spain as a "marketing problem" addressed by allowing any and all settlers to acquire land, provided that "they swear allegiance to Mexico and convert to Catholicism.")[26] Yet, despite claims to accuracy, Hancock altered the layout of the Alamo compound so that the chapel façade would always be visible when filming inside. He also chose to have Crockett be executed by Santa Anna, in accordance with the diary account of José Enrique de la Peña, instead of the traditional representation of Crockett as having died fighting.[27] Rather than a measure of accuracy, Hancock's Alamo movie creates new mythologies, drawing on available historical information to shape a story for consumption by a twenty-first-century commercial audience.

The vast majority of the press on the movie addresses not its cinematic flaws (of which there are many), but its historical importance. *Village Voice* writer Jessica Winter makes a connection between the appearance of Disney's *Alamo* and the state of George W. Bush's presidency at that moment. She asserts that Disney's film, which mirrors Bush's tattered "mission accomplished" image, works in much the same way that Wayne's *Alamo* did for Kennedy's troubled foreign policy in 1960.[28] She postulates that presidents have used the Alamo story to help refocus their shaky policies in an attempt to get audiences to look beyond present (needless) sacrifices to future victories. The idea that a contemporary commander-in-chief might use a film about the most famous battle of the Texas Revolution to bolster his position in a time of crisis speaks volumes about the political power of Texan cultural memory and Texan identity in the United States.

The linking of the Alamo to the political arena reflects not only the current cultural perception that "everything is political" but also the recent understanding of the role that politics played in the Texas Revolution, in the struggles between the Provisional Government and Gen. Sam Houston. The Alamo legend may be heroic, but the Alamo story makes visible the political aspects of the history, memory, and performance of Texan cultural identity. These two blend in the figure of the Alamo's most celebrated actor, David/Davy Crockett, "king of the wild frontier." An experienced tracker and Indian fighter, Crockett was elected to the Tennessee legislature in 1821 and again in 1823, and held a seat in the U.S. Congress from 1827 to 1831 and again from 1833 to 1835. He was a public figure long before his foray into politics, and his stories about backwoods life were published in 1834 in his autobiography, *A Narrative of the Life of David Crockett of the State of Tennessee.* In its day, a narrative functioned less as a piece of literature than as a performative event: "Crockett's contemporary reader would have entered the *Narrative* in much the same way he prepared to see a strolling actor, watch a stage comedian, hear a political orator, or participate in a joke and story session: on guard, willing to play the game, and with disbelief suspended for the moment" (see Photo 19).[29]

The fascination with Crockett was present even before his death. *Colonel Crockett's Exploits and Adventures in Texas, "Written by Himself"* (1836) fueled interest in him as a character. A work of fiction loosely based on letters Crockett wrote back east, the book was wildly popular and spurred the sales of its predecessor, *An Account of Colonel Crockett's Tour to the North and Down East* (1835). Despite the revelation that the text was written by Robert Penn Smith, *Colonel Crockett's Exploits* remained in print for decades, in altered forms, and was followed by similar stories after Crockett's death.[30]

However, it is in a stage play that Crockett's Lone Star persona makes its earliest appearance. In 1831, the same year that Crockett was defeated in a reelection bid, the James Kirke Paulding play *The Lion of the West* debuted at the Park Theatre in New York. *Lion* was remarkable not only because it was "the first American comedy to use an uncouth frontiersman as its central character,"[31] but also because that character, Col. Nimrod Wildfire, is ostensibly based on Crockett, despite the author's protestations to the contrary. Crockett accepted the denial of the play's relationship to his life, but he also enjoyed the resulting attention that the play gave to his flagging political career (references to his defeat soon appeared in performances). While many of the speeches that Paulding uses had appeared in various sources at least twenty years before *Lion* premiered,[32] their inclusion in the play links them indelibly to Crockett and his backwoods persona, helping to commodify both the frontiersman in general and Crockett in particular as a brand to be consumed on stage.

Crockett rode Wildfire's buckskin coattails back into public office, drawing on the public's association of him with the character in the popular press. In 1833, shortly after his reelection to Congress, James Hackett (the actor who portrayed Wildfire) came to Washington, D.C., to perform in a benefit. Benjamin Perley relates in *Reminiscences of Sixty Years in the National Metropolis* that Hackett performed *The Lion of the West* at Crockett's special request, and that Crockett was escorted to a front-row seat in front of a roaring crowd. Hackett then appeared on stage, in costume, and bowed first to the audience, then to Crockett, who returned the nod. The audience responded with cheers and applause.[33]

The Lion of the West centers on Mrs. Amelia Wollope, a visitor from England who comes to New York determined to "ameliorate" the manners of the country, a thinly disguised hit at Mrs. (Frances) Trollope, whose *Domestic Manners of the Americans* (1832) caused outrage in the United States for its criticism, the quality of which is indicated in this passage from the play:

> Mrs. Wollope: To ameliorate the barbarism of manners in America has been the ruling wish of my life; my husband, the only obstacle to its fulfillment, by his death has provided me with the means, and the plan I have concerted is founded, I conceive on a true knowledge of the national character. The root of all the evils of this country is familiarity—where everyone is equal, everyone is familiar.[34]

Her scheme is to charge five hundred dollars per share for her lessons in civilizing behavior: "a national social academy for refinement of manners and elegant exchange for the cultivation of taste."[35] Meanwhile, her brother, Percival Jenkins, has disguised himself as the late Lord Granby and is competing for the hand of Freeman's daughter, Caroline. Wildfire is the nephew of Freeman, an American merchant whose wife longs for a type of society that she associates with British gentry. Wildfire's "trip to New York" intersects the arrival of these two schemers, who are each foiled in their respective plans and depart.

Wildfire is the stock frontiersman character, the "Kentuckian." Like the Bowery Boy Mose or the noble savage Metamora, he lends some local color to the "Trip to New York" (the play's British title) and its resulting intrigues.[36] Col. Nimrod Wildfire, can, in his own words "jump higher—squat lower—dive deeper—stay longer under and come up drier" than "all of the [other] fellers either side of the Allegheny hills."[37] His rough-and-ready ways provide the perfect foil to the off-putting airs of Mrs. Wollope and Mrs. Freeman and allow him to ensure a happy ending for the romantic couple, Percival and Caroline.

The "lionization" of Crockett gained strength when his Nimrod impersonator, Hackett, returned to the States in 1833 in a revised, more successful, version of the play. Crockett, about to lose his congressional seat, gained renewed strength as a public icon, a performative effectiveness that would easily transfer into his "role" at the Alamo.

Crockett left for Texas when he was defeated in an 1835 reelection bid. That same year, two ghostwritten Crockett books were published: *Col. Crockett's Tour to the North and Down East,* and the *Life of Martin Van Buren,* a satire produced by the Whig Party.[38] The first Crockett almanac also appeared (an annual event from Crockett's death until 1856) in "Boston, New York and other cities." The almanacs contain "not only old anecdotes about him but many new ones about travels and adventures of his that took place years after the Alamo fell."[39] Musical tributes to Crockett were especially popular after his death. About 1837, *Colonel Crockett's Free and Easy Song Book* appeared, full of songs about his life and some that he would have liked,[40] and, in 1839, came "The Alamo, or the Death of Crockett," set to the tune of "The Star-Spangled Banner."

The cult of Crockett continued to grow after the Civil War. Crockett dime novels became popular between 1871 and 1896,[41] and Frank Murdock and Frank Mayo's play, *Davy Crockett: Or, Be Sure You're Right, Then Go Ahead,* debuted in 1872 with Mayo in the lead, and was performed regularly until 1896, when Mayo died. On stage, the Crockett myth merged with the Alamo myth, branding the Davy Crockett character as a Texan hero and imparting Crockett's political and cultural power in the United States to the men of the Alamo. Texas' hero had become America's hero. Crockett's political legacy had gained a similar national scope, shifting from Tennessee to the Union.

So viewed, the Alamo became a struggle of heroic proportions, an appropriate ending to Crockett's life. The Crockett and Alamo film craze began in 1909, when Charles K. French starred in the first Crockett film, the silent one-reeler *Davy Crockett—in Hearts United,* and he is featured prominently in all of the early Alamo films, though his character's motives and presentation vary greatly from picture to picture.[42]

Interest in Crockett surged again in the 1950's, when the specter of Communism created the need for heroes who embodied patriotism and American values. Crockett was an immediate favorite, "the highest ideal of American heroism and virtue."[43] The twentieth-century Crockett craze built up the branding of Crockett as the quintessential Texan, exemplifying individualism, bravery, and a tough-guy ethos. The Texan brand reduced him to an immobile stereotype of heroic behaviors. Walt Disney Studio's *Davy Crockett, Indian Fighter,* starring Fess Parker (a native Texan), debuted on the *Disneyland* television show on December 15, 1954, and its theme song, "The Ballad of Davy Crockett," was first aired then. In January, the *Disneyland* show featured "Crockett Goes to Washington," followed by the February broadcast, "Davy Crockett at the Alamo." That same year, Disney edited the three episodes into a theatrical release, *Davy Crockett, King of the Wild Frontier,* and Bill Hayes' version of "The Ballad of Davy Crockett" reached number one on the Billboard charts. Thirty years later, in 1986, David/Davy Crockett had lost none of his appeal and was celebrated on the occasion of the 150th anniversary of his death, which coincided with the sesquicentennial of the fall of the Alamo. As with the Centennial Celebration of 1836, "ten thousand special events, ranging from visits by two or three presidents to an oatmeal cook-off and a bike race in Oatmeal, Texas, presided over by Miss Bag of Oats," marked the occasion throughout Texas.[44]

Scholars have long agreed that the Crockett we know today, in any form, bears little if any resemblance to the man who lived long ago. As one scholar wrote in honor of Crockett's two hundredth birthday,

> Crockett was no warrior chieftain—neither Hector nor Achilles. As a youth he had tasted war and quickly come to view it as the cruel obscenity that it is. So contemptuous was he of the soldier's craft that in his autobiography he falsely claimed part in a mutiny and readily admitted that he had hired a substitute to finish out his term of enlistment. He

> came to Texas, like so many others, in search of economic and political opportunity. He died in search of that opportunity, not lusting after the blood of his fellow man.[45]

Despite the truth of the man, the function of Crockett in the master Texan narrative is to embody the loner, the confident, self-sufficient man. Two hundred years after the Alamo, Crockett's death had rendered the Texan an authentic American, even though Crockett, like many of the heroes of the Texas Revolution, was not, technically, a Texan. No matter; his death in the Lone Star State, not his life and accomplishments in Tennessee, is what his hero status requires. Casting actual Texans to play the Crockett role (Fess Parker in the 1950's and Billy Bob Thornton in 2004) adds a whiff of authenticity to their portrayals, linking the historical figure's presence at the historic battle to a transcendental Texan-ness in Crockett's—and his impersonators'—attitudes and behaviors.

THE POLITICS OF MARKETING TEXAS: THE TEXAS CENTENNIAL CELEBRATION AND THE CONTROL OF UNDESIRABLES, PART 2

The marketing strategies that would make best use of the Crockett brand predate Disney Studios but not Crockett's stage plays or early movies about him and the Alamo. Those strategies were developed in the years leading up to the Texas Centennial Celebration of 1936, which grew out of an economic crisis that fueled an identity shift in Texan cultural memory. Prior to the Centennial, most Americans' knowledge of Texas came from fictional accounts that focused on the Alamo and the image of the cowboy. Texans were depicted as plainspoken and honest (on the positive side) but illiterate and uncultured (on the negative). The Centennial set out to change the perception of Texas as the home of, as William Ragsdale phrases it, "Indians, longhorn cattle, illiterate cowboys, and wealthy ranchers."[46] In order to produce a counterimage, the Centennial's creators and marketers retained aspects of Texan cultural identity, such as ten-gallon hats and the Texas Rangers, while carefully crafting a message of economic prosperity and political acumen to rival that of the Midwest and East. These performances, grand in scope and educational in nature, were designed to appeal to families and contained enough information about the state's resources and accomplishments to dispel the stories of rattlesnakes and tumbleweeds.

Planning for the Texas Centennial started in the 1920's. With the onset of the Great Depression, however, politicians in both Washington, D.C., and Austin, Texas, questioned the need for a grand blowout when much of the population was unemployed. In the end, economic considerations were, indeed, the decisive factor in determining the shape and scope of the Centennial. Rather than planning, as originally envisioned, a series of commemorative events on the local and regional levels, the Texas Centennial Committee used the state's hundredth birthday as an excuse to, as they put it, market Texas to the rest of the country. After a fierce debate, Dallas was chosen as the site for the Texas Centennial Central Exposition, a 185-acre extravaganza of food, exhibits, and presentations which showcased the "mighty storehouse of information" which could be found within the state.[47] In an address to the Texas Senate, then-governor Miriam A. Ferguson said that "the Texas Centennial will bring in my opinion ten million new people to Texas, which will spend an average of Ten Dollars each for the manufactured products of our natural resources . . . No matter how you figure the Centennial it means a Hundred Million Dollars [of] new money turned loose in Texas. I am for it."[48]

The fair was a marvel of its time: it contained the largest open-air theatre in existence (Casa Mañana, still in use) and the largest Shakespearean theatre of its day, and featured the first use of air-conditioning at an exposition of any kind. To ensure that visitors and exhibitors were kept abreast of the exposition's success in terms of attendance, a huge, building-size cash register tallied attendance by the hour.

Businesses also used the Centennial to demonstrate the investment viability of the state, particularly in a time of economic downturn. Locally owned companies attracted business and spectators through clever combinations of the economic and the historical. The Humble Oil and Refining Company's Hall of History, for example, used fourteen dioramas to illustrate the state's history and eight huge relief maps to illustrate its geology.[49]

Despite its display of the riches of modern Texas, the focus of the Centennial remained grounded in the Texan revolutionary cultural identity. There were six twenty-foot cast stone art deco statues representing the six flags that had flown over Texas. Nowhere was the presence of revolutionary pedagogy more obvious than in the *Cavalcade of Texas,* an open-air drama depicting the history of the state "from galleon to oxcart and presidio to mission."[50] The *Cavalcade* offered Texas as central not only to its own history but also to that of the United States. The drama declared in its opening lines, "Out of the pages of history comes the story of the Cavalcade of Texas, marching onward through four hundred years up the steep peaks of empire. A mighty commonwealth has been robbed out of the vast wilderness of the Southwest."[51] Now (ostensibly) a state like any other, Texas presented itself as a unique entity by foregrounding its contributions to the civilization of the American Southwest.

The *Cavalcade of Texas* domesticated Texas history in a seventy-five-minute extravaganza of singing and patriotism that played two shows a night and became the Centennial Exposition's major success. The offstage narrative of the Centennial Exposition added a savvy blend of domestication and consumption, measured not in dollars (the entire fair finished deeply in debt) but in the number of people who attended and how many bottled drinks and sandwiches they consumed. The *Cavalcade* offered family-oriented, educational entertainment in an environment in which the more rough-and-tumble exploits of Davy Crockett or Jim Bowie were out of place. The grandeur of the drama's staging reinforced traditional notions of patriotism, strength, and honor as typically Texan.

A leading feature of the exposition's commercializing culture was the Centennial Rangerettes, a group of pretty young beauty queens who were to serve as hostesses. Clad in chaps, ten-gallon hats, and British riding pants (women's blue jeans did not yet exist), these ambassadors of the Centennial combined the visual cues of the Lone Star cowboy with feminine decorum and domestic behavior.

The exposition included the contributions of non–Lone Star types only as minor characters.[52] There were no tributes or exhibits devoted to Mexican Americans, though foreigners were given room in the amusement section of the fairgrounds, which included a Black Forest German village with an ice show skating rink, a "City of China," and a "Streets of Paris" show, with a club featuring nudity.[53] The absence of representations of Hispanics signaled the economic and political triumph of the Lone Star brand. As Joseph Roach observes, cultures perform themselves by performing "what and who they thought they were not. By defining themselves in opposition to others, they produced mutual representations from encomiums to caricatures, sometimes in each [other's] presence, at other times behind each other's backs."[54] Excluding representations outside of the Texan brand made clear who was not a part of Texan cultural identity: Hispanics and blacks. The traditional roles allotted women by Centennial organizers, except as simulacra of men (e.g., "cowboy" Rangerettes), also negated their importance to the construction of the Texan brand.

The invisibility of non-Texans at the Centennial precipitated the further economic and political disenfranchisement of (particularly) Hispanics within the state. Before the Texas Revolution began, Hispanics had become a minority in Texas, prompting the opening of Texas to Anglo colonization. The requirement that Anglo settlers become Mexican citizens and convert to Catholicism played on already existing religious and ethnic prejudices against native, immigrant, and slave populations. As the Anglo presence in Texas grew, continued Anglo loyalty to the United States rather than to Mexico led to the closing of American immigration in 1830. Those who were arriving from the United States were perceived to bring with them, in the words of one author, "an alien and degenerate race with dubious humanity."[55]

The Texan brand which emerged at the time of the Centennial reflects a complex web of political, economic, and cultural factors that had emerged by the early twentieth century. It is a facet of what Richard Flores calls "Texas Modern," or "how the forces of modernity wreaked havoc on Mexicans and Mexican Americans as they were displaced through the forces of technology, industrialization, and capitalism, or social production more generally."[56] The Texan brand was a part of this "social production," a performance of positive Texan characteristics in counterpoint to negative imagery relating to Mexicans. That imagery had, ultimately, legitimated the use of violence and other tactics to disenfranchise the Hispanic population. The "police arm" of the state had a long history of dispensing unequal justice by allowing "Anglos who murdered *mexicanos* to go unpunished."[57] That history predated the Texas Revolution and is on view in Juan Seguín's 1875 protest against the seizure of his land and that of other Tejano heroes of the Revolution, most of whom faced violence when they attempted to hold or reclaim their property. Farm- and ranchlands legally owned by Mexicans/Tejanos were seized by Texan courts and lawyers, and extortion was common, for example, charging a Tejano cattle owner with rustling (a crime punishable by death) and then pressuring his widow to sell.[58]

The disenfranchisement of the Hispanic population helped to bolster the image of the Texan as decidedly non-Hispanic. Traditions such as the presence of women at gaming tables and the prevalence of the fandango (a vigorous dance that exposed women's legs) were marked as signs of Mexican immorality during the decades leading up to the Centennial Celebration.[59] Performances of the "Mexican" became the ethnic counterpoint to performances of the "Texan";[60] indeed, the Mexican concept of machismo was singled out for ridicule as a sign of backward behavior (even as Texan men engaged in similar behavior).[61] The creation in the latter part of the nineteenth century of a "dual wage" and colonial labor system (which segregated workers into different classes of work and different pay scales based on ethnicity) separated nonwhite workers economically from their Texan counterparts. So did the segregation of Mexican Americans into their own schools, which operated (until found unconstitutional in 1948) without even the pretense of the "separate but equal" conditions found in black and white schools.[62] The formation of a "Chicano labor reserve," which ensured that labor was cheap and plentiful, set the boundaries of Texan identity in the first half of the twentieth century firmly outside the Hispanic community. Despite disenfranchisement, Texas was the destination Mexican immigrants chose by an overwhelming margin in the years 1910–1929, until the creation of the Border Patrol in 1924 began to limit migration.[63]

The Alamo began to be used as a symbol of political power. Attempts to save the mission pitted Adina De Zavala against Clara Driscoll, with Driscoll coming out the winner in her privileging of the mission as the real Alamo site. At the same time, as we have seen, movie images of the Alamo battle continued to depict the Mexican army in general and Santa Anna in particular as a force of evil. The doctrine of exclusion represented by the Texan brand, in its attempts to "own" the Alamo and to repress Hispanic Texans culturally, educationally, and economically, helped create resistance in the Hispanic community, as the formation of labor unions and advocacy groups such as LULAC attest. Resistance included teaching skills that enabled Hispanics to make a living, the buyback of old land (or purchase of new land), and advocating against economic and political discrimination. While these organizations confronted performances of an Anglo-constructed Mexican, they did little to interact with earlier twentieth-century formations of the predominantly white and male Texan. By 1950, the lines of demarcation between commercialized Texan cultural identity and the people it was designed to efface—those not conforming to the "correct" racial and gender norms—were drawn.

Over the next decades, part of maintaining the continued domestication of the brand involved the weeding out of undesirables. Disney's Davy Crockett played a large role in this process during the 1950's, but the process itself continued long after that decade. Indeed, the Texan became progressively more focused around issues relating to political power. At first, the brand depicted conflict with the need to weed out undesirables, exemplified by Sheriff Ed Earl Dodd in the musical *The Best Little Whorehouse in Texas* (1978). Based on the true story of Texas' last brothel, the Chicken Ranch outside of La Grange, the musical depicts the closing of the establishment due to pressure from a religious fanatic, Melvin J. Thorpe, and a scandal involving college football players.

Ed Earl is a good ole boy, a Lone Star, whose ideas play into the racial and ethnic biases prevalent in the state:

> SHERIFF: I'd just picked up three Meskin kids—they'd stole theirselves a goat from old man W. B. Starr and was throwin' theirselves a barbeque . . . I parked my car in a ditch and snuck up on them little greasers—they was barbercuin' that goat on a mesquite tree spit, and sloshin' on the barbeque sauce enough for LBJ. That proved it was pre-med-i-ta-ted, them havin' that sauce, don't you see? So we got 'em for Goddamn *felons.*[64]

Ed Earl's "funny" treatment of the "Meskins" in his custody—he "just slapped the cuffs on them little peckerwoods and marched 'em in lockstep back to the car"—and his stereotypical Texan language and attitudes reflect the power of the brand even when it tells against Anglos, because it distinguishes them from Hispanics. The distinction, however negative, helps maintain the sovereignty of the brand and, by extension, of Texan cultural identity.

One form of Texan bigotry comes up against another when the sheriff encounters the religious fanatic Thorpe, who uses his media savvy to create and sustain the existence of the Chicken Ranch as an issue of interest to the entire state. Ed Earl is quite aware of the political aspects of his job, even as he tries to balance them with the desire to keep Miss Mona's Chicken Ranch open:

> SHERIFF: I've stuck my neck out from hell-to-Georgia protecting you and there's some folks just might get to thinkin' its because of them campaign contributions you give me.
> MONA (teasingly): Ed Earl, we both know that ain't even half the story.
> SHERIFF: Me and you knows that sure . . . but what about them forty-six hunnerd voters out there? An office-holder's gotta make ends meet just like ever'body else . . . but the public don't unnerstand how politics works, no better than pigs unnerstands kissin'.[65]

Despite his political savvy, Ed Earl's very down-home qualities cause trouble when he cusses out Thorpe, who catches the incident on tape and broadcasts it on television. It is this incident, and not the existence of the Chicken Ranch, which initially polarizes the town:

> RUFUS: Ed Earl, ya can set up speed traps to catch the tourists, you can look the other way when the wrong kid swipes a car to go joy-ridin', hell,

you can even allow Mona to run her place out there. But the one thing you can't get away with, Ed Earl, is broadcasting gutter talk on TV!
SHERIFF: I didn't know he was takin' pitchers.
DOATSEY MAE: What did you figger the camera was for?[66]

The domestication of the Texan brand by the small town is not enough in this instance; Texan domestic values must be backed up by a paradigm of decorum. While the play never depicts Thorpe as a hypocrite, his fanatical pursuit of Mona without regard for her or her girls as people makes him a less-likeable character than the well-meaning, bigoted Ed Earl.

The character in *The Best Little Whorehouse,* however, who embodies the greatest scope in the performative range of the Texan is the waffling governor, whose signature song, "The Sidestep," sums up political acumen—to speak much but say nothing:

GOVERNOR (singing): Fellow Texans / I am proudly standing here to humbly say / I assure you / and I mean it / now who says I don't speak out as plain as day / and fellow Texans / I'm for progress / and the flag, long may it fly / I'm a poor boy / come to greatness / so it follows that I cannot tell a lie.[67]

Though weak in virtue, the Governor is politically savvy:

GOVERNOR (singing): OOOOOOOOOOO! I love to dance the little sidestep / now they see me, now they don't / I've come and gone . . . / and OOOOOOOOOOO! I love to sweep around a wide step / cut a little swath / and lead the people on.[68]

Whorehouse's Governor is an empty shell waiting to be filled with content, a fact he revels in and sees as central to his success. The Governor's use of the Texan brand underlines the emptiness of a Texan politics shorn of the "domesticated" virtues visible in other small-town Texan plays. Forty-two years after the Texas Centennial began to remove "undesirables" from the Texan brand, *The Best Little Whorehouse in Texas* reinserted them by presenting Anglo stereotypes of the brand. Nationally marketed, the branding of Texan cultural identity has lost the markers that first created it. The blending of "unique" and "common" reflected in the cultural brand, by 1978, needed a new take on power and politics. Fortunately, new recreations of Crockett were waiting in the wings.

THE NEW/OLD TEXAN BRAND

The characters who now appeared to carry the Texan brand through the twentieth century and across the globe each brought a unique rubric to the table. Larry Hagman's J. R. Ewing played the Texan to the world between 1978 and 1991. Rich, powerful, ruthless, and underhanded, though always deceptively charming, it was the picture of J. R. Ewing, resplendent in cowboy boots and Stetson, that most identified the Texan at that time. Hagman, who was born in Texas, brought J. R. to life and gave him his slickness as a Texan. It was easy to picture J. R. Ewing as one of the original investors in the Centennial: a wealthy man with power and influence who desired to market his product to the world. In the case of *Dallas,* which ran for thirteen seasons, J. R. was the product, the lynchpin of the show's popularity and appeal. The Texan was center stage. America's obsession with Texas and, more specifically, the Texan, grew during this time, much as it had during the days of Fess Parker. Texan cultural identity as a distinct performance of regionality could be emulated, although never duplicated, by viewers around the world.

Dallas was not the only television show to capitalize on the Texan brand to bring in audiences. In the 1990s, Chuck Norris' Cordell Walker, of *Walker, Texas Ranger,* redefined the Lone Star as the straightlaced (and straight-faced) Texas Ranger with superior fighting skills and mystical abilities (bestowed on him as a child by American Indians). If J. R. Ewing was the dark side of the Texan, then Walker was the other end of the spectrum. Branding permits and encourages this kind of range, far from the Lone Star's original grounding in the actions of Crockett, Bowie, and Travis, because the purpose of a brand is to be memorable. Equally white and male, J. R. and Walker could each carve out a definition of the independent, freedom-loving, larger-than-life Texan and carry the version to new, global sites. Because of this wider context, it was easier for the Lone Star to appear in previously unrealized places, provided that the portrayers still met the basic criteria of the brand: white and male.

Enter a political figure who met the criteria and was a perfect receptacle for the political power of the Lone Star brand, provided from outside of the character itself: George W. Bush. The perception of the Texan in politics received a new spin in the blending of J. R. Ewing, Cordell Walker, and Ed Earl Dodd into a performance of the Bush/Shrub/"W" brand of Texan developed by, for, and from George W. Bush.

The linking of the Texan to political power is particularly obvious at a time when the president of the United States casts himself in the role of the quintessential Texan. Rather than retreating to Camp David, President Bush entertains foreign dignitaries at his ranch in Crawford. In turn, he has been feted with barbecue dinners and ten-gallon hats during state visits abroad. As governor of Texas, he was often perceived as shaping Texas government by "sidestepping" like the Governor in *The Best Little Whorehouse in Texas*. Speaking much, but saying nothing, long a feature of political satire, is adroitly combined in George W. Bush's Texan, with earlier Texan attributes of the plainspoken and down-home characteristics of the cowboy (also represented by Calvin Armstrong in *Texas!*).

Comparison of Pres. George W. Bush to a cowboy, however, is as slippery a performance as sidestepping blended with plain speaking. Cowboys do not wear "$300 designer cowboy boots, a $1,000 cowboy hat and [own a] 1,600-acre . . . ranch,"[69] nor are they sons and grandsons of millionaires or graduates of Yale University. Neither does George W. Bush emblematize the spirit of honesty, magnanimity, and fair play that dominates early 1950's movies, when Gene Autry, Roy Rogers, and the Virginian were the role models of choice. Indeed, like Davy Crockett, George W. Bush is not a native Texan (he was born in New Haven, Connecticut).

Bush's representation of the Texan, then, is an inherited brand, characterized by what has been called a "faux-Texas accent and gunfighter strut,"[70] a brand anyone might assume and perform. Though it appears that political and economic forces have detached the Texan brand from revolutionary pedagogy and brought it into a new arena, making Texan cultural identity synonymous with his values, beliefs, and ideas, George W. Bush's performance of the Texan is, in fact, an effective (and thus practiced) performance of that pedagogy which appeals to the (now international) aspects the Texan brand represents. This is no "one man's Texan" or "perversion of the code." Rather, the political Texan brand of the early-twenty-first century has taken what it needs from Texan cultural identity and abandoned less-useful aspects. In this way, Indians have become cowboys; Europeans, J. R. Ewing devotees; and George W. Bush, like the "Texan" Davy Crockett before him, a brand for liberty and home rule.

Such brands are developed to identify and be remembered. George W. Bush's version of the Texan is interesting for what it admits and omits. Several writers, including columnist Molly Ivins, have commented that, "in Texas, 'intellectual' is often used as a synonym for 'snob.'"[71] Alamo movies portray William Barret Travis as an educated man who looked down on the men under his command and, more important, the members of the militia under the command of Jim Bowie (the regular guys). In Disney's

The Alamo, for example, Travis apologizes to Bowie for insulting the men under the latter's command; Bowie replies, "They didn't even understand what you were saying." Because he is outside the realm of comprehension of common "Texians," it is up to Travis to become "plainspoken."

George W. Bush also marked this shift in his successful 2000 presidential campaign when he distanced himself from the seemingly more educated (and therefore aloof) Al Gore. During an interview with Oprah Winfrey in 2000, Bush replied to a question concerning self-doubt caused by his lack of experience: "There's a lot of folks in my state that—whose judgement and instincts and common sense I respect a lot. They may not even have ever gone to college."[72] According to one analyst, "Bush deftly used the question . . . to portray himself as a regular guy who found himself out of place among the sons of the elite at Andover but quickly discovered that his lack of book learning did not signal a lack of intelligence."[73]

Since the 1990's, George W. Bush has honed his down-home Texan political persona to an art, first as governor of Texas, then as president. From the beginning, he has cast himself as the plainspoken, not-too-educated (never mind Andover and Yale) good ole boy who can get the job done. He has played this role not only for the American public but for Europeans, as well. Long before "freedom fries" and the conflict with France over the Iraq invasion, President Bush was criticized by the European press for using what one reporter called "frontier lingo . . . [feeding] the images overseas of Mr. Bush as a hopelessly inarticulate, trigger-happy cowboy."[74] Armed with the Texan tradition associating articulate, educated speech with aloofness and snobbery, an unabashed Bush makes good use of the brand's appeal to "regular guys" who value both plain speech and "frontier" forthrightness.

Take, for example, an editorial cartoon from the Belgrade daily *Danas* from July 2003. There, on the front page, is an image of George W. Bush in ten-gallon hat, kerchief, and cowboy boots. He is positioned in a hole in a brick wall which just lines up with the outline of a large, mythological-appearing beast, which he appears to be riding. The symbolism is plain: Bush is represented as the Texan, which is now the American brand (the cartoon is criticizing the invasion of Iraq). The conflation is natural enough: Bush is a Texan and he is also the president of the United States; thus, the brand, at this time, simultaneously represents both spaces. What is notable in the conflation is that the Texan, in becoming a brand, has been emptied of the history and culture it once represented and now references only itself, a situation evoking a statement George W. Bush made prior to the 2000 election: "Actually, I—this may sound a little West Texas to you, but I like it. When I'm talking about—when I am talking about myself, and when he's talking about myself, all of us are talking about me."[75] As a global brand, the Texan enters the realm of what Baudrillard calls a "simulation," a sign which communicates the absence of what it represents, much as a signature machine represents the sign of the absent boss who signed, but did not sign, a paycheck.[76]

The Bush administration has never denied its use of stagecraft to sell the president's ideas and, in fact, is proud of its ability to continually create backdrops and scenarios deemed appropriate to the situation, as with the now-infamous "'Top Gun' landing on the deck of the carrier Abraham Lincoln" in 2003 to announce the end of formal combat in Iraq.[77] Given President Bush's identification with the Texan brand, leaders and countries outside of the United States have begun to see the American as the Texan and Bush's attitudes as those of all Americans. In addition, as Molly Ivins puts it, all Texans get painted with the "Bush brush,"[78] and, indeed, the Texan brand is a fungible trope that works as well at the local as at the global level.

Part of effective branding is the "identify and buy relationship," which requires performing (buying) what is recognized (the brand); thus the Texan is currently what the brand representative (George W. Bush) does. What is missing from this equation is the other thing a good brand is supposed to cause us to do: to remember the brand and what it represents. By reducing the brand to George W. Bush, the sign of the Texan implies what it used to remind us of. What remains is the performance of characteristics, a show of shows.

Christopher Hitchens, the narrator of the documentary *Texas: America Supersized,* observes that George W. Bush is "a man for whom the word cowboy carries no insult."[79] He is happy to enact the cowboy, and his performance of the Texan harkens back to the stage representations of Crockett. Indeed, "W's" brand is a conflation of two nineteenth-century theatre stereotypes: the stage Yankee, and the stage frontiersman. In his study of George W. Bush's Texan image, Michael Lind claims that "the swaggering Texan is nothing more than the Scots-Irish frontiersman—a more recent version of the stereotypical 'Kaintuck' portrayed in early nineteenth century American literature and popular drama, before the Texan cowboy became a cliche. The career in fact and legend of David Crockett . . . symbolizes the westward movement of this Scots-Irish archetype. The imagery of the Texan cowboy may be that of northern Mexico (the cowboy or vaquero costume, the lariat and horse, the ranch), but the spirit is that of the mountaineers of the Appalachians and Ozarks."[80] Lind depicts the political mind-set currently represented by George W. Bush as a kind of mental contaminant, the result of Scots-Irish immigrant culture combining with southern Protestant fundamentalism and Old South racism to create a landscape awash in power, money, and conservatism. Lind, a fifth-generation native Texan, attempts to counter this political trend with the more "enlightened" historical viewpoints of other "native" Texas politicians, such as Lyndon B. Johnson and H. Ross Perot.[81]

Lind's is a critique of authenticity, a "battle of the brands," in which one person's performance must emerge as more "real" than another's, as in the days of the Daughters of the Republic of Texas' battle over the Alamo. Such contests serve only to legitimate the existence of the brand and to control its performance; indeed, George W. Bush's critics claim that he is mainly the performer of scripts written by people making the real decisions (Deputy White House Chief of Staff Karl Rove, Vice President Dick Cheney). Self-scripted or not, it is brand performance that creates loyalty in the world of identify and buy. That is what consumers remember, absent what cultural identity demands of its presentations: history, myth, and memory.

CHALLENGING THE BRAND

There are performances which intersect with the Texan brand and problematize its seemingly placid façade. When they occur, these performances have also provided some of the most cutting critiques of the claims to authenticity of political narratives. Ruth Margraff's *Centaur Battle of San Jacinto* (1997), "an extended barroom brawl" in nine scenes, presents archetypal characters who simultaneously represent both generic Texans and such famous revolutionary figures as Stephen F. Austin, Davy Crockett, Sam Houston, and Santa Anna. Perhaps the most incongruous character in the play is Crazy Horse, an Oglala Sioux chief who, according to Margraff's notes, was "not born yet during this battle, which makes him even more innocent."[82] The scenes move through the previously articulated historical spaces of the Revolution layered with the "muscular vernaculars of the 1830's, classic cinematic posturing and threat, undocumented exhalations of the casualties, [and] ancient Anglo verbal combat (warcries/precedents) inscribing the monuments and money of this brave new world . . . [and] inspiring the Texan behavior at the battle of San Jacinto . . . and hereafter."[83] In her narrative, Margraff problematizes the traditional "heroic" performance of revolutionary pedagogy by Anglo characters and, by extension, the Texan historical memory which employs its practices.

An unusual addition to Margraff's drama is the character of the Yellow Rose—proprietor of the saloon in which the brawl occurs and based on the character of Emily Morgan/West (see Chap. 2). Maragraff centers her drama around the usually elided (and oft-thought-fictitious character) of the Yellow Rose. Maragraff capitalizes on the ambivalence of Morgan/West as a symbol in another play, *Centaur Battle of San Jacinto.* The Yellow Rose not only "dallies" with Santa Anna (fulfilling her legendary role), but they have sex onstage, during which Santa Anna claims her as his "bauble," a woman so ignorant that she "can't even tell a ring from a spoon."[84] In the end, however, the Yellow Rose is the only one left standing, as the men destroy one another in a vain attempt to achieve the status of archetype. She smears something, "possibly warpaint," on her face and remarks, "[you] hate me harder everyday. But you sing up in my ear all night that I'm the yellow rose of Texas."[85] The Yellow Rose is able to appropriate the Texan brand for herself, then destroys it and all of its representations and counter-representations to create a new series of performance practices that will allow for a wider variety of voices to participate in the political arena.

There have been other, momentary, interactions with the Lone Star brand that call into question its presuppositions. Many of these moments occur in performance art pieces that center on the Alamo and other Texan images. Guillermo Gómez-Peña and La Pocha Nostra's collaboration with San Antonio's Jump-Start Performance Co., *Epcot: El Ala-MALL* (2004), puts on display a series of ethnic stereotypes and then, as with most of Pocha Nostra's work, stages strategic interventions around them. The context of the performance is an exhibit of "provocative specimens for human consumption" staged by a multinational media corporation, SpikNN—CC. Stereotypes such as Selena, la Chola, the Daughters of the Republic of Texas, el Vato, the seductive *señorita,* and the Chicano Secret Service Sellout are part of the pantheon of characters who represent those artifacts of Texan cultural identity which are undesirable. The aim of the piece is to present these subjects in their domesticated forms so that "audiences [can] safely experience a range of abhorrent bodies, skins, minds, and ideologies."[86] The result is an interactive environment in which audience members, continually recontextualizing the presence of stereotypes within the piece, are invited to exhibit their own aberrations within the larger framework of the displays. *Epcot: El Ala-MALL* promotes those whose stories fall outside the heroic exploits of Crockett, creating a space where those stories that have been rendered politically undesirable because of race, ethnicity, gender, and so on, are put on display. It is a kind of counter-Centennial Exposition, where the exhibits are designed to show the viewer what is not part of the Texan brand.

The installation was shown in San Antonio, the home of Texan cultural identity—the Alamo—and drew on the image of the site for its logo and decor. The audience, as was the authors' intent, was enthusiastic and interacted eagerly with the "exhibits," in some cases, becoming part of the installations themselves.

Some of the performers served as "moving personas" who circulated through the spectators. One such character, "Viva Maxine, the last of the DIRT (Daughters in the Republic of Texas)," was a man dressed as a middle-aged woman in tennis shoes, recalling Carliner's characterization of the DRT in the *Viva Max!* confrontations at the Alamo. Maxine's job is to represent the traditional view of Texas as white and (covertly) male. As the show progressed, Maxine's position was undercut by her interaction with the—in her mind—"inferior" characters around her, and she began to enforce her viewpoint through progressively more violent means, accosting characters physically who did not conform to her image of appropriate Texan identity. By evening's end, she/he (having lost her wig during the fighting) was transformed into a man in drag engaged in a slow-motion, sadomasochistic sex simulation with the "enemy," a character by the name of El Aztec Loco Tech. Maxine's journey from stereotypical Texas "lady" to a character whose appearance and behavior was completely outside of the Texan brand helped to undercut the brand's supremacy and showed how even the most secure of Texan images—the DRT—could be co-opted for the purpose of subverting Texan cultural identity's dominant white, male narrative.

Other subversive performance events have circulated on the World Wide Web. The first scene of Tony Kushner's *Only We Who Guard the Mystery Shall Be Unhappy* (2004), part of a larger work which gained popularity in an on-line form and was published in *The Nation* magazine, features First Lady Laura Bush, who "speaks with a gentle Texas drawl."[87] In a satire of a *Reading Rainbow* moment, Laura Bush reads to dead Iraqi children and reveals (what is portrayed as) her true inner feelings about the war, the civilian casualty count, her husband's actions, and the role of religious faith in promoting totalitarianism. The text is one of her favorite books, "The Grand Inquisitor" section of Dostoyevsky's *The Brothers Karamazov* ("he would have *gotten* me, I think, you know?)."[88] Laura Bush links the work to a larger sphere of Texan cultural discourse—"Fyodor Mikhailovich Dostoyevsky was I think . . . sometimes I think the only man who could really understand me, and many, many women feel this way. At least in Texas we do"—tying her own desires and needs to that larger Texan identity through which things in her life assume or lose importance. Her descriptions of the president, or "Bushie," as she calls him, position him as the Dread Spirit come to claim his victims. Even though she is the wife of a Texan whose views and policies are otherwise, Kushner's Laura Bush positions herself as a spokesperson for the other, now little heard, voice of political Texas: liberal, peace loving, democratic, horrified by the deeds perpetrated by her country and, more specifically, her husband. Like Emily Morgan/West, the Yellow Rose of Texas, this First Lady of the Republic transgresses the pedagogical boundaries of revolutionary discourse. Despite Laura Bush's alterity, the ending of this scene is ambiguous. As she kisses the children to whom she will read, she is reminded of the end of the story:

> LAURA BUSH: The kiss glows in my heart. That's from *The Brothers Karamazov* . . . In fact, now that I think of it, it's something Ivan says about the Grand Inquisitor . . . Here it is: "The kiss glowed in his heart. But the old man adhered to his ideas."
> (She closes the book. She looks troubled. She smiles at the children.
> They smile at her.)
> LAURA BUSH: The kiss glows in my heart.
> But.
> I adhere to my ideas.[89]

The implication is that, in the end, the Texan is unswerving in his (or her) beliefs, though the satirical nature of Kushner's text sets up a moment in which those whose political performances fall outside of the reigning Texan brand interrogate what signification has come to represent.

All three of the performances challenging exclusive readings of the Texan brand have either been small-scale affairs, performed in independent theatres for short runs and with little or no publicity, or performed on the Internet with only a virtual audience. Their presence, however, underscores Bhabha's construction of the Janus-faced discourse in which narratives counter to the dominant one enter into the larger discourse, not through a large-scale intervention, but at a grassroots level, drawing in people locally and building them into a critical mass.[90] It is in this way that Texan cultural identity is represented, contested, and inverted and showcases the absence of and need for history, myth, and memory in the Texan brand.

CONCLUSION

The Texan brand has been in a constant state of transformation since the historical event producing its foundational myth, the Texas Revolution of 1836, occurred. Various political agendas have used the myth to advance their own purposes. The brand created from that myth retains the myth's image, replayed as a Texan agenda that got its political power by privileging certain enactments of race and gender over others. Grounded in the historical exploits of characters like Crockett, Bowie, and Travis, as well as the behaviors found in small-town Texas, the Texan myth has functioned to keep Texan cultural identity relatively stable and Texan cultural memory selective.

The demand for a return to the history, myth, and memory cultural identity demands is visible not only in the performances of undesirables but also through opposition within the ranks traditionally identified as closest to filling the brand's criteria. The *Lone Star Iconoclast,* a Crawford, Texas, paper, for example, endorsed John Kerry in the 2004 election campaign.[91] Cries of outrage from local residents gave that opposition national visibility through the work of *Doonesbury* creator Garry Trudeau, who featured the article in his daily comic strip (October 15, 2004).[92]

National newspapers also covered the "runaway Democrats" in the 2003 Texas House of Representatives who, when faced with a Republican-driven redistricting plan that would have given the GOP a clear majority in the Texas House, fled to Oklahoma and deprived that body of the quorum needed to vote on the measure. This action was seen by many in the news media as a throwback to the heroic days of the Republic, with the Democrats playing the "Texians" and the Republicans, the "Mexicans" (or vice-versa, depending on media allegiances).[93] Again, the episode received national news attention (including a series of articles in the *New York Times*), and, again, it was cast as an incident that could only happen in the state which had produced Pres. George W. Bush.

Politically, the Texan brand, like a flag to be captured, can represent a variety of performances. A brand is a fixed but appropriable depiction of what it represents, a simulation at the end of a long movement away from the historical event that gave birth to the cultural identity the Texan brand both captures and mocks. Emptied of their cultural signifiers, cultural brands retain imitable characteristics, signs like the events and behaviors commemorated in foundational myths, but up for sale to those who identify with and remember what the brand impersonates. The Texan as a brand enables wearers of it, like George W. Bush, to put on the characteristics the brand impersonates, like cowboy boots on the feet of wealthy women shopping on Rodeo Drive in California. Such impersonations always draw attention back to what is represented, mocking acquired claims to the real and turning the brand entity into the true sign of the ability to purchase and display it. Commodified identity represents only itself and testifies to a claim to authenticity where nothing authentic can be found.

SIX

CONCLUSION

"Our Flag Still Waves Proudly from the Walls"

Where memory is, theatre is.

HERBERT BLAU

Texan cultural identity works on a variety of levels to construct and maintain its particular parameters and representations.[1] Actual sites where historical events occurred are appropriated for the reenactment of Texan cultural memory, a space for occupation and shaping through the use of history, nature, and the "museumization" of culture. The reshaping of actual sites produces a recognizable pedagogy which promotes an ideological stance about events in the Texas Revolution and their interpretation; this sets a text about "Texan"-"Mexican" relations in place. These teachings about macro events at the micro level in turn encourage Texan behaviors visible in the performance of the beliefs, ideas, and attitudes by average Texans in small towns and in plays and other works about small Texas towns. The political Texan allows history, reenactment, and ideology to localize a global stage through the commodification of the Texan into a brand which is then marketed nationally and internationally.

The preceding chapters have shown the depth and breadth of Texan performance and its relationship to various spaces of cultural memory. One does not have to be "culturally aware" to be persuaded by the image, and even the critically minded may take the Texan as normative. As Robert Bryce has said, "Whether you are buying gasoline for your car, listening to the radio, or even casting your vote for president, the Lone Star State is probably affecting your experience."[2] Texans seem to be everywhere, from actual residents who sport "Texan by birth" bumper stickers to the "Texas passport" gag gift given to those outside the Lone Star State. The Internet now offers a tremendous amount of historical information from sources as reputable as the Texas State Archives, thereby creating ranks of "virtual" Texans who further identity claims with the Lone Star State. Texan cultural identity has moved beyond the brand into the realm of the virtual, confounding the meaning of events such as the bestowal by George W. Bush, himself a created Texan, of "honorary Texan" status on foreign dignitaries.[3]

The power of the performance of regionality is, paradoxically, reinforced by the interest of outsiders: those who live outside of Texas seek ways to understand and experience Texan-ness. As René Girard notes, "order, peace and fecundity depend on cultural distinctions; it is not these distinctions but the loss of them that gives birth to fierce rivalries and sets members of the same family or social group at one another's throats."[4] The performance of regionality is exemplified by the crafting of Texan cultural identity into a distinct brand which privileges a certain race, gender, and historical lineage. Taken side by side with other forms of cultural distinction, the performance of regionality becomes a powerful tool for marking the boundaries between states: states of being, geographic states, and conflicting states of affairs.

The practice of Texan cultural memory reverses the Orwellian concept of "rectification," in which the past is continually brought up to date to reflect the present. In the case of the Texan, the present must in some way bring itself into alignment with the past. The brand is one way in which this goal has been accomplished. The architectural framework of state monuments, parks, and museums provides a space in which the brand can exist, and historical pedagogy provides grounding for it, as do plays that depict culturally defined behaviors identified primarily as small town. The primary function of the brand is political-economic, but the overall function of historical memory is to ensure the uniqueness of the Texan as opposed to residents of any other state in the Union. As Sonja Kuftenic asserts, such identities are not preformed but performed and, as a result, have a fluidity that their surface permanence attempts to obscure.[5] The more that historians, politicians, and residents of the state attempt to hold onto a unilateral idea of what constitutes Texan cultural identity, the more that identity shifts, changes, and avoids attempts to codify its multifaceted parts.

The architectural, historical, behavioral, and political aspects of Texan cultural identity work together to keep the culture itself intact. This interweaving is vital to the culture's survival and growth. It reinforces the ideas of Raymond Williams, who states that "a culture, while it is being lived, is always in part unknown, always in part unrealized. The making of a community is always an exploration, for consciousness cannot precede creation, and there is no formula for unknown experience. A good community, a living culture, will, because of this, not only make room for but actively encourage all and any who can contribute to the advance in consciousness which is the common need."[6]

The shifting parameters of Texan cultural identity keep the community growing but also keep the various cultural groups in their respective places. Texan cultural identity uses stereotypical behaviors and historical mindsets to maintain its boundaries, despite constant conflict with ethnographic artifacts—people, stories, and performances—which fall outside of those parameters yet demand to be included. These demands are all the more ironic because, while they seek to move "real" Texas history back to American Indians, the arrival of the French pirate Jean Laffite, the establishment of Spanish missions, the Texas Revolution, or the Confederacy, they validate the appropriateness of seeking an originary point for a history which predates the culture "Texan" seeks to identify.

The population of Texas has increasingly shifted to cosmopolitan centers. In addition to the high-population centers of Dallas and Houston, the state includes San Antonio, now the ninth-largest city in the United States by population, and Laredo, the city with the ninth-largest overall population growth in the 1990s.[7] Contemporary performers, such as Guillermo Gómez-Peña, have used the existence of a cosmopolitan audience to challenge the perceptions of the Texan (and all Hispanics) in Texas projected by traditional depictions such as *The Best Little Whorehouse in Texas,* the *Tuna* plays, and many films. The small-town Texan now joins the revolutionary Texan in traditional depictions as a nostalgic glimpse back to a past slipping beyond recall.

The Texan as a sign of the common performance of regionality provides us with a new and diverse perspective on how Americans perform their cultural identity because of the Texan's history and prominence as a unique identity within American culture. To be an identity within an identity, "part of a pluralistic world," as Gianni Vattimo observes, "means to experience freedom as a continual oscillation between belonging and disorientation."[8] The performance of Texan and similar cultural identities helps to provide some sense of grounding for Americans within a maelstrom of global movement, yet each identity is a construct, not a reality, and represents choices from among available beliefs, attitudes, and ideologies. In this way, the Texan brand represented by George W. Bush demonstrates how cultural identity functions and what it means at this historical moment. The ability of any region—great or small, city or state—to create, enact, and document cultural identity produces an archive of cultural representations that has generated performances and theatrical practices which the region, in turn, reflects. What we learn from the Texan is the importance of performance in creating and maintaining a cultural identity that, both powerful and fragile, constantly repeats and changes our understanding of history, myth, and memory—and of identity itself.

NOTES

CHAPTER I

1. Quotation in the epigraph retrieved November 25, 2005, from http://politicalhumor.about.com/library/blbushisms2000.htm.

2. The organization, founded in December 1995, had, until the siege, contented itself mostly with issuing proclamations in support of American Indian tribes attempting to reclaim land from the U.S. government and announcing formal diplomatic relations with newly emerging nations.

3. Chuck Lindell, "McLaren Lays Down Arms," *Austin American-Statesman* (May 4, 1997). Two others who had initially surrendered fled instead into the Davis Mountains. One was killed in a shootout with police, and the other was arrested four months later near New Waverly, Texas (Chuck Lindell, "Rangers End Hunt for Second Fugitive," *Austin American-Statesman* [May 7 [8?], 1997]; Terri Langford, "Republic of Texas Fugitive Keyes Caught," *Austin American-Statesman* [September 20, 1997]). McLaren was tried later that year and sentenced to ninety-nine years in prison. He is currently incarcerated in the federal penitentiary at Huntsville, Texas.

4. Although the movement was nearly destroyed by the publicity caused by the siege and McLaren's trial, not to mention Republic president Archie Lowe's indictment on contempt charges (Associated Press, "Legal Problems Deepen Rift Splitting Republic of Texas," *Victoria Advocate* [May 27, 1997]), the Republic of Texas continued to exist as two separate organizations throughout the late 1990's and the early 2000's. However, the two sides reunited under the leadership of Daniel Miller at a General Council meeting on June 17, 2002 ("Republic News: FLASH!!! GREAT NEWS!!!" [http://www.republic-of-texas.org/news.htm]; retrieved August 1, 2002). The Republic has since established its capital in the East Texas town of Overton and continues to recruit members (Simon Romero, "In Small Town, the Fight Continues for Texas Sovereignty," *New York Times on the Web* [February 13, 2005], http://www.nytimes.com/2005/02/13/national/13overton.html?ex=1108962000&en=55f728a380a6e274&ei=5070; retrieved February 13, 2005).

5. Texas' tenuous claim to sovereignty stems from the reintegration of the Confederacy into the United States following the Civil War (see Chap. 4); however, the Republic of Texas movement traces its assertions back to the treaty of annexation in 1845.

6. Mike Tharp and William J. Holstein, "Mainstreaming the Militia," *U.S. News and World Report* (April 21, 1997).

7. The current state of Hawai'i was a kingdom until its territory was annexed by the United States in 1893 (http://www.pixi.com/~kingdom/; retrieved May 22, 2007).

8. The full explanation of the Republic's stance and its interpretation of the 1845 annexation treaty can be found at http://www.republic-of-texas.net/q&a.shtml#Is%20this%20legal; retrieved August 1, 2002.

9. Francis Barker, *The Culture of Violence* (Chicago: University of Chicago Press, 1993), 233.

10. Homi K. Bhabha, "Introduction," *Nation and Narration* (New York: Routledge, 1990), 3.

11. Barbara Kirshenblatt-Gimblett, *Destination Culture: Tourism, Museums, and Heritage* (Berkeley & Los Angeles: University of California Press, 1998), 17–18.

12. Other states, such as Maine, rely more on landscape and activities such as lobster fishing to create a unique regional identity.

13. Allen R. Myerson, "They Remember the Alamo Differently" (*New York Times;* reprinted in *Minneapolis Star-Tribune* [March 30, 1994]). More about this attempt will be revealed in Chapter 2.

14. Diana Taylor, *The Archive and the Repertoire: Performing Cultural Memory in the Americas* (Durham, N.C.: Duke University Press, 2003), xvi.

15. The Lone Star nickname is derived from the state's flag: "A single star was part of the Long Expedition (1819), Austin Colony (1821) and several flags of the early Republic of Texas. Some say that the star represented the wish of many Texans to achieve statehood in the United States. Others say it originally represented Texas as the lone state of Mexico which was attempting to uphold its rights under the Mexican Constitution of 1824. At least one 'lone star' flag was flown during the Battle of Concepcion and the Siege of Bexar (1835). Joanna Troutman's flag with a single blue star was raised over Velasco on January 8, 1836. Another flag with a single star was raised at the Alamo (1836) according to a journal entry by David Crockett. One carried by General Sam Houston's Texian army (which defeated Mexican General Santa Anna at the Battle of San Jacinto) may have been captured and taken to Mexico. Another 'lone star' flag, similar to the current one but with the red stripe above the white, was also captured the following year (1837) and returned to Mexico. The 'David G. Burnet' flag, of 'an azure ground' (blue background) 'with a large golden star central' was adopted by the Congress of the Republic of Texas in December of 1836. It continued in use as a battle flag after being superseded in January of 1839. The 1839 design has been used to symbolize the Republic and the 'Lone Star State' ever since" (http://www.50states.com/bio/nickname5.htm); retrieved May 13, 2004.

16. According to the 2000 Census, all persons who identified as Hispanics made up 32 percent of the state's total population. Of that number, 76 percent were Mexican in origin (U.S. Census Bureau, Census 2000, Summary File 1 and unpublished data).

17. This perception of performance, to Goffman, is not due simply to a person's conscious decision to embody certain character traits; it also stems from the fact that, "when an individual enters the presence of others, they commonly seek to acquire information about him or bring into play information about him already possessed." This is so that, in Goffman's view, "the others will know how best to act in order to call forth a desired response from him" (*The Performance of Self in Everyday Life* [New York: Anchor, 1959], 1).

18. Dwight Conquergood, "Rethinking Ethnography: Towards a Critical Cultural Politics," *Communication Monographs* 58 (June 1991): 190.

19. Michel de Certeau, *The Practice of Everyday Life* (Berkeley & Los Angeles: University of California Press, 1944), xviii–xix.

20. Marvin Carlson, *Performance: A Critical Introduction* (New York: Routledge, 1996). For an excellent synopsis of just how complicated is the relationship between theatre and performance (and their attendant adjectives, performativity and theatricality), see Janelle Reinlet, "The Politics of Discourse: Performativity Meets Theatricality," *SubStance* 31 (2002): 201–215.

21. Judith Butler, *Excitable Speech: A Politics of the Performative* (New York: Routledge: 1997), 51, emphasis hers.

22. Dwight Conquergood, "Performing as a Moral Act: Ethical Dimensions of the Ethnography of Performance," *Literature in Performance: A Journal of Literary and Performing Art* 5.2: 2.

23. The use of such stereotypes was typical in the theatre of the time, as the "Kaintuck" and "Bowery Boy" characters popular on the American stage indicate. The Kaintuck, based on Davy Crockett, will be discussed in Chapter 5. For more on the Bowery Boy and other stage representations of American types, see Rosemarie K. Bank, *Theatre Culture in America, 1825–1860* (New York: Cambridge University Press, 1997).

24. Edward Tabor Linenthal, *Sacred Ground: Americans and Their Battlefields,* 2nd ed. (Urbana: University of Illinois Press, 1993), 3.

25. Kenneth E. Foote, *Shadowed Ground: America's Landscapes of Violence and Tragedy* (Austin: University of Texas Press, 1997), 5.

26. The hyperreal is defined by Jean Baudrillard as "the product of an irradiating synthesis of combinatory models in a hyperspace without atmosphere" ("Simulacra and Simulations, *Selected Writings,* ed. and intro. Mark Poster [Stanford, Calif.: Stanford University Press, 1988], 167). It is the manifestation of the emptiness of the real, of the lack of reality itself, implicit in its very representation. To Baudrillard, "America . . . is a hyperreality . . . because it is a utopia which has behaved from the very beginning as though it were already achieved (*America,* trans. Chris Turner [New York: Verso, 1988], 28).

27. Joseph Roach, *Cities of the Dead: Circum-Atlantic Performance* (New York: Columbia University Press, 1996).

28. For example, American Indians were Texas' allies in the Civil War. Chickasaw, Choctaw, Creek, and Cherokee were fighting with the Tenth Cavalry on the side of the Confederacy and were recognized for their contributions to the cause by their inclusion in the design of the unit's flag (Robert Mayberry, *Texas Flags* [College Station: Texas A&M University Press, 2001], 67–68).

29. The constitution recognized by the Republic of Texas is the March 17, 1836, document, which states that anyone who has lived within Texas' boundaries for at least six months can apply to become a citizen of the Republic of Texas ("Citizenship in the Republic of Texas" [http://www.republic-of-texas.com/citizen.html; retrieved October 11, 1997]). This is a liberal interpretation of Article I, Section 4, of the 1836 Constitution, which deals with election to the Texas House of Representatives and reads, "No person shall be eligible to a seat in the house of representatives until he shall have attained the age of twenty-five years, shall be a citizen of the republic, and shall have resided in the country or district six months next preceding his election ("The Constitution of the Republic of Texas, March 17, 1836" [http://www.republic-of-texas.com/cons1836.htm; retrieved October 13, 1997]).

30. Perhaps the most notorious example of this is the 1969 film *Viva Max!* which stars Peter Ustinov as an inept Mexican general who attempts to retake the modern-day Alamo. The filming of the movie caused an uproar, which will be discussed in detail in Chapter 3. For more information on the film, see Frank Thompson, *Alamo Movies* (Plano, Tex.: Wordware Press, 1991), 85–90.

31. Barker, *Culture,* 220.

32. Southwestern Writers Collection, Special Collections, Albert B. Alkek Library, Texas State University Archives, San Marcos, Box 118, Folder 1. More details about the impact of this pronouncement appear in Chapter 4.

33. See William C. Davis, *Three Roads to the Alamo: The Lives and Fortunes of David Crockett, James Bowie, and William Barret Travis* (New York: HarperCollins, 1998), for an example of this new type of biographical perspective.

CHAPTER 2

1. The quotation in the epigraph comes from the officer in charge of overseeing Texas during Reconstruction. For more information on Philip Sheridan, see "Sheridan, Philip Henry," *Handbook of Texas Online* (http://www.tsha.utexas.edu/handbook/online/articles/view/SS/fs6.html). The quotation is a famous one and can be found in numerous on- and off-line sources, including http://en.thinkexist.com/quotes/philip_henry_sheridan/. Both retrieved June 15, 2007.

2. Phil Rosenthal and Bill Groneman, *Roll Call at the Alamo,* Source Texana Ser. 1 (Ft. Collins, Colo.: Old Army Press, 1985), 50–57.

3. Myerson, "They Remember the Alamo."

4. For an overview of the DRT's perspective, see Marjorie Parsons, "Chipping Away at the Alamo," *Gonzales Inquirer* (March 21, 1995). This article in a small-town weekly Texas paper was written by a member of the local DRT chapter and lambasts the Texas Legislature for its attempts to bring the Alamo under the jurisdiction of the Texas Parks and Wildlife Department.

5. James Duncan and David Ley, eds., *Place/Culture/Representation* (New York: Routledge, 1993); Foote, *Shadowed Ground;* Linenthal, *Sacred Ground;* and Kirk Savage, "The Past in the Present," *Harvard Design Review* (Fall 1999): 14–19.

6. Michael Kammen, *Mystic Chords of Memory: The Transformation of Tradition in American Culture* (New York: Knopf, 1991), 3.

7. Paul Connerton states that "our experiences of the present largely depend upon our knowledge of the past, and our images of the past commonly serve to legitimate a present social order" (*How Societies Remember* [New York: Cambridge University Press, 1989], 3).

8. Connerton, *How Societies Remember,* 72.

9. For a more in-depth reading of how specific Texas battle sites have been configured, see Foote, *Shadowed Ground,* chap. 7; and Linenthal, *Sacred Ground,* chap. 2.

10. The use of "landscape" here has a double meaning: that of the actual geography of the state, as well as "the discursive terrain across which the struggle between the different, often hostile codes of meaning construction has been engaged" (Stephen Daniels and Denis Cosgrove, "Spectacle and Text: Landscape Metaphors in Cultural Geography," in Duncan and Ley, *Place/Culture/Representation,* 59).

11. Foote, *Shadowed Ground,* 10.

12. Many of the people I have met during my trips to the Alamo over the years state that they are visiting for the second, third, even tenth time, usually to honor an ancestor who fought in the Texas Revolution (if not necessarily at the Alamo). The Alamo is the site of the annual "Alamo Heroes Day" commemoration, on March 6. Also, each year, around April 21 (San Jacinto Day), the first day of San Antonio's Fiesta, the DRT holds a pilgrimage to the Alamo to commemorate the battle. The Alamo Chapter of the DAR (Daughters of the American Revolution) is but one of the groups that participates in this event (http://www.texasdar.org/chapters/Alamo/; retrieved June 11, 2007). The advent of blogs has given visitors who would remain invisible a chance to be seen; Texas Representative Aaron Peña created a blog entry about his visit to the shrine (November 7, 2005) in which he said, "I have called this march a pilgrimage because that's what I believe it is. For me it is more than a 222 mile journey to Texas greatest historical shrine now known as the Alamo, but rather a sacred journey to a little shrine known as Mission San Antonio de Valero w[h]ere we seek the blessing and grace of our Lord on this noblest of missions" (http://www.acapitolblog.com/search?q=222+mile+journey; retrieved June 11, 2007).

13. Bob Greene, "Remember the Alamo? It's Still Deep in the Heart of Texas, across from Woolworth's," *Esquire* (April 1984).

14. A small stone on the Alamo grounds, donated to the DRT in 1914 by Japanese professor Shigetaka Shiga, likens the Battle of the Alamo to the Japanese battle of

Nagashino in 1575 and commemorates the heroes of both conflicts. In 1989, it was the focal point of a ceremony which applauded not only the spirit of goodwill which accompanied the original gift but also the desire for recognition of common heroic traits in former enemies and as an important aspect of the remembrance of World War II tragedies like Pearl Harbor and Hiroshima.

15. The full text reads, "The Daughters of the Republic of Texas, by virtue of the authority delegated by the State of Texas, is the custodian of the Alamo, Shrine of Texas Freedom, and the French Legation Embassy in the days of the Texas Republic. These ancient structures, requiring continuing renovations, are maintained as museums solely by gifts and efforts of the Daughters, who are dedicated to the perpetuation of the memory and spirit of those who achieved the Independence of Texas. DRT encourages and provides for historical research, maintaining a library at the Alamo. It fosters the publication of historical documents and records and preserves relics of early Texas in the Republic of Texas Museum in Austin" (http://www.drt-inc.org/General-Information.html; retrieved September 25, 1997).

16. Robert L. Ables, "The Second Battle of the Alamo," *Southwestern Historical Quarterly* 70 (January 1967): 372–413.

17. According to the *Handbook of Texas,* a Tejano, "derived from the Spanish adjective *tejano* or (feminine) *tejana* (and written in Spanish with a lower-case *t*), denotes a Texan of Mexican descent, thus a Mexican Texan or a Texas Mexican." The term was used as early as 1824 in the Mexican Constitution but gained more widespread use toward the end of the twentieth century, when it shifted its meaning to a regional identity that included "cultural manifestations in language, literature, art, music, and cuisine." Traditionally, the *Handbook* states, "historians have applied the term specifically, perhaps anachronistically, to those Mexican Texans in Spanish Texas, to distinguish them from residents of other regions, and in Texas from the end of the Spanish era in 1821 to Texas Independence in 1836, in contradistinction to the Texian or Anglo-American residents of that time and of the Republic of Texas" ("Tejano," *Handbook of Texas Online,* http://www.tsha.utexas.edu/handbook/online/articles/TT/pft7.html; retrieved June 11, 2007).

18. American Heritage presents *The Alamo,* prod./dir. Arthur Drooker, narr. Tom Berenger (History Channel Video, 1996).

19. Richard Flores, *Remembering the Alamo: Memory, Modernity, and the Master Symbol* (Austin: University of Texas Press, 2002), 75.

20. These stories can be found in, among other sources, Adina De Zavala, *History and Legends of the Alamo and Other Missions in and Around San Antonio,* ed. Richard Flores (Houston, Tex.: Arte Público Press, 1996). While the book does contain transcripts of Travis' famous letter from the Alamo, "To the People of Texas and All Americans in the World," as well as maps of the battle site, lists of those killed, and other Texas revolutionary documents, these pieces are positioned as part of a larger overall narrative that stretches back to the founding of the mission, its work with American Indians, and the legends and stories that grew up around the site as a result.

21. Along with private donations (solicited on http://www.thealamo.org/main.html; retrieved May 24, 2007), the money from the sale of souvenirs and memorabilia in the Alamo museum gift shop is the major source of revenue for the upkeep of the site. The DRT receives no state funding. To do so, the organization feels, would require it to acquiesce to demands from the Legislature about how the site is constructed.

22. At this height, the San Jacinto Monument is not only the tallest public monument in the United States—the Washington Monument in Washington, D.C., stands only 555 feet, 5/8 inches (http://www.tourofdc.org/monuments/washington-monument/; retrieved May 24, 2007)—it is also the tallest monument column in the world, according to the Guinness Book of World Records, a fact that the museum proudly touts on its Web site (http://www.sanjacinto-museum.org/; retrieved May 24, 2007).

23. I use the term "Texian" to distinguish the historical events of the Revolution from the contemporary performance of Texan cultural memory.

24. *Texas Forever!! The Battle of San Jacinto,* San Jacinto Museum of History Association (http://www.sanjacinto-museum.org/show.html; retrieved January 25, 2003; copy in author's collection).

25. According to the *Handbook of Texas,* "the term Runaway Scrape was the name Texians applied to the flight from their homes when Antonio López de Santa Anna began his attempted conquest of Texas in February 1836." More information about the scope of the flight can be found at "Runaway Scrape," *Handbook of Texas Online* (http://www.tsha.utexas.edu/handbook/online/articles/RR/pfr1.html; retrieved June 11, 2007).

26. *Texas Forever!! The Battle of San Jacinto,* prod./dir. San Jacinto Museum of History Association, narr. Charlton Heston, viewed April 20, 2002.

27. "Goliad Massacre," *Handbook of Texas Online* (http://www.tsha.utexas.edu/handbook/online/articles/GG/qeg2.html; retrieved May 24, 2007).

28. "Alavez, Francita," *Handbook of Texas Online* (http://www.tsha.utexas.edu/handbook/online/articles/AA/fal53.html; retrieved May 24, 2007). More will be said about Alavez and her role in Texan national narrative formation in Chapter 3. In 2004, a statue of Alavez erected in memory of her efforts to save Texian prisoners was dedicated at Presidio La Bahía as part of the recently completed Angel of Goliad [Walking] Trail (Robin M. Foster, "Angel of Goliad Trail," *Victoria Advocate* [December 5, 2004]).

29. In addition to the monument erected on the grave site in 1936, there is a monument on the site of the Coleto Creek battlefield and a Fannin memorial in the town of Goliad. Ironically, this last statue was one of the very first memorials erected to commemorate the Revolution in the state of Texas (Foote, *Shadowed Ground,* 222–223, 229).

30. In addition to candlelight tours, a memorial service, and a pilgrimage to the Fannin memorial, the Presidio La Bahía Living History Program has inaugurated a two-day reenactment of both the Battle of Coleto Creek and the Goliad Massacre, held on March 29–30 (http://www.presidiolabahia.org/living_history.htm; retrieved May 24, 2007). This feature of the Goliad memorial site will be covered in more depth in Chapter 3.

31. "Alamo Cenotaph," *Handbook of Texas Online* (http://www.tsha.utexas.edu/handbook/online/articles/AA/gga2.html; retrieved May 24, 2007).

32. Fernando Urissa/Uriyza, as told to Nicholas Labadie, "San Jacinto Campaign," *Texas Almanac (1859)*; also in James M. Day, *The Texas Almanac 1857–1873—A Compendium of Texas History* (Waco, Tex.: Texian Press, 1967), 174.

33. Although there are no exact numbers, later accounts of the Scrape acknowledge that "added to the discomforts of travel were all kinds of diseases, intensified by cold, rain, and hunger. Many persons died and were buried where they fell" ("Runaway Scrape," *Handbook of Texas Online* (http://www.tsha.utexas.edu/handbook/online/articles/RR/pfr1.html; retrieved May 24, 2007).

34. Peter Vergo, ed., "Introduction," *The New Museology* (London: Reaktion, 1989), 1–2.

35. Vergo, "Introduction," 2.

36. Michael Barnes, "All Texas, All the Time," *Austin American-Statesman* special commemorative section (April 22, 2001).

37. The Bob Bullock Archives are located at Baylor University in Waco (http://www3.baylor.edu/Library/BCPM/Bullock/biography/bullock_chronology.htm; retrieved May 25, 2007).

38. "About Bob Bullock," Bob Bullock Texas State History Museum (http://www.thestoryoftexas.com/the_museum/special/about_bob_bullock_web.html; retrieved May 25, 2007).

39. "Did You Know?" Bob Bullock Texas State History Museum (http://www.tspb.state.tx.us/TSHM/About/Didknow.htm; retrieved December 9, 2002; copy in author's collection).

40. For an in-depth review of the museum's then–cutting edge approach, see Walter R. Buenger, "'The Story of Texas'? The Texas State History Museum and Forgetting and Remembering the Past," *Southwestern Historical Quarterly* CV, no. 3 (January 2002): 481–493.

41. Barnes, "All Texas," 4.

42. http://www.thestoryoftexas.com/showtimes/special/star_of_destiny.html; retrieved May 25, 2007.

43. *Davy Crockett in Texas,* starring Douglas Taylor and Ken Webster; dir. Catherine Berry. Texas Spirit Theater, Bob Bullock Texas State History Museum, March–August 2002.

44. Svetlana Alpers, "A Way of Seeing," *Exhibiting Cultures: The Poetics and Politics of Museum Display,* ed. Ivan Karp and Steven D. Lavine (Washington, D.C.: Smithsonian Institution Press, 1991), 31.

45. Alpers, "A Way of Seeing," 32.

46. Kirshenblatt-Gimblett, *Destination Culture,* 17–18.

47. Centennial map, Barker Texas History Collection, Center for American History, University of Texas at Austin.

48. http://www.thc.state.tx.us/markerdesigs/madmark.html; http://www.thc.state.tx. us/faqs/faqpdfs/HistProgFactSheet.pdf; both retrieved May 25, 2007.

49. Subject Markers, Texas Historical Commission (http://www.thc.state.tx.us/markerdesigs/madsubmarker.html; retrieved May 25, 2007).

50. Recorded Texas Historic Landmarks, Texas Historical Commission (http://www.thc.state.tx.us/markerdesigs/madrthl.html; retrieved May 25, 2007).

51. Gilles Deleuze, "Rhizome vs. Trees," *The Deleuze Reader,* ed. and intro. Constantin V. Boundas (New York: Columbia University Press, 1993), 29.

52. Deleuze, "Rhizome vs. Trees," 29–31.

53. Paul Green, *Texas; A Symphonic Outdoor Drama of American Life* (New York: Samuel French, 1967), 3.

54. Green, *Texas,* 67.

55. Green, *Texas,* 20.

56. "Dateline Texas: Musical Drama Texas Updated for Accuracy," *Houston Chronicle* (May 26, 2002).

57. http://www.heritageent.com/content.asp?tpl=prod_leg; retrieved August 8, 2002; copy in author's collection. The Canyon, Texas, Chamber of Commerce (http://www.canyonchamber.org/) can provide more information.

58. Daniels and Cosgrove, "Spectacle and Text," 59.

59. Savage, "The Past," 17.

60. "The famed mission in San Antonio where a gallant band fought and fell to the Mexican army in 1836 is under attack once more by an enemy force. A tiny but persistent enemy force" ("Morning Edition Returns: Dismember the Alamo," *Morning Edition,* National Public Radio, March 6, 2003 (http://www.npr.org/templates/story/story.php?storyId=1185064); retrieved June 11, 2007).

CHAPTER 3

1. Epigraph from Jon Winokur, "Curmudgeon," *Funny Times* 17.2 (December 2002): 6.

2. "Mexican Officials Lose Alamo Flag," *Austin American-Statesman* (December 19, 1994).

3. "Artifacts beneath the Alamo," *Chronicle of Higher Education* (March 10, 1995).

4. The Revolution's actual causes and aims are themselves contradictory. It was not a simple case of Anglo versus Mexican or even Texas against Mexico, because Texas was part of Mexico (the province of Coahuila y Tejas). The Revolution started out as a battle by federalist government supporters throughout Mexico (including Stephen F. Austin) to restore the Mexican Constitution of 1824 after Santa Anna and his centralist supporters ousted democratically elected president Anastacio Bustamante (Flores, *Remembering the Alamo,* 22–24). Santa Anna quelled several federalist uprisings in other provinces before proceeding to Texas. However, the arrival of American immigrants after Santa Anna seized power and ended immigration turned the war into one for independence from Mexico entirely. There are three first declarations of independence: the Tejano one (¡Viva Tejas!); the one at Goliad; and the "official" one signed at

Washington-on-the-Brazos on March 2, 1836. For more information, see the most popular histories of Texas in general and the Alamo in particular: Walter Lord, *A Time to Stand: The Epic of the Alamo* (New York: Bison, 1978); Lon Tinkle, *13 Days to Glory: The Siege of the Alamo* (1958; College Station: Texas A&M University Press, 1985); Stephen L. Hardin, *Texian Iliad: A Military History of the Texas Revolution* (Austin: University of Texas Press, 1994). The politics of the Revolution will be discussed in greater depth in Chapter 5.

5. These types of "pedagogical procedures," according to Michel de Certeau, "make up the apparatus which, by realizing the ancient dream of enclosing all citizens and *each one* in particular, gradually destroys the goal, convictions and the educational institutions of the Enlightenment" (Certeau, *The Practice,* 166). Enlightenment educational institutions are those which draw primarily from the scientization of history, not from the romanticization of it or attempts to craft a history that reflects a particular national spirit.

6. René Girard, *Violence and the Sacred,* trans. Patrick Gregory (1972; Baltimore, Md.: Johns Hopkins University Press, 1977), 42.

7. Other regions have their own historical dramas: North Carolina has Paul Green's *The Lost Colony* (the longest-running outdoor drama) and Kermit Hunter's *Unto These Hills,* as well as numerous smaller historical dramas depicting the struggles of Daniel Boone in the American Revolution (*Horn in the West*), the Quakers (*The Sword of Peace*) and the Waldenses (*From This Day Forward*). Other long-running historical dramas include Ohio's *Trumpet in the Land* (the Moravians) and *Tecumseh!* (based on the life of the Shawnee nation's leader), Oklahoma's *Trail of Tears* (the Cherokee nation's removal), and Kentucky's *Stephen Foster: The Musical* (based on the life of the composer). All of these outdoor dramas except *From This Day Forward* and *Trail of Tears* were still being performed as of May 2007 (http://www.unc.edu/depts/outdoor/dir/history.html). In each instance, the drama serves a pedagogical function—to educate tourists about the lives and events of historical importance in the region—and contributes to the formation of a distinct regional identity within its specific area.

8. According to David Glassberg, pageantry "movements" were primarily a Progressive Era phenomenon that culminated with *The Pageant and Masque of St. Louis* in May 1914 (*American Historical Pageantry: The Uses of Tradition in the Early Twentieth Century* [Chapel Hill: University of North Carolina Press, 1990], 160). This trend was due to the link between pageantry as an expression of civilization and "the art of democracy," which characterized the Progressive Era (p. 199). However, such pageantry "movements" were primarily limited to the Northeast and Midwest. By the time pageantry became a major performance force in the South and West (of which Texas falls somewhere between), it had become primarily amateur and individualized, focused more on educating schoolchildren and the general public in historical subjects than reflecting the will of a community to celebrate its progress and development (p. 231). It is this amateur type of pageantry that primarily constituted the types of pageants found in the years leading up to the Texas Centennial and the body of historical plays which followed.

9. According to the Web site for Disney's Alamo movie, "there have been some 11+ movies created about the Alamo since man [*sic*] first started using a motion picture camera. The first Alamo movie was shot in 1911 and was called *The Immortal Alamo.* It starred Francis Ford (the older brother of John Ford) and several other silent movie stars that time has forgotten. No copies of this film are known to exist" (http://www.thealamofilm.com/alamo-movies.shtml). For more information on the history and construction of the Alamo narrative on film, see Thompson, *Alamo Movies.*

10. While perhaps more widely known as a Civil War–related phenomenon, battle reenacting extends into most major conflicts throughout history, from Christian versus Aztec reenactments from the 1500's to contemporary events that reenact World War II. Tony Horwitz's Pulitzer Prize–winning *Confederates in the Attic: Dispatches from the Unfinished Civil War* (New York: Vintage, 1998) gives a popular-culture view of these events and those who participate in them. There have been scholarly studies of various types of reenacting cultures, such as Jenny Thompson's *War Games: Inside the World of 20th-Century War Reenactors* (Washington, D.C.: Smithsonian Books, 2004). More on battle reenactments will be said later in this chapter.

11. A 2004 study by the National Endowment for the Arts "reported that book reading has dropped sharply in the United States during the past 10 years" (Les Christie, "Endangered: The American Reader," CNNMoney.com [http://money.cnn.com/2004/07/09/news/bookreading/; retrieved May 25, 2007]). The study, entitled "Reading at Risk," shows that "the percentage of adults who read literature has dropped . . . from 56.9% in 1982 to 46.7% in 2002" (ALA News, www.ala.org). The study says that younger adults (age eighteen to thirty-four) have shown the greatest decline. The study focused on books it defined as "literature," meaning that current-events books and other best sellers were not included, but the overall trend still suggests that today's citizens are more likely to get their history from a performative source (such as the History Channel) than a written one, making the need to scrutinize exactly what is being depicted and how it is being depicted of primary importance.

12. Kirshenblatt-Gimblett, *Destination Culture,* 149.

13. In fact, the phrase "reality effect" is a translation of the French *l'effet de réel,* or "the effect of the real," which is (visually on the page) also the effect of the (English) "reel."

14. Lord suggests that everyone "follow the advice of J. K. Beretta . . . [a defender of the line story, who said,] 'Is there any proof that Travis didn't draw the line? If not, then let us believe it'" (Lord, *A Time to Stand,* 204).

15. This conflict can be seen most clearly in the turmoil surrounding the creation of *Alamo: The Price of Freedom,* an IMAX film version of the Battle of the Alamo. (More about this film and the controversy surrounding it later in this chapter.) The conflict was so great that it even made news outside the state. See Charles Hillinger, "Is the New 'Alamo' Film History or Is It an Insult to Latinos?" *Los Angeles Times* (December 19, 1987), Gregory Curtis Papers, DRT Library, the Alamo, San Antonio, Texas.

16. Kenneth B. Ragsdale, *Centennial '36: The Year America Discovered Texas* (College Station: Texas A&M University Press, 1987), 100.

17. Glassberg, *American Historical Pageantry,* 199.

18. According to Naima Prevots, "The artist members of the APA [American Pageant Association, founded in 1913] saw pageants as a catalyst to develop audiences and introduce dance, theatre, and music originating in American rhythms and energies. Civic leaders saw the productions as a way of bridging barriers between the rich and poor and also inculcating patriotic values" (*American Pageantry: A Movement for Art and Democracy* [Ann Arbor, Mich.: UMI Research Press, 1990], 3).

19. Glassberg, *American Historical Pageantry,* 290.

20. Most Texas history pageants elide representations of Texas' role in the Confederacy during the Civil War, either by not representing it at all or by limiting its representation to the showing of the Confederate flag.

21. Ed R. Bentley, *Texas under Six Flags: An Historical and Patriotic Pageant, Depicting in a Symbolical Way, in Story, Song, Dance and Tableaux, the History of the Lone Star State* (1921), Barker Texas History Collection, University of Texas at Austin, 9–10. This is the only pageant that recognizes Troutman's contribution to the Revolution by drawing a clear allusion to her American revolutionary counterpart, Betsy Ross.

22. Bentley, *Texas under Six Flags,* 11–12.

23. Mary Ann Zuber, "An Escape from the Alamo," *Texas Almanac of 1873, and Emigrant's Guide to Texas* (Galveston, Tex.: Richardson, Belo, and Co., 1872), 691–697. The story does not appear in any of the accounts of known Alamo survivors such as Susanna Dickinson or Enrique Esparza (son of Gregorio, one of the six Tejanos to die at the Alamo) until the end of the century. Historians are divided on whether or not the event actually occurred. Walter Lord believed that Rose, if he existed, invented the story of the line in the sand (*A Time to Stand,* 201–204).

24. Many of these documents have been collected and published in Timothy M. Matovina, *The Alamo Remembered: Tejano Accounts and Perspectives* (Austin: University of Texas Press, 1995).

25. This statistic is found in several sources, most recently, "Westward Expansion: The Texas Revolution," *Digital History,* University of Houston Web-based textbook (http://www.digitalhistory.uh.edu/database/article_display.cfm?HHID=312; retrieved June 1, 2007).

26. http://www.tsl.state.tx.us/treasures/republic/alamo/travis-full-text.html; retrieved June 1, 2007.

27. Bessie Lee Dickey Roselle, *The Messenger of Defeat: A Play Presenting the Siege of the Alamo in Three Scenes, Dramas of Daring Deeds Depicting Texas History* (San Antonio, Tex.: Naylor, 1936), 20.

28. Bentley, *Texas under Six Flags,* 8.

29. Rebecca Washington Lee, *Following the Lone Star: A Pageant of Texas* (Fort Worth: Texas Christian University, 1924), 2.

30. Flores, *Remembering the Alamo,* 160.

31. Flores, *Remembering the Alamo,* 161.

32. Bentley, *Texas under Six Flags,* 9.

33. Delza Harvick Stone, *Indian Paintbrush: A Pageant* (San Antonio, Tex.: 1936), 6 (my pagination).

34. Birdie Brenoltz Gambill, *We Are Texas: A Texas Pageant* (Dallas, Tex.: Banks Upshaw, 1936), 15–16.

35. Sam DeShong Ratcliffe, *Painting Texas History to 1900* (Austin: University of Texas Press, 1992), xv.

36. In a letter to Texan painter Henry McArdle dated November 18, 1874, "Reuben Potter . . . declared that the Alamo, not San Jacinto, had marked the birth of the Republic of Texas" (Ratcliffe, *Painting Texas History,* 43). Potter had participated in the Texas Revolution and the Civil War and was considered an expert on both conflicts. His articles on the Revolution were published in Texas and "back East." For a brief overview of Potter's life, see "Potter, Reuben Marmaduke," *Handbook of Texas Online* (http://www.tsha.utexas.edu/handbook/online/articles/view/PP/fpo30.html; retrieved June 1, 2007).

37. Even the recent discovery of a letter which proves that Huddle's depiction of Sam Houston's wound is on the incorrect leg cannot blunt the didactic power of this picture (Mark Babinek, "Lone Star Leg Twister Unraveled," *[Baton Rouge] Advocate* [April 21, 2002]). The painting shows Houston wounded in the right leg; the letter, written by Houston to his wife, Margaret, on January 11, 1853, says that the "San Jacinto wound" was in his left.

38. Bentley, *Texas under Six Flags,* 8–9.

39. Bessie Lee Dickey Roselle, *The March of the Immortals: A Pageant of Texas Heroes, Pageants and Plays of Pioneers Commemorating the Centennial of Texas* (San Antonio, Tex.: Carleton Printing Co., 1935), 98.

40. Roselle, *The March,* 100, 101.

41. Roselle, *The March,* 102.

42. In addition to the other pageants referenced in this chapter, see depictions of Santa Anna in Virginia Bradford, "Ghosts Walk and Talk on the Old Spanish Trail," *Phantoms of the Chaparral* (San Antonio, Tex.: Naylor, 1936), 10; and Ilanon Moon, *Texas, Land of the Strong* (Austin, Tex.: Steck, 1936). There are also representations of "generic" Mexicans, equally unflattering, in May Ingham Perry, *Texas, Land of Romance* (New York: A. S. Barnes, 1929), 7; Bradford, "The Run-Away Scrape," 47; and Bessie Lee Dickey Roselle, "The Turn of the Tide," *Dramas of Daring Deeds Depicting Texas History* (San Antonio, Tex.: Naylor, 1936),

43. Stone, *Indian Paintbrush,* 5 (my pagination).

44. Mrs. Frankie Guthrie, *Did You Call Me?,* in *Let's Go to Texas* (San Antonio, Tex.: Naylor, 1936), 28. Even Santa Anna's historical memory is incorrect; it was General Urrea who commanded the Mexican troops that captured and executed Fannin and his men at Goliad.

45. Guthrie, *Call,* 30.

46. Several Centennial-era pageants, including *Centinela: An Epic Drama of Texas* (1936), *Indian Paintbrush* (1936), *We Are Texas* (1936), and *Gran Cueriva* (1938), include

scenes of Indian life and/or Indian characters. These representations, however, are mostly pantomimed tableaus of "war dances" (the text of *Indian Paintbrush* says that "any good Indian dance may be substituted if preferred" [p. 4]) and stereotypical gestures and dialogue. These scenes occur at the beginning of the dramas and are used mostly to encourage the colonization of Texas by the Spanish and French, not to depict Indian life before or treatment after colonization began. No Indian character is present in any pageant that I have seen once the events leading to the Revolution begin; it is as if they simply ceased to exist.

47. "Alavez, Francita," *Handbook of Texas Online* (http://www.tsha.utexas.edu/handbook/online/articles/view/AA/fal53.html; retrieved June 1, 2007). Little is known about her, including her real first name (which is listed in various sources as "Francita," "Panchita," or "Pancheta") or surname (Alavez, Álvarez, or Alevesco). After being deserted by Alavez in Mexico City following the Revolution, she returned to Texas and lived out her life on the King Ranch. Her descendants travel to Goliad each year to commemorate her role in the Revolution.

48. Mabel Claire Thomas, *The Angel of Goliad* (Dallas, Tex.: Tardy Pub., 1936), DRT Library, the Alamo, San Antonio, Texas, Vault 812 T459a: 1.

49. At the Battle of Coleto, Fannin and his men negotiated a surrender with Urrea that stipulated that the soldiers would be sent to New Orleans, even though Urrea knew of Santa Anna's orders to execute all who raised arms against the Mexican army. Some of the Mexican army officers considered it unethical and a violation of the rules of combat to then turn around and execute Fannin's men. See "Coleto, Battle of," *Handbook of Texas Online* (http://www.tsha.utexas.edu/handbook/online/articles/CC/qec1.html; retrieved June 1, 2007).

50. Thomas, *The Angel,* 3.

51. Thomas, *The Angel,* 8.

52. Thomas, *The Angel,* 7.

53. Thomas, *The Angel,* 15.

54. Thomas, *The Angel,* 17.

55. Thomas, *The Angel,* 20.

56. Paul Baker, "Introduction," in Ramsey Yelvington, *A Cloud of Witnesses: The Drama of the Alamo* (Austin: University of Texas Press, 1959), 8.

57. Baker, "Introduction," 8.

58. Ramsey Yelvington, *A Cloud of Witnesses: The Drama of the Alamo* (Austin: University of Texas Press, 1959), 44.

59. Baker, "Introduction," 8.

60. Paul Green, *The Lone Star: A Symphonic Drama of the Texas Struggle for Independence* (1977; New York: Samuel French, 1986), 3. As with most Paul Green dramas, the action is site specific. It takes place primarily in the area between San Felipe and San Jacinto (near Houston) in the southeastern part of the state. The play was written to be performed at the Mary Moody Northen Amphitheatre in Galveston Island State Park, whose stage resembles that of another Paul Green outdoor drama, North Carolina's *The Lost Colony.*

61. Green, *The Lone Star,* 60.

62. Green, *The Lone Star,* 86.

63. Green, *The Lone Star,* 20.

64. Green, *The Lone Star,* 29–30.

65. Green, *The Lone Star,* 48.

66. Mike Tolson, "Emily Morgan Isn't Inn Name for Hotel," *San Antonio Light* (May 23, 1985).

67. *William Bollaert's Texas,* ed. W. Eugene Hollon (1956; Norman: University of Oklahoma Press, 1989), 108n.

68. Letters, clippings, and photographs relating to Susanna Dickinson, Francita Alavez, and Emily Morgan/West, vertical files, DRT Archive, the Alamo, San Antonio, Texas. Donald C. Cutter, handwritten note to Henry Guerra, Bexar County Historical Commission chair, on speech manuscript of Mrs. Thelma Cade Perdue, dated June 20, 1985, Emily Morgan vertical file, DRT Library, the Alamo, San Antonio, Texas.

69. Henry Guerra, chairman, Bexar County Historical Commission, letter to Robert Pincus, August 28, 1985, Emily Morgan vertical file, DRT Library, the Alamo, San Antonio, Texas.

70. Dr. Margaret Swett Henson, "Emily D. West: AKA Emily Morgan and the Yellow Rose of TX," manuscript, rev. April 1995, pg. 2, Emily Morgan vertical file, DRT Library, the Alamo, San Antonio, Texas.

71. James E. Crisp, "Did the 'Yellow Rose of Texas' Really Exist or Is This Just Another Story from Texas Lore?" "The War Room," *Alamo de Parras* (http://www.tamu.edu/ccbn/dewitt/adp/central/warroom/warroom12.html; retrieved June 1, 2007).

72. Though the hotel name remained the Emily Morgan, the owners have used the legendary sexual liaison as a tool of subjection, an object of titillation for prospective guests. A visit to the hotel's Web site (http://www.emilymorganhotel.com/) reveals a series of pictures in which prospective guests say, "That's her" or "So, she's the one." The overviews of rooms and amenities are named "Emily's Rooms" and "Emily's Amenities," sexualizing the space with a feel that, in the end, fulfills Perdue's fear that the place would sound like a "prostitute hotel."

73. Many free blacks immigrated to Texas to escape slavery in the United States. Some served in the Texian army or in more indirect ways during the Revolution; many slaves fought alongside their masters. The first casualty in the Revolution was a free black soldier named Samuel McCulloch, who was disabled during the storming of the Mexican-held Presidio La Bahía at Goliad on October 9, 1835 ("McCulloch, Samuel, Jr.," *Handbook of Texas Online* [http://www.tsha.utexas.edu/handbook/online/articles/view/MM/fmc36.html; retrieved June 1, 2007]).

74. Darrell Flint, "Our Yellow Rose Isn't Blighted," *San Antonio Express-News* (April 25, 1995); photocopy, Emily Morgan vertical file, DRT Library, the Alamo, San Antonio, Texas.

75. Following the establishment of the Republic, the Legislature gradually eroded the rights of free blacks, culminating in the passage of a law in 1840 which required all free blacks to leave the Republic by January 1, 1842 (Alwyn Barr, *Black Texans:*

A History of African-Americans in Texas, 1528–1995, 2nd ed. [1973; Norman: University of Oklahoma Press, 1996], 6–9).

76. Andrew Forest Muir, "The Free Negro in Harris County, Texas," *Southwestern Historical Quarterly* 46 (January 1943): 218.

77. Ben Durr (with Anne Corwin), *Miss Emily, the Yellow Rose of Texas: A Novel* (Santa Fe, N.M.: Sunstone, 2001), 308–312.

78. Lugones defines "ethnocentrism" as "the disrespective, lazy arrogant indifference to other cultures" characterized by stereotyping or lack of appreciation of those cultures' unique aspects. She defines racism as "lack of awareness or blindness to being racialized" through the "structures and mechanisms of the racial state." Taken together, "ethnocentric racism" illustrates the reflection of cultural myopia in the structures which create and maintain ethnic and racial inequality and the inability of the dominant culture to understand its complicity in maintaining those structures (María Lugones, "Hablando cara a cara/Speaking Face to Face: An Exploration of Ethnocentric Racism," *Making Face, Making Soul: Creative and Critical Perspectives by Feminists of Color,* ed. Gloria Anzaldúa [San Francisco, Calif.: Aunt Lute Foundation Books, 1990], 48–49).

79. "Q and A," *San Antonio Express-News* (December 22, 1996); Francita Alvarez file, DRT Library, the Alamo, San Antonio, Texas.

80. Ruth Maragraff, *Centaur Battle of San Jacinto* (Austin, Tex.: Vanguard Press, 1997), 28 (emphasis hers). The presence of Crazy Horse, a late-nineteenth-century figure, in this mid-century narrative, is an anachronism which reinforces the totalizing Anglo narrative of Texas revolutionary pedagogy by showing the all-inclusive racism of the victorious Texans.

81. Maragraff, *Battle,* 35.

82. Mrs. Frankie Guthrie, *Texas Was Mine,* in *Let's Go to Texas* (San Antonio, Tex.: Naylor, 1936), 35.

83. Maragraff, *Battle,* 4. More about Maragraff's play will be said in Chapter 5.

84. A full listing of and links to reviews of the film can be found at http://www.imdb.com/title/tt0318974/externalreviews; retrieved June 1, 2007.

85. *The Alamo* was Wayne's first directorial venture. He had originally intended to play the cameo role of Sam Houston, but the nervous executives at United Artists insisted that he take on one of the central characters to ensure sufficient box-office draw as a condition of funding the production (F. Thompson, *Alamo Movies,* 71).

86. *Alamo Visitors Guide* (San Antonio, Tex.: R. Jay Cassell, 1981).

87. *Seguin,* dir. Jesús Treviño, *American Playhouse* (January 26, 1982).

88. F. Thompson, *Alamo Movies,* 112–113.

89. Not all Anglos sided with the Texians and not all Tejanos sided with the Mexicans during the Revolution, and not all were enemies afterward, despite the difficulties faced by Tejanos in the Republic. In her essay on the Tejanos of Victoria County, Ana Castillo Crimm highlights the disparate treatment received from their Anglo neighbors by two Tejano ranchers who acted in almost identical ways during General Urrea's

march through the area ("Finding Their Way," in *Tejano Journey, 1770–1850,* ed. Gerald E. Poyo [Austin: University of Texas Press, 1996], 120).

90. Mary Ann Noonan Guerra, "Chronology," in *Viva Tejas: The Story of the Tejanos, the Mexican-born Patriots of the Texas Revolution,* ed. Rubén Rendón Lozano (1936; San Antonio, Tex.: Alamo Press, 1985), 66–67 (my pagination). See also "Zavala, Lorenzo De," *Handbook of Texas Online* (http://www.tsha.utexas.edu/handbook/online/articles/view/ZZ/fza5.html; retrieved June 1, 2007).

91. Although his unit (the Second Regiment of Texas Volunteers, 9th Company) was the only Tejano army unit to fight at the Battle of San Jacinto, and he was elected mayor of San Antonio twice, Seguín declared himself "a foreigner in his own land" after his ranch was burned to the ground. He took his family to Mexico for six years (1842–1848) to escape threats on his life (Guerra, "Chronology," 73; "Seguín, Juan Nepomuceno," *Handbook of Texas Online,* http://www.tsha.utexas.edu/handbook/online/articles/view/SS/fse8.html; retrieved June 1, 2007).

92. Guerra, "Chronology," 73–78; also see Arnoldo De León, *The Tejano Community, 1836–1900* (1982; Dallas, Tex.: Southern Methodist University Press, 1997), 23–49.

93. Arnoldo De León, "Tejanos and the Texas War for Independence," *New Mexico Historical Review* 61 (April 1986): 139–140; also see Thomas Lloyd Miller, "Mexican Texans at the Alamo," *Journal of Mexican American History* 2 (Fall 1971): 33–41.

94. Rudolfo Acuña, quoted in De León, "Tejanos," 143–144.

95. James Lehrer, quoted in F. Thompson, *Alamo Movies,* 85. Lehrer is the author of the book on which the film is based. The first view we get of the Daughters in the film is in a voice-over in which one of them is reading Travis' famous letter aloud in a tone bordering on orgasmic. The camera pans around to show the reader, a middle-aged white woman, instructing a group of tourists in the importance of the document and the site on which they stand (the chapel).

96. Scarborough, quoted in F. Thompson, *Alamo Movies,* 85. For more about the *Viva Max!* controversy, including its resolution, see F. Thompson, *Alamo Movies,* 85–90.

97. Ustinov, quoted in F. Thompson, *Alamo Movies,* 88.

98. For more about the formation of the Pedro and Pancho stereotypes and their roles in Texas-Mexican border culture for the past 150 years, see Américo Paredes, *Folklore and Culture on the Texas-Mexican Border* (Austin: University of Texas Center for Mexican American Studies, 1993), 33.

99. Herb Qedi, *Viva Max!* comment page, Internet Movie Database (IMDb) (http://us.imdb.com/CommentsShow?0065184; retrieved June 3, 2007). The IMDb has very few recorded comments for *Viva Max!* so the film is relatively obscure. Another comment is from a native Texan who appreciates the send-up of what she terms the "Texas Mystic" and says the film will "mean more" to those who have visited the Alamo (although the interior of the Alamo compound in the film is as much a fabrication as the film itself). It is out of production on VHS and has not been transferred to DVD.

100. The claim of providing a "realistic" experience had been removed from the Web site; now, the site invites the audience to "relive history's unforgettable thirteen days

of glory as 189 Texian and Tejano defenders fight for Texas Independence. IMAX puts you in the middle of this historic action with its six-story screen and six-track stereo sound" (http://www.imax-sa.com/alamo.html; retrieved June 3, 2007).

101. The film won the 1988 Wrangler Award for Best Historic Western Film from the National Cowboy Hall of Fame, which recognizes attempts to "preserve the stories of the West" (http://www.nationalcowboymuseum.org/fs1_e.html). This was the third time Kieth Merrill had won the award for his IMAX and documentary film work (http://www.ldsfilm.com/directors/Merrill.html; http://www.nationalcowboymuseum.org/e_awar_winn_spec.html; both retrieved June 3, 2007).

102. Susie Phillips, "Critics Can Scan New Alamo Film," *San Antonio Express-News* (September 22, 1987). Martínez is quoted as saying, "I am interested in every single scene that portrays a Tejano."

103. John Rosales, "Rough-cut 'Alamo' Version Leaves a Tough Impression," *San Antonio Light* (December 23, 1987); Susie Phillips, "Group Wants Film Scrapped," *San Antonio Express-News* (December 31, 1987); Susie Phillips, "DRT Waits for Action to Decide on Movie," *San Antonio Express-News* (January 1, 1988); Kevin R. Young, "Letter to the Editor," *San Antonio Light* (January 2, 1988); Rick Casey, "Martyrdom Needed to Beat Alamo Myth," *San Antonio Light* (January 3, 1988); R. M. Dryer, "Letter to the Editor," *San Antonio Light* (January 6, 1988); all in Gregory Curtis Papers, DRT Library, the Alamo, San Antonio, Texas.

104. Susie Phillips, "Controversy over Alamo Movie to Focus on Flag," *San Antonio Express-News* (January 7, 1988); Susie Phillips and Rolando Martínez, "Coalition Says Alamo Film and Its Makers Are Frauds," *San Antonio Express-News* (January 9, 1988).

105. For two more detailed accounts of the controversy caused by *Alamo . . . The Price of Freedom,* see Linenthal, *Sacred Ground,* 75–78; and F. Thompson, *Alamo Movies,* 100–109. Also, the Gregory Curtis Papers at the DRT Library at the Alamo collect newspaper articles about the dispute as well as Curtis' eventual sidebar—not a full article, and certainly not a cover story—on the situation for *Texas Monthly.*

106. Musketeer Battle Club, *The Musketeer Battle Club Fighting Manual* (http://www.varmouries.com/mbc/manual.html; retrieved June 3, 2007).

107. Catherine Wilson, "Rally 'Round the Reenacted Civil War," *[Minneapolis] Star-Tribune.com* (August 31, 2003) (www.StarTribune.com/dynamic/story; retrieved April 6, 2005).

108. Jenny Thompson, "Playing Wars Whose Wounds Are Fresh," *New York Times on the Web* (June 5, 2004) (www.nytimes.com/2004/06/05/arts/05ENAC.html; retrieved June 3, 2007).

109. Gene Fogerty, "To Arms! The Hobby of Re-enacting" (http://www.thealamofilm.com/article_toarms.htm; retrieved May 5, 2003).

110. The ones in San Antonio reenact only the events leading up to the battle, including the grand marches of both armies, Santa Anna's council of war, and living history first-person dramatizations, not the battle itself (San Antonio Living History Association, "Remembering the Alamo" weekend, March 4–5, 2006).

111. "Come and Take It" was the motto of the Gonzales residents who refused to return a small cannon given to them by the Mexican government. According to the *Handbook of Texas Online,* "The Gonzales or 'Come and Take It' flag was designed and painted by Cynthia Burns and Evaline DeWitt and was allegedly used at the battle of Gonzales in October 1835" (http://www.tsha.utexas.edu/handbook/online/articles/FF/msf2.html; retrieved June 3, 2007).

112. Newton Warzecha, telephone interview with the author, March 18, 2003.

113. Although de la Garza's rescue of Nicholas Fagin is the only one depicted during the reenactment, he is also credited with saving the lives of John Fagin, James W. Byrnes, Edward Perry, Anthony Sideck, and John B. Sideck (Crimm, "Finding Their Way," 120).

114. Don DeLillo, *White Noise* (New York: Penguin, 1984), 12–13.

115. Fogerty, "To Arms!"

116. "Texas Pride," *Austin American-Statesman* (March 2, 1998).

117. For more information on the efforts of these individuals and others to determine the authenticity of the Alamo's re-presentations in revolutionary history, see the History Channel's *The Alamo.*

118. Bentley, *Texas under Six Flags,* 8–9.

119. Deleuze, "Rhizome vs. Trees," 44.

CHAPTER 4

1. Epigraph from Jaston Williams, Joe Sears, and Ed Howard, *Greater Tuna* (New York: Samuel French, 1983), 58.

2. Nelson Algren, "If You Must Use Profanity," *The Texas Stories of Nelson Algren,* ed. and intro. Bettina Drew (Austin: University of Texas Press, 1995), 45.

3. Two notable departures from these small-town representations is *The Two Towns of Jasper* (a.k.a. *A Texas Murder in Black and White,* 2002), a cable movie chronicling the aftereffects of the murder of James Byrd Jr.; and *Jasper, Texas* (2003), another film with similar intent. However, *The Two Towns of Jasper* is built around the murder and the responses of the black and white citizens of Jasper and depicts small-town life only from the perspective of the murder.

4. Certeau, *The Practice,* 108.

5. Certeau, *The Practice,* 106.

6. Certeau, *The Practice,* 106.

7. Ragsdale, *Centennial '36,* 37.

8. Ragsdale, *Centennial '36,* 100.

9. Texas Centennial Celebrations, "Centennial Year Calendar" (Dallas), revised to March 7, 1936.

10. Ragsdale, *Centennial '36,* 120.

11. Although towns like Gonzales did build their celebrations around their revolutionary identity, this was the exception, not the rule.

12. Molly Ivins, "Lone Star Strange," *The Nation,* reprinted in *Utne Reader* (March–April 2004).

13. From the Barnes and Noble review of the first-season DVD release (http://video.barnesandnoble.com/search/product.asp?EAN=24543069911&x=2116709; retrieved June 3, 2007).

14. Episode K08, "Shins of the Father" (March 23, 1997) (http://www.fox.com/kingofthehill/episodes/index.htm; retrieved June 3, 2007). This is not Peggy's only foray into latent feminism; see also K22, "Peggy's Turtle Song" (May 10, 1998). I use the term "latent" because her "feminist" ideas come from a misinterpretation of "real" ideals by other characters.

15. K12, "Meet the Manger Babies" (January 11, 1998).

16. KH714, "I Never Promised You an Organic Garden" (April 13, 2003).

17. K10, "Bobby Slam" (December 14, 1997).

18. K01, "Pilot" (January 12, 1997); K19 "Junkie Business" (April 26, 1998).

19. K22, "Peggy's Turtle Song" (May 10, 1998).

20. K03, "The Order of the Straight Arrow" (February 2, 1997).

21. The irony is that Peggy is no different from the historical Texans discussed in Chapter 3; she is originally from Montana (KH822, "A Rover Runs through It" [November 7, 2004]).

22. *King of the Hill* has aired one episode that directly deals with Texas revolutionary history (KH814, "How I Learned How to Stop Worrying and Love the Alamo" [April 18, 2004]), in which Bobby is taking his required Texas history class. To Hank's horror, Bobby's Texas history textbook is a tome "in which the story of the Alamo has been replaced with the history of Mexican fashions, the planting of poinsettias and the tragedy of Selena."

23. Marco Lanzagorta, "The Land of Redemption," *Pop Matters* (March 31, 2003) (http://www.popmatters.com/tv/reviews/k/king-of-the-hill.shtml; retrieved June 3, 2007).

24. Five seasons into the show, Bobby was still attending Tom Landry Middle School (K07, "What Makes Bobby Run" [December 10, 2000]). Matt Groening's *The Simpsons* enjoys a similar freedom in its ability to tackle issues.

25. Most family situation comedies, such as *Family Matters, Full House,* and *Family Ties,* face this dilemma; as the children age, story lines seem forced to deal with adolescent issues and the children's eventual departure from home. Because Bobby is not maturing, or at least is maturing at a highly restricted pace, the writers have been able to deal with numerous issues relating to his character that might not be possible in shows in which the actors, and thus the characters, age.

26. Don Shirley, "Preston Jones, Regional Hero," *Washington Post* (April 25, 1976), Preston Jones Collection, Texas State University, San Marcos, Box 98, Texas Trilogy folder.

27. Jones, "The Place," in *A Texas Trilogy* (New York: Hill & Wang, 1976), 1.

28. Jones, *Graduate,* 305.

29. Jones, *Magnolia,* 109–110.

30. Jones, *Magnolia,* 85.

31. Jones, *Magnolia,* 114.

32. Shirley, "Preston Jones."

33. Shirley, "Preston Jones"; David Richards, "Deep in the Hate of Texas, *Washington Star* (May 3, 1976); David Richards, "Can 'Trilogy' Survive N.Y. Last Word?" *Washington Star* (August 31, 1976); all in Preston Jones Collection, Texas State University, San Marcos, Box 98, Texas Trilogy folder.

34. Jerry Parker, "Prairie Fire Heads for Broadway," part 2, *Christian Science Monitor* (September 19, 1976), Preston Jones Collection, Texas State University, San Marcos, Box 99, Folder 10.

35. Clive Barnes, "Stage: The Last of 'Texas Trilogy,'" *New York Times* (September 24, 1976), Preston Jones Collection, Texas State University, San Marcos, Box 99, Folder 10.

36. Walter Kerr, "The Buildup (and Letdown) of 'Texas Trilogy,'" *New York Times* (October 3, 1976), Preston Jones Collection, Texas State University, San Marcos, Box 99, Folder 10.

37. Eileen Hillary, review, *East Side Express* (October 7, 1976); Robert C. Roman, "'Texas Trilogy' and Tidbits," *Irish Echo* (October 16, 1976); Joan T. Nourse, "Positive Values of a Texas Trilogy," *Catholic News* (October 14, 1976); Robb Baker, "Uptown/Downtown," *Soho Weekly News* (October 7, 1976); "In einer kleinen Stadt in Texas," *N.Y. Staats-Zeitung und Herold* (October 9–10, 1976), Wochenend-Magazin; all in Preston Jones Collection, Texas State University, San Marcos, Box 99, Folder 1.

38. Clifford Ridley, "Myopia Is Killing Broadway," *National Observer* (October 23, 1976); Richard L. Strout, "Provincial New York," *Christian Science Monitor* (November 5, 1976); both in Preston Jones Collection, Texas State University, San Marcos, Box 99, Folder 1. See also Victor Volland, "'Texas Trilogy' a Big Success Everywhere West of Broadway," *St. Louis Post-Dispatch* (January 23, 1977); Patrick Kelly, "Theatre Review: A Texas Trilogy," *The Alternative: An American Spectator* (January 1977); John Neville, "Trilogy's Fate," originally published in *Dallas Morning News,* reprinted in *The Prompter,* Midland Community Theatre (December 1976); all in Preston Jones Collection, Texas State University, San Marcos, Box 98, Texas Trilogy folder.

39. Robert Whitehead, a producer of the *Trilogy,* wrote an article at the behest of the *New York Times* challenging what he termed Barnes' "disinterest" in the trilogy due to its regional focus, but the article was never published (Preston Jones Collection, Texas State University, San Marcos, Box 99, Folder 1).

40. The other two plays in the trilogy, *A Tuna Christmas* and *Red, White and Tuna,* continue the story lines of the major characters and introduce a few new ones. One significant plot twist is the inclusion of a romance for Baptist, bible-thumping Bertha with radio announcer Arles Struvie during the town's annual Christmas celebrations. The newest installment, *Red, White and Tuna,* takes place at the annual Fourth of July Tuna High School reunion and ties up several of the main stories, such as what ever happened to Stanley Bumiller when he left town, while introducing us to even more of the town's current, and former, inhabitants.

41. The use of men in drag to play female parts ties *Tuna* to a classical performance tradition typified most recently by the Ridiculous Theatre of Charles Ludlam. The use of men in drag provides a critique of the construction of masculinity and feminity in contemporary society.

42. The script for *Greater Tuna* states that, while having the roles played by two people "greatly increases the fun of the show," the decision whether or not to cast the roles individually "is left up to the individual producer" (Williams, Sears, and Howard, *Greater Tuna,* 8).

43. See Diane Holloway, "Tuna-ites Dive into Fiesta," *Austin American-Statesman* (suppl.) (April 25, 1993).

44. Mel Gussow, "Theatre: *Greater Tuna,* Comedy," *New York Times* (October 24, 1982).

45. Michael Feingold, "The Way We Are," *Village Voice* (November 9, 1992).

46. Michael Barnes, "New York Critics Melt over 'Tuna Christmas,'" *Austin-American Statesman* (December 19, 1994).

47. Holloway, "Tuna-ites." Holloway considers the ads, which feature Tuna residents Vera Carp, Pearl Burras, and Bertha and Charlene Bumiller, "so funny you don't realize you're being sold a bag of groceries."

48. Williams, Sears, and Howard, *Greater Tuna,* 30.

49. Williams, Sears, and Howard, *Greater Tuna,* 56. This sentiment mirrors almost exactly that of a line from Jones' *Magnolia,* in which the characters see themselves as dedicated "to doing the [Lord's] work" (p. 56).

50. Williams, Sears, and Howard, *Greater Tuna,* 46.

51. Several studies highlighting how discourses of "whiteness" in American culture serve to reinforce traditional dominant power structures. See Martin A. Berger, *Sight Unseen: Whiteness and American Visual Culture* (Berkeley & Los Angeles: University of California Press, 2005); Robert Jensen, *The Heart of Whiteness: Confronting Race, Racism and White Privilege* (San Francisco, Calif.: City Lights, 2005); and María DeGuzmán, *Spain's Long Shadow: The Black Legend, Off-Whiteness, and Anglo-American Empire* (Minneapolis: University of Minnesota Press, 2005).

52. Wharton is located about sixty miles west-southwest of Houston, on U.S. Highway 59. It is the county seat of Wharton County. The U.S. Census produced a population count of 9,237. See *http://www.whartontexas.com/; http://www.city-data.com/city/Wharton-Texas.html;* all retrieved June 5, 2007.

53. Laurin Porter, *Orphan's Home: The Voice and Vision of Horton Foote* (Baton Rouge: Louisiana State University Press, 2003), 4.

54. Gerald C. Wood, *Horton Foote and the Theatre of Intimacy* (Baton Rouge: Louisiana State University Press, 1999), 2.

55. In chronological order, the plays in the *Orphan's Home Cycle* are *Roots in a Parched Ground, Convicts, Lily Dale, The Widow Claire, Courtship, Valentine's Day, 1918, Cousins,* and *The Death of Papa.*

56. *Roots in a Parched Ground* introduces us to twelve-year-old Horace Robedeaux, whose father, a lawyer, has drunk himself to death. To support herself and her infant

daughter, Horace's mother moves to Houston, leaving Horace behind, supposedly in the care of relatives but, in essence, an orphan. *Convicts* covers thirteen-year-old Horace's first job as a shop boy for a plantation owner. *Lily Dale* deals with twenty-year-old Horace's visit to his remarried mother's house and his interactions with his stepfather and flighty sister (for whom the play is named). *The Widow Claire* covers Horace's brief flirtation with a local widow as he leaves for business school; *Courtship* covers the beginning of his relationship with Elizabeth Vaughn, eldest daughter of the last scions of Harrison; *Valentine's Day* covers the reconciliation between the lovers and her parents following their elopement; *1918* is the story of the Texas flu epidemic of that year, which took the life of Horace and Elizabeth's eldest child (at the end of this installment, Elizabeth is pregnant again, this time with Young Horace, the character based on Foote's father). *Cousins* introduces some missing members of Horace's family from his father's side, and *The Death of Papa*, the final installment, deals with the death of Elizabeth Vaughn's father and the passing of the pater familias role to Horace.

57. Horton Foote, *Courtship; Valentine's Day; 1918: Three Plays from "The Orphan's Home Cycle"* (New York: Grove Press, 1987), 83.

58. Horton Foote, *Roots in a Parched Ground; Convicts; Lily Dale; The Widow Claire: The First Four Plays of the Orphan's Home Cycle* (New York: Grove Press, 1988), 94.

59. H. Foote, *Convicts,* 149.

60. H. Foote, *Convicts,* 101–102.

61. H. Foote, *Convicts,* 131.

62. H. Foote, *Convicts,* 103.

63. See the discussion of the reviews of Pauline Kael, John Simon, and Richard Corliss in Porter, *Orphan's Home,* 3.

64. Porter, *Orphan's Home,* 3.

65. Samuel G. Freedman, "From the Heart of Texas," *New York Times Magazine* (February 9, 1986), 61.

66. Charles S. Watson, *Horton Foote: A Literary Biography* (Austin: University of Texas Press, 2003), 160–161.

67. Wood, *Horton Foote,* 19.

68. Paul Auster, "The Book of Memory," *The Invention of Solitude* (1982; New York: Penguin, 1988), 122.

69. Terry Eagleton, *The Idea of Culture* (London: Blackwell, 2000), 37.

70. Marsha Norman, "Interview," *In Their Own Words: Contemporary American Playwrights,* ed. David Savran (New York: TCG, 1988), 183.

71. Barker, *Culture,* 213.

72. As noted earlier, this phenomenon is what Homi Bhabha would call a "Janus-faced" discourse; see Homi K. Bhabha, "Narrating the Nation," *Nation and Narration* (New York: Routledge, 1990), 3.

73. Williams, Sears, and Howard, *Greater Tuna,* 41–42.

74. I served as properties coordinator for a production of *Greater Tuna* for Kent State University's Porthouse Theatre Company in the summer of 1990. My job was to procure "authentic" Texas properties for the show: Lone Star beer cans, Texas signs, and

the like. As a native Texan, I was seen to have inside knowledge of what was needed to make the show really reflect the state.

75. Peggy Hailey, "My Texas" (www.bookpeople.com/infobook.num.isbn—09-484119; retrieved May 5, 2001).

76. Gianni Vattimo, "The Postmodern: A Transparent Society?" *The Transparent Society,* trans. David Webb (Baltimore, Md.: Johns Hopkins University Press, 1992), 7–10.

CHAPTER 5

1. Epigraph from Kinky Friedman, *Guide to Texas Etiquette* (New York: Cliff Street, 2001), 26.

2. Lianne Hart, "No Messing around with Texas' Slogan" (*Los Angeles Times on the Web* [July 6, 2004]) (http://www.latimes.com/news/nationworld/nation/la-na-texas6jul06.story; retrieved July 6, 2004).

3. Garrison Keillor, himself a prime example of the "Minnesotan" cultural identity, slams Texas no fewer than three times in *Homegrown Democrat: A Few Plain Thoughts from the Heart of America* (New York: Viking, 2004), 131, 197, 232. Keillor's distaste for Texas appears to run beyond his political sentiments: he speaks of Manhattanites who "belong to a world of theater and books and street life and freedom of thought and the democracy of the subway" as "part of a world utterly different from that of George W. Bush's Texas" (p. 232).

4. Eagleton, *Idea of Culture,* 59.

5. This idea of culture supposes that it comes about as the result of nation-state formation and is inherently materialistic. Groups such as tribes, which contemporary nation-states would label as "native" or "primitive," nonetheless have cultures of their own. Since Texan cultural identity is heavily grounded in the modern concept of the nation-state and rejects or obfuscates traditionally marginalized cultural groups (Hispanics, African Americans, Native Americans), Eagleton's limited definition is an effective representation of the way in which Texan cultural identity functions within the larger American cultural landscape.

6. Two of the last three presidents—and three of the last eight—have been Texans. Two of these were oilmen. And all three fought major ground wars. For more information on this aspect of Texan politics, see Robert Bryce, *Cronies: Oil, the Bushes, and the Rise of Texas, America's Superstate* (New York: Public Affairs, 2004), 3.

7. The show, which runs in syndication on FOX stations, centers around Judge Larry Joe Doherty, a "real-life Texan"(who is white and male) and his African American bailiff, William M. Bowers, who dispense "Texas justice" in a courtroom fraught with temper tantrums and other bad behavior. According to one watcher/blogger, "Bailiff William M. Bowers often has to help out if things get out of control. He takes guests into his 'closet' for a good talking to, before allowing them back into court" (http://www.geocities.com/entertalkmentsite/texasjustice.html; retrieved October 21, 2004).

8. "Horse neglect draws bread-and-water sentence" (http://www.msnbc.msn.com/id/5164349/ [June 8, 2004]; retrieved June 6, 2007).

9. James Bennet, "Sharon Laments 'Occupation' and Israeli Settlers Shudder," *New York Times on the Web* (June 1, 2003) (http://select.nytimes.com/search/restricted/article?res=F0061FFF3E540C728CDDAF0894DB404482; retrieved June 6, 2007).

10. See http://www.lonestarbeer.com/; retrieved August 7, 2007.

11. Unlike other Texas-brewed beers, such as Shiner Bock, Lone Star is sold only within the State of Texas, making it a regional beer, not a nationally marketed one.

12. Many contemporary commercials—particularly tourist-oriented ones—and other forms of advertising feature Texas as a multicultural state by showcasing a wide variety of genders and ethnicities; however, the historical figure of the Texan does not often appear in these commercials. History is usually relegated to pictures of the Alamo's façade.

13. "And It Doesn't Break Down for Traveling," *Field & Stream* (November 1999): 18.

14. Alessandra Stanley, "Just Skimming Texas Means Considerable," *New York Times on the Web* (August 6, 2004) (http://movies2.nytimes.com/mem/movies/review.html?res=940CE6D6153CF935A3575BC0A9629C8B63; retrieved June 6, 2007).

15. Stanley, "Just Skimming."

16. One viewer's summary of the show states that it "was set in Dallas and chronicled the exploits of wealthy Texas oil millionaires" (Tad Dibbern, http://www.imdb.com/title/tt0077000/plotsummary; retrieved June 6, 2007), providing implicit support for the branding of the show's characters as forms of the Lone Star.

17. For more about this conflict, see William C. Davis, *Lone Star Rising: The Revolutionary Birth of the Republic of Texas* (New York: Free Press, 2004), chap. 10.

18. H. W. Brands, *Lone Star Nation: How a Ragged Army of Volunteers Won the Battle for Texas Independence—and Changed America* (New York: Doubleday, 2004), 202–208. The Brands and Davis books are part of a library of Texas history texts that attempt to re-present the events of the Revolution and Republic as less than glorious, though, in the end, they see the Revolution and the republic—and the fighting spirit of the Lone Stars which made them possible—as positive events for the people and the United States.

19. http://www.tsl.state.tx.us/ref/abouttx/annexation/marc845.html; http://www.lsjunction.com/docs/annex.htm; both retrieved June 6, 2007.

20. The basis for that claim comes from the documents that readmitted Texas to the United States following its secession during the Civil War. According to those documents, "[n]o requirement exists—either in the Reconstruction Acts governing the rebel states or in the document readmitting Texas to full statehood—for the governor of Texas to sign a document reaffirming Texas' position as a state within the United States republic. The only ongoing requirement of Texas government was that no constitutional revision should deny the vote or school rights to any citizen of the United States" (http://www.tsl.state.tx.us/ref/abouttx/secession/20aug1866.html; quotation retrieved July 3, 2004; Web site accessed June 6, 2007). Since the original order of secession

from the Union specifically states that Texas no longer recognizes the U.S. government or Texas' status as a state and no clause is included in the readmission articles that mandates recognition, Texas, as well as the other Confederate states, claimed that they retained the right of secession from the United States following the Civil War.

21. Barr, *Black Texans,* 5–9.

22. *The Alamo,* dir. John Lee Hancock, starring Billy Bob Thornton, Jason Patric; Touchstone Pictures, 2004.

23. Earlier films may have expressed doubt about the success of the endeavor or, like Wayne's Crockett, been torn between his duty and his feelings for the Mexican woman Flaca, but none ever overtly stated that, given the chance, someone would leave. In fact, leaving was portrayed as the role of the coward Moses Rose, discussed in Chapter 3.

24. Eric Hoover, "Myth Understood," *Chronicle of Higher Education* 16 (April 2004): A17.

25. Bronson Tate, "Remembering the Alamo," Smithsonian Magazine (April 2004) (http://www.smithsonianmag.com/issues/2004/april/alamo.php?page=1; retrieved June 6, 2007).

26. Tate, "Remembering the Alamo," 2.

27. José Enrique de la Peña, *With Santa Anna in Texas: A Personal Narrative of the Revolution,* trans. and ed. Carmen Perry (College Station: Texas A&M University Press), 53. The diary is a heavily disputed document, with hard-core Crockett supporters claiming the manuscript to be a forgery. The best known of the latter is Bill Groneman; see *Defense of a Legend: Crockett and the de la Peña Diary* (Plano: Republic of Texas Press, 1994). Other scholars, however, believe that the document's authenticity and veracity have been proven through paper testing and comparison of other entries in the diary with outside sources (David B. Gracy, "'Just As I Have Written It': A Study of the Authenticity of the Manuscript of José Enrique de la Peña's Account of the Texas Campaign," *Southwestern Historical Quarterly* 55 [October 2001]: 255–291).

28. Jessica Winter, "Bush-era Frontier Epics Express Timely Doubts about American Imperialism," *Village Voice* (April 5, 2004) (http://www.villagevoice.com/issues/0414/winter3.php; retrieved June 6, 2007).

29. Richard Boyd Hauck, *Crockett: A Bio-Bibliography* (Westport, Conn.: Greenwood, 1982), 8.

30. Hauck, *Crockett,* 51. An example of this latter phenomenon is a volume entitled *Life of David Crockett, the Original Humorist and Irrepressible Backwoodsman, comprising his early history, his bear hunting and other adventures; his early service in the Creek War; his electioneering speeches and career in Congress; with his triumphal tour through the Northern states and services in the Texan war, An Autobiography, to which is added an account of his glorious death at the Alamo while fighting in defence of Texan independence,* with an introduction by G. Mercer Adam (New York: Perkins, 1903). The identity of the author of the "addition," however, is never revealed.

31. James N. Tidwell, "Introduction," *The Lion of the West: Retitled The Kentuckian, or A Trip to New York,* by James Kirke Paulding (Stanford, Calif.: Stanford University

Press, 1954), 7. Coincidentally, John Augustus Stone, the author of *Metamora, or The Last of the Wapanagoes,* was hired by James Hackett, the actor who played Wildfire, in the fall of 1831 to revise *The Lion of the West.*

32. Hauck, *Crockett,* 58. In his *Sketches* (1833), Mathew St. Clair Clarke states that Crockett, not Wildfire, originated the speeches, including the famous line, "I'm half horse, half alligator" [in Hauck, *Crockett,* 45–46].

33. For a synopsis of the event, see Tidwell, "Introduction," 7–8; Hauck, *Crockett,* 47.

34. James Kirke Paulding, *The Lion of the West: Retitled The Kentuckian, or A Trip to New York,* ed. James N. Tidwell (Stanford, Calif.: Stanford University Press, 1954), 31.

35. Paulding, *Lion,* 41.

36. Tidwell, "Introduction," 8–9.

37. Paulding, *Lion,* 35.

38. Hauck, *Crockett,* 149.

39. Walter Blair, "Introduction," *Crockett at Two Hundred: New Perspectives on the Man and the Myth,* ed. Michael A. Lofaro and Joe Cummings (Knoxville: University of Tennessee Press, 1989), 3.

40. Charles K. Wolfe, "Crockett and Nineteenth Century Music," in Michael A. Lofaro and Joe Cummings, eds., *Crockett at Two Hundred: New Perspectives on the Man and the Myth* (Knoxville: University of Tennessee Press, 1989), 83–85. It is possible, says Wolfe, that the songbook was in print during Crockett's lifetime.

41. Blair, "Introduction," 3–4.

42. According to Frank Thompson, "David Crockett is a solemn ex-congressman in *Davy Crockett at the Fall of the Alamo* (1926), a grizzled-yarn spinner in *The Last Command* (1955) and a rather raucous thug itching for a fight in *Heroes of the Alamo* (1937) (*Alamo Movies,* 13).

43. F. Thompson, *Alamo Movies,* 51.

44. Blair, "Introduction," 1.

45. Paul Andrew Hutton, "An Exposition on Hero Worship," in Lofaro and Cummings, *Crockett,* 37.

46. Ragsdale, *Centennial '36,* 142.

47. Ragsdale, *Centennial '36,* 252.

48. Journal of the Senate of Texas, Forty-third Legislature, 21–23.

49. Other local oil companies were equally clever, if not as historically minded: Sinclair Oil Company, for example, used mechanical dinosaurs to attract visitors to its exhibit.

50. Ragsdale, *Centennial '36,* 249. Admission to the *Cavalcade* was an additional forty cents, yet between sixty thousand and seventy thousand people per week paid the extra money to see the show (p. 251).

51. Ragsdale, *Centennial '36,* 251.

52. There was an appeal by A. Maceo Smith, a Dallas high school teacher, for a "Negro" display as part of the Centennial Exhibition, but these efforts came to nothing (Ragsdale, *Centennial '36,* 65).

53. Ragsdale, *Centennial '36,* 258.

54. Roach, *Cities,* 5.

55. De León, *The Tejano Community,* 10–11.

56. Flores, *Remembering the Alamo,* 154.

57. Robert J. Rosenbaum, *Mexican Resistance in the Southwest: "The Sacred Right of Self-Preservation"* (Austin: University of Texas Press, 1981), 39. The Cortina Affair, which began in 1859 after the slaying of an Anglo law officer who "was pistol-whipping a vaquero," was the beginning of the postannexation Anglo-Mexican border wars, and its end result "saw Anglos, principally the [Texas] Rangers, retaliate indiscriminately against all mexicanos in a fit of bloody terrorism" (pp. 42–43). The LULAC Web site reports that "more Mexicans were lynched in the Southwest between 1865 and 1920 than Blacks in other parts of the South and cases of Mexicans being brutally assaulted and murdered were widespread" (http://www.lulac.org/Historical-Files/Resources/History.html; retrieved May 4, 2004).

58. Rosenbaum, *Mexican Resistance,* 41.

59. De León, *The Tejano Community,* 13.

60. Paredes, *Folklore,* 33. These performances include the "Mexican car wash (leaving your car out in the rain), Mexican credit card (a piece of hose to siphon gasoline out of other people's cars), Mexican overdrive (driving downhill in neutral), Mexican promotion (an increase in rank without a raise in pay), [and] Mexican two-step (dysentery)." None of these tags are indigenous to the area, but the proliferation of them reinforces the ethnic binary and further solidifies the surface images of good (Anglo-inferred) and bad Mexican.

61. Paredes, *Folklore,* 215–234. Paredes believes that machismo in both Mexicans and Anglos is a sign of nostalgia: "the North American *macho* acts as if the Wild West had never come to an end; the Mexican *macho* behaves as if he is still living in the times of Pancho Villa" (p. 234).

62. LULAC was formed February 17, 1929, out of three civic organizations whose job it was to advocate for the rights of Mexican Americans, and it was instrumental in the 1948 school desegregation ruling (http://www.lulac.org/Historical-Files/Resources/History.html; retrieved May 4, 2004); see also John R. Chávez, *The Lost Land: The Chicano Image of the Southwest* (Albuquerque: University of New Mexico Press, 1984), 116.

63. Barrera, 67, 74.

64. Larry L. King and Peter Masterson (book), Carol Hall (music and lyrics), *The Best Little Whorehouse in Texas* (New York: Samuel French, 1978), 88. This speech was deleted from the 1982 film version.

65. King, Masterson, and Hall, *Whorehouse,* 42–43.

66. King, Masterson, and Hall, *Whorehouse,* 50.

67. King, Masterson, and Hall, *Whorehouse,* 65–66.

68. King, Masterson, and Hall, *Whorehouse,* 66.

69. Erik Baard, "George W. Bush Ain't No Cowboy," *Village Voice* (September 28, 2004) (http://www.villagevoice.com/news/0439,baard,57117,1.html; retrieved June 7, 2007).

70. Carol V. Hamilton, "Being Nothing: George W. Bush as Presidential Simulacrum," *C-Theory* 27.1–2 (July 13, 2004) (http://www.ctheory.net/articles.aspx?id=427; retrieved June 7, 2007).

71. Molly Ivins, "Is Texas America?" *Who Let the Dogs In? Incredible Political Animals I Have Known* (New York: Random House, 2004), 144. She goes on to state that "George W. Bush perfectly exemplifies that attitude."

72. *Oprah,* September 19, 2000.

73. Paul Waldman, *Fraud: The Strategy Behind the Bush Lies and Why the Media Didn't Tell You* (Naperville, Ill.: Sourcebooks, 2004), 19.

74. Among others, see Maureen Dowd, "W.'s Spaghetti Western," *New York Times on the Web* (May 29, 2002) (http://www.nytimes.com/2002/05/29/opinion/29DOWD.html; retrieved June 7, 2007); David E. Sanger, "To Some in Europe, the Major Problem Is Bush the Cowboy," *New York Times on the Web* (January 24, 2004) (http://www.globalpolicy.org/security/issues/iraq/attack/2003/0124cowboy.htm; retrieved June 7, 2007). "Frontier lingo" quotation from Baard, "George W. Bush."

75. George W. Bush, on *Hardball,* MSNBC (May 31, 2000) (http://politicalhumor.about.com/library/blbushisms2000.htm; retrieved June 7, 2007).

76. Jean Baudrillard, "Simulacra and Simulations," *Selected Writings,* ed. and intro. Mark Poster (Stanford, Calif.: Stanford University Press, 1988), 167.

77. Elisabeth Bumiller, "Keepers of Bush Image Lift Stagecraft to New Heights," *New York Times on the Web* (May 16, 2003) (http://www.nytimes.com/2003/05/16/politics/16IMAG.html?ex=1368417600&en=72949a566ce1e8c6&ei=5007&partner=USERLAND; retrieved June 7, 2007).

78. Molly Ivins, "Blushing for Bush," *Who Let the Dogs In? Incredible Political Animals I Have Known* (New York: Random House, 2004), 202.

79. The documentary was part of the month (August 2004) of Texas-related material shown on Britain's Trio channel, including screenings of such perennial Texas film favorites as *The Dallas Cowboys Cheerleaders* and *Debbie Does Dallas* (only the dramatic scenes of this pornographic film were shown, lasting a half hour). Specials and additional material included a documentary entitled *Business, Texas Style,* made following the Enron collapse (http://www.slate.com/id/2104849; retrieved June 7, 2007).

80. Michael Lind, *Made in Texas: George W. Bush and the Southern Takeover of American Politics* (New York: Basic, 2003), 29–30.

81. In an interview on National Public Radio's *Here and Now* (February 12, 2003) the interviewer gave Lind authority, and he invoked said authority as a "fifth-generation native Texan" who can trace his heritage back to the 1840's.

82. Ruth E. Margraff, *Centaur Battle of San Jacinto* (Austin, Tex.: Salvage Vanguard Press, 1997), 3.

83. Margraff, *Centaur Battle,* 4. The author also says that the play is "an inquiry of my own behavior after living 6 months in the 'State of Texas,' climbing into the dome of the [capitol] taller than the white house and looking down on the five-pointed lonestar."

84. Margraff, 24.

85. Margraff, 38.

86. Program notes, *Epcot: El Ala-MALL,* Jump-Start Performance Co., in collaboration with Guillermo Gómez-Peña and La Pocha Nostra, San Antonio, Texas, June 18–20, 2004.

87. Tony Kushner, *Only We Who Guard the Mystery Shall Be Unhappy* (http://www.thenation.com/doc/20030324/kushner; retrieved June 7, 2007). Performed as a staged reading at Louisiana State University on December 15, 2004, dir. Leon Ingulsrud.

88. Kushner, *Only We.*

89. Kushner, *Only We.*

90. Bhabha, "Introduction," 3.

91. See http://lonestaricon.com/2005/Columns/2004/editorial40.htm; retrieved June 7, 2007.

92. Garry Trudeau, *Doonesbury, Baton Rouge Advocate* (October 15, 2004). In the last frame of the strip, the character Mark replies to Joanie's assertion that the article (from the *Lone Star Iconoclast*) is "totally iconoclastic" with "Well, they have to *protect the brand*" [emphasis mine].

93. "But this Mexican, er, Texas standoff is for high stakes" is an example of one such comment during the newspaper coverage of the event ("The Eyes of Texas," *Wall Street Journal* [May 15, 2003]; retrieved from Pro Quest database May 16, 2004). Signs outside the Holiday Inn in Ardmore, Oklahoma, where the House members stayed, read, "Thank heaven these Democrats weren't defending the Alamo" [Ken Hoffman, "Democrats Find Fame and Infamy in Ardmore," *Houston Chronicle* [May 16, 2003] (http://www.chron.com/CDA/archives/archive.mpl?id=2003_3654690; retrieved June 7, 2007).

CHAPTER 6

1. Epigraph from Herbert Blau, *The Audience* (Baltimore, Md.: Johns Hopkins University Press, 1990), 382.

2. Bryce, *Cronies,* 7.

3. "'Texan' Bruton Upbeat about New Role" (http://www.ireland.com/newspaper/world/2004/1210/2162844062FR10BRUTON.html; retrieved June 11, 2007). This story reports that the newly appointed European Union ambassador to the United States, John Bruton, was made an honorary Texan "some years ago" by then-governor Bush. Bruton, however, "has accumulated other honorary American titles, such as "Citizen of Sioux City, Iowa," "Ambassador of Agriculture of South Carolina," and "General of Washington State," which, according to the article, "should help somewhat in his stated goal of improving relations between Europe and the United States."

4. Girard, *Violence,* 49.

5. For more on this concept, see Sonja Kuftenic, *Staging America: Cornerstone and Community-based Theatre* (Carbondale: Southern Illinois University Press, 2003), chap. 7.

6. Raymond Williams, *Culture and Society, 1780–1950* (New York: Columbia University Press, 1958), 334.

7. For 2000 figures, see http://proximityone.com/plc100.htm; http://www.censusscope.org/us/metro_rank_popl_growth.html; both retrieved June 11, 2007. For 2005 figures, see http://factfinder.census.gov/servlet/ACSSAFFFacts?_event=Search&geo_id=&_geoContext=&_street=&_county=&_cityTown=&_state=04000US48&_zip=&_lang=en&_sse=on&pctxt=fph&pgsl=010; retrieved June 11, 2007.

8. Gianni Vattimo, "The Postmodern: A Transparent Society?" *The Transparent Society,* trans. David Webb (Baltimore, Md.: Johns Hopkins University Press, 1992), 10.

INDEX

Abilene, TX, 79, 83

An Account of Colonel Crockett's Tour to the North and Down East, 100

Acuña, Rudolf, 61, 62

African Americans: and Confederacy, 57; representations of, 50, 80–81, 88–89; and Texan identity, 4, 9, 11–12, 47, 55, 56, 57, 97; and Texas Revolution, 56–57, 59. *See also* free blacks/persons of color; mulattos; slavery

the Alamo (mission), 1, 7, 12, 15, 16–21, 28, 31, 36, 55, 67, 70, 75, 129n12; and American identity, 3, 16; and American Indians, 37, 40, 130n20; archeological dig at, 37; as archive, 19; and Cenotaph, 14, 20, 23, 40; chapel at, 17, 18–19, 20, 52, 60, 62, 99; DRT and, 4, 14, 17, 18–20, 37, 39, 115, 129n4, 129n12, 130n15, 131n21; and DRT Library, 17, 18, 130n15; façade of, 20–21, 26, 30; in film, 62–63, 99; funding of, 21, 39, 131n21; Hispanics and, 9, 18–19, 40, 108; Hugo-Schmelzer building at, 19; jurisdiction of, 4, 14, 39–40, 129n4; Long Barrack at, 17, 18–19, 20; LULAC and, 4, 40, 108; monuments at, 17–18, 129–130n14; museum and gift shop at, 17, pedagogical purpose of, 17, 20–21, 63; Plaza at, 37, 62, 64; political power and, 108; "reclamation" of, 14, 18–20; as RTHL, 29; siege and fall of, 42, 47, 53–54; as shrine, 4, 16, 17, 18–19, 20, 37, 39, 56, 62–63, 67, 129n12, 130n15; as tourist site, 14, 16–17, 20–21, 72; Wall of History at, 20, 21. *See also* Mission San Antonio de Valero

The Alamo (1960 film), 3, 8, 13, 60, 63, 67, 99, 140n85, 150n23; and authenticity, 60, 63; and Kennedy presidency, 100

The Alamo (2004 film): and Bush presidency, 99–100; Disney and, 60, 99–100, 135n9; representation of Bowie and Travis, 112–113; representation of Davy Crockett, 99, 100

the Alamo, Battle of, 17, 22, 23, 38, 129–130n14; accounts of, 9–10, 43–44, 136n23; and Anglo/Mexican binary, 45; as birthplace of the Republic of Texas, 137n36; and Bonham, James, 49; and Bowie, James, 47–48, 64, 65; and Crockett, Davy, 10, 27, 47, 48, 60, 64, 70, 103–104; and cultural geography, 7; dramatic representations of, 51–52; in film, 12, 13, 60–61, 62–65, 99–100, 103, 104, 108, 128n30; flag of, 37, 126n15; heroes of, 10–11, 17, 19, 20, 47–48, 93–94, 129–130n14; and the Immortal Thirty-Two, 18, 25; in pageants, 44–45; political uses of story of, 99–100, 108; reenactments of, 64, 67, 68, 142n110; and revolu-

the Alamo, Battle of (*continued*)
tionary history, 46, 100; and Santa Anna, 43, 108; Tejanos and, 61; Texians and, 10, 18–19, 23; and Travis, William Barrett, 43–44, 45, 47–48, 62, 64, 70, 136n23
"The Alamo, or the Death of Crockett" (song), 102
Alamo . . . The Price of Freedom (IMAX film), 13, 62, 64–65, 67, 141–142n100; authenticity of, 64; and the Esparza brothers, 64, 65; and flag controversy, 65, 135n15; and National Cowboy Hall of Fame, 64, 142n101; protests against, 65
Alamo-as-event, 44, 45, 62, 63
"Alamo Heroes Day," 129n12
Alamo Village. *See* Happy Shahan's Alamo Village
Alavez, Captain Telesforo (husband of Francita), 22, 58, 59
Alavez, Francita (Panchita), 57–58, 70, 138n47; as "Angel of Goliad," 22, 23, 59, 131n28
Algren, Nelson, 71, 88
Álvarez, Telesforo. *See* Alavez, Captain Telesforo
American identity: and regional identity, 82; and Texan identity, 1, 41, 44, 94, 100, 113–114
American Indians: and Alamo, 37, 40, 122, 130n20; in Bullock Museum, 26; Cherokee Nation, 33, 134; and Civil War, 128n28; dramatic representations of, 50, 58, 59; Ogala Sioux, 115; and Republic of Texas, 125n2; stereotypes of, 49, 59; and Texas identity, 9, 47, 70; and "Trail of Tears," 33. *See also specific people and tribes*
American Playhouse (television series), 60
The Angel of Goliad (drama), 50–51, 59
Anglo/Mexican binary, 23, 37, 43, 44, 45, 47, 54, 55, 65, 107–108, 120, 152n60
annexation, 2, 18, 21, 42, 98, 126n5, 126n8
architectural space: archival function of, 14–15, 19, 24; and branding, 121; and landscapes, 96; natural space, 31–32, 35–36; and performance of identity, 1, 71; and power, 26
archival spaces, 4, 16
artifacts, 7, 21, 26, 27; cultural artifacts, 16, 24; ethnographic artifacts, 4, 26, 36, 122
Auster, Paul, 90
Austin, J. L., 6
Austin, Stephen F., 115; dramatic representations of, 41, 58; as "Father of Texas," 42; imprisonment of, 26; in pageants, 48, 49; in Texas Revolution, 133n4
Austin, TX, 11, 25, 71, 86
Austin American-Statesman, 69
Autry, Gene, 112
"average" Texan, 73, 75–76, 90, 93–94, 120

Baker, George Pierce, 40
"The Ballad of Davy Crockett" (Hayes), 103
Barker, Francis, 2, 11, 91
Barnes, Clive, 11, 82, 83, 145n39
battles. *See specific battles*
battle sites: and commemoration, 7–8, 23–24; configuration of, 129n9; as location of cultural memory, 15; patriotic function of, 7; pedagogical function of, 7–8, 16, 24, 36. *See also specific battles*
Baudrillard, Jean, 8, 127n26; and "simulation," 114, 119
Baylor University, 63
Baytown, TX, 21, 68
Bennet, James, 96
The Best Little Whorehouse in Texas, 12, 57, 108, 110, 112; and domestication of the Texas brand, 108–110; and racial

biases, 109, 122; and Texan stereotypes, 109–110
The Best of Texas (Hart), 35
Bexar County Historical Association, 55, 56
Bhabha, Homi K.: on national narratives, 3, 118, 147n72
Bissinger, Buzz: *Friday Night Lights*, 71
blacks. *See* African Americans
Blau, Herbert, 120
Bob Bullock Texas State History Museum, 25–28, 31; and cultural memory, 15; *Davy Crockett in Texas* at, 27; and excess, 25–26; Goddess of Liberty at, 26; history of, 25; IMAX Theater at, 25, 26; and spectacle, 16; "The Star of Destiny" at, 26–27; "The Story of Texas" at, 25, 26, 36; and Texan identity, 12, 27–28; Texas Spirit Theater at, 15, 25, 26–27; as tourist attraction, 28
Bollaert, William: *William Bollaert's Texas*, 55
Bonham, James, 42, 49
Border Patrol, 97, 108
borders, 5, 6–7, 9, 60, 141n98, 152n57
Bowie, James, 9, 80, 90, 106, 111, 119; representations of, 42, 47, 48, 49, 52, 64, 65, 99, 112–113
Braches House (Gonzales), 31
Brackettville, TX, 60
branding, 97, 111, 113–114; and Anglo male dominance, 111; and anti-intellectualism, 112–113; and Bush, 111–115; global branding, 111; politics and, 111, 118–119. *See also* "Lone Star"
Broadway: regional bias towards, 83, 145n39; and *Texas Trilogy*, 11, 80, 82–83
Bryce, Robert, 120
Bull, John, 40, 42
Bullock, Bob, 25
Bush, George W., 1, 9, 10–11, 12, 13, 25, 94, 95, 96, 97, 100, 122; and authenticity, 112, 119; as bestower of "honorary Texan" status, 121, 154n3; as cowboy, 112, 114; influences on identity of, 114; and new Texas brand, 111–115
Bustamante, Anastacio, 133n4
Butler, Judith, 6
Byrd, James Jr., 143n3

Calgary, Alberta, 65
Carliner, Mark, 62–63, 117
Carlson, Marvin, 6
cattlemen, 32, 34–35
Centaur Battle of San Jacinto (Margraff): archetypal characters in, 115; and challenge to revolutionary pedagogy, 115–116; Crazy Horse as character in, 58, 59, 115, 140n80; Yellow Rose character in, 115–116
Centennial Celebration, 9, 20, 21, 26, 44, 73–75, 104–107; and Centennial Commission, 28–29, 74; and historical dramas, 50; and historical markers, 28–29, 79; and marketing of Texas, 104–107; and pageants, 32, 34, 40–41, 44, 46, 48, 49, 50; regionalism and, 73–74; small towns and, 74–75, 89; and *Texas Centennial Review*, 74
Centennial Central Exposition, 9, 26, 74, 105, 106, 116; and Casa Mañana, 105; and *Cavalcade of Texas*, 13, 105–106; and Centennial Rangerettes, 106; exclusion of blacks and Hispanics from, 106; and Humble Oil and Refining Company's Hall of History, 105; and representation of non-Texans, 106
challenges to Texan identity, 4–5, 9, 11, 13, 15, 21, 22–23, 34, 40, 55, 59, 115–116
Cheney, Dick, 115
Chicken Ranch (La Grange, TX), 12, 108–109. See also *The Best Little Whorehouse in Texas*
Chisholm Trail, 29, 31
Chronicle of Higher Education, 37

Circle on the Square (New York), 85
Civil War: 8, 26, 46, 67, 102, 126n5, 136n20, 137n30, 149–150n20; and American Indians, 128n28; in pageants, 41; reenactments of, 66, 135n10
A Cloud of Witnesses (Yelvington), 51–52, 59
Coahuila y Texas, 61, 98, 133n4. *See also* Mexico
Coleman, Ron, 48
Coleto Creek, Battle of, 21, 22, 24, 50, 131n29, 138n49; battle site of, 8, 16, 22–24; compared to Little Bighorn, 22; defeat at, 23; and de Urrea, José, 22; and Fannin, James, 22; reenactments of, 67; surrender at, 22. *See also* Goliad Massacre
Colonel Crockett's Exploits and Adventures in Texas, "Written by Himself" (Smith), 100
Colonel Crockett's Free and Easy Song Book, 102
Colonel Crockett's Tour to the North and Down East, 102
Colonial Williamsburg, 15
colonization, 17, 60, 107, 138n46
"Come and Take It": and battle, 25, 30; and cannon, 16, 26, 27; celebration of, 8, 13, 67, 74; as motto of Gonzales, 67, 143n111; reenactment of, 67. *See also* Gonzales, Battle of
commemoration, 23–24, 29, 31, 74, 129–130n14; ceremonies of, 15, 20, 23; pageants as, 40, 44; performances as, 32; reenactments as, 39, 40, 66
Communism, 103
Confederacy, 122, 126n5; American Indians and, 128n28; and readmission of Texas to U.S., 149–150n20; in reenactments, 66; representations of, 41; Texas under, 58
Confederates in the Attic: Dispatches from the Unfinished Civil War (Horowitz), 135n10
Confederate States of America. *See* Confederacy
Connally, John, 62
Conquergood, Dwight, 6
The Constitution of the Republic of Texas, 128n29
Convicts (Foote), 88–89, 146n55, 147n56
Corpus Christi, TX, 37
Cortés, Hernán, 49
Cotton Bowl, 26, 74
Courtship (Foote), 146n55, 147n56
Cousins (Foote), 146n55, 147n56
cowboy, 112; Anglo versus Mexican identity for, 114; Bush as cowboy, 112, 114
Crawford, TX, 9, 94, 119; and Bush's "Camp David," 112; and *Lone Star Iconoclast* endorsement of Kerry, 119
Crazy Horse. See under *Centaur Battle of San Jacinto* (Margraff)
Crisp, James E., 56
Crockett, Davy (David), 95, 90, 106, 112, 115, 119, 151n42; at Alamo, 7, 10, 15, 27, 47, 70, 126n15; and almanacs, 102; and autobiography and other accounts, 100; and "The Ballad of Davy Crockett," 103; as brand, 103–104; and Bush, 114–115; Colonel Nimrod Wildfire based on, 99, 101–102; compared to Cumberland's West Indian, 7; dime novels about, 102; dramatic representations of, 42, 48, 49, 58, 64, 100–102; execution of depicted in de la Peña's diary, 150n27; and exhibit at Bob Bullock Museum, 27; in film, 17, 80, 99–103; and ghostwritten books, 102; as "king of the wild frontier," 100; merging with Alamo myth, 102–103; and Morris, Quincy, 6; Parker, Fess, as, 7, 17, 103; political career of, 100; reality of vs. myth of, 104; as Scots-

Irish frontiersman, 114; and sesquicentennial commemoration of death, 103; song tributes to, 120; stereotypes based on, 127n23; on television, 103; as Texian, 9, 33; Thornton, Billy Bob, as, 99; Wayne, John, as, 3, 7, 17, 60, 150n23
Cuidad Acuña. *See* Del Rio/Cuidad Acuña
cultural memory, 17, 20–21, 23, 24, 28, 37, 42, 45, 56, 60, 63, 70, 82, 83; and architectural space, 14–15, 24, 36; and performance, 34, 35, 39, 50, 120; political power of, 100; shift in, 104
cultural narrative, 33, 40, 72, 73

Dallas (television series), 9, 13, 97, 111, 149n16. *See also* Ewing, J. R.
Dallas, TX: 71, 97, 122; as Centennial city, 29, 74, 105
Dallas Cowboys, 76, 77
Dallas Theater Center, 79, 82, 83
Danas (Belgrade), 113
DAR (Daughters of the American Revolution), 129n12
Dare, Virginia, 33
Daughters of the Lone Star State (Shores), 81
Daughters of the Republic of Texas. *See* DRT
Davis Mountains, 125n3
Davy Crockett—In Hearts United (French), 103
Davy Crockett, Indian Fighter (television feature), 103
Davy Crockett, King of the Wild Frontier (1955), 5, 17, 103
Davy Crockett: Or, Be Sure You're Right, Then Go Ahead (Mayo), 102
Davy Crockett in Texas (one-man show), 27
The Death of Papa (Foote), 146n55, 147n56
de Certeau, Michel, 134n5; on local authorities, 73; on pedagogical procedures, 134n5; on "the practice of everyday life," 6; on "Walking the City," 72–73
de la Garza, Carlos, 68
de la Peña, José Enrique, 99; authenticity of diary of, 150n27
Deleuze, Gilles, 30
DeLillo, Don: *White Noise*, 69
Del Rio/Cuidad Acuña, 60
demographics, 122, 127n16
de Urrea, José, 22, 140–141n89
De Zavala, Adina: and the Alamo, 18–20, 108; *History and Legends of the Alamo and Other Missions in and Around San Antonio*, 130n20
de Zavala, Emily, 56
de Zavala, Lorenzo, 23, 42, 53, 61, 62
Dickinson, Almeron (husband of Susanna), 43
Dickinson, Angelina, (daughter of Susanna), 57
Dickinson, Susanna, 9–10, 12, 43, 44, 45, 47, 57–58, 136n23
Did You Call Me? (pageant), 49
Disneyland (television series), 103
Disney Studios, 17, 60, 104, 135n9; and Alamo, 99–100; and Davy Crockett, 103, 108
diversity, 21, 34, 42, 77
Dodd, Sheriff Ed Earl, 108–111. See also *The Best Little Whorehouse in Texas*
Doherty, Larry Joe: *Texas Justice*, 96, 148n7
Domestic Manners of the Americans (Trollope), 101
Doonesbury (Trudeau): cartoon about Crawford, 119
Dracula (Stoker), 7
Driscoll, Clara: and the Alamo, 19–20, 108; *In the Shadow of the Alamo*, 19

DRT (Daughters of the Republic of Texas): and the Alamo, 4, 14, 17, 18–20, 37, 39–40, 115, 129n4, 129–130n14, 130n15, 131n21; and Driscoll, Clara, 18–20; and De Zavala, Adina, 18–20; and French Legation Embassy, 130n15; and LULAC, 4, 40; and Republic of Texas Museum, 130n15; and Texas legislature, 40, 129n4; and *Viva Max!*, 62–63

Eagle Pass/Piedras Negras, 60
Eagleton, Terry, 90, 96, 148n5
Eggleston House (Gonzales), 30, 31
Emily Morgan Hotel (San Antonio), 55–56, 139n72
Epcot: El Ala-MALL (Gómez-Peña), 116–117
Esparza, Enrique (son of Gregorio), 136n23
Esparza, Gregorio, 10, 23, 53, 63
Esparza, Victoria (wife of Gregorio), 53
Esparza brothers, 64, 65
ethnicity, 12, 15, 21, 23, 40, 38, 50, 69; and binaries, 45, 54 (*see also* Anglo/Mexican binary); and conflict, 61; and the Other, 57; and reenactments, 68; and sexuality, 57; and stereotypes, 54
ethnocentrism, 140n78
ethnography, 6
everyday life: and Texas identity, 72, 73, 80, 83, 92; "practice of everyday life," 6; Wal-Mart and, 85
Ewing, J. R., 9, 10, 75, 97, 111, 112. See also *Dallas*; Hagman, Larry

Fagin, Nicholas, 68, 143n113
family: and Texas identity, 90–91
Fannin, James: Battle of Coleto, 22, 50, 58, 68, 137n44, 138n49; representations of, 49
Fannin Memorial Monument (Goliad), 23, 131n29
Fat City (television series), 97
Feingold, Michael, 85
Ferguson, Miriam A.: Governor of Texas, 105
festivals, 1, 4, 67, 74
films. *See specific titles and subjects*
Flores, Richard, 19, 45; on "Texas Modern," 107
Fogarty, Gene, 66, 69
Following the Lone Star: A Pageant of Texas (Washington Lee), 44–45
football, 24, 72, 76, 108
Foote, Horton, 12, 94; *Orphan's Home Cycle*, 72, 87–90; *Tender Mercies*, 87; *The Trip to Bountiful*, 87; and Wharton, TX, 87, 146n52
Foote, Kenneth E., 8, 16
Ford, Francis: *The Immortal Alamo*, 135n9
Fort Davis, TX, 2
Fort Worth, TX, 97
Foxworthy, Jeff, 84
France: Texas under, 41, 58; and Iraq invasion, 113
free blacks/persons of color, 56; in Republic of Texas, 98, 139n75; in Revolution, 139n73
freedom, 23, 52
French, Charles K., 103
French Legation Embassy, 130n15
Friday Night Lights (Bissinger): film, 72; television show, 71
"Friendship" (state motto), 34

Galveston, TX, 26–27, 53, 138n60
gender, 5, 9, 12, 13, 15, 56; and feminization of Texas, 42, 48, 52; stereotypes of, 56. *See also* challenges to Texan identity; masculinity; women
geographic space: and Texas identity, 3, 6–7, 13, 15, 29, 30, 32, 33, 36, 53
Gettysburg, Battle of, 16, 67
Giant (1956), 26
Girard, René: on violence, 37–38, 121

Glassberg, David, 40, 134n8
Glover, William, 11
Goffman, Erving, 6
Goliad Campaign. *See* Coleto Creek, Battle of; Goliad Massacre
Goliad Massacre, 22, 58, 59; reenactments of, 50, 131n30; representations of, 50–51. *See also* Coleto Creek, Battle of
Goliad Monument, 22–24, 31, 36, 131n29; and repositioning national narrative, 23–24
Gómez-Peña, Guillermo: *Epcot: El Ala-MALL*, 116, 122
Gonzales, Battle of: 21, 22, 43; battle site of, 8; monument to, 74. *See also* "Come and Take It"
Gonzales, TX, 30–31, 143n11; and "Come and Take It" celebration, 8, 13, 74; and Gonzales Chamber of Commerce, 30; and Gonzales County, 31; and the Immortal Thirty-Two, 18, 25; as the "Lexington of Texas," 67, 74; and the Runaway Scrape, 31
Gonzales Memorial Museum, 24, 25
Gore, Al, 113
Gottfried, Martin, 82
Great Depression, 13, 105
Greater Tuna (play), 13, 71, 83–86, 93, 147n74; humor in, 85; performance in New York, 85. See also *The Tuna Trilogy*
Greek drama, 38, 45, 51–52
Green, Paul: *The Lone Star: A Symphonic Drama of the Texas Struggle for Independence*, 138n60; *The Lost Colony*, 33; *Texas! A Symphonic Outdoor Drama of American Life*, 32–33, 35, 50, 53
Groesbeck-Mexia, TX: Fort Parker, 74
Gulf Coast, 87
Gussow, Mel, 85

Hackett, James: as Colonel Nimrod Wildfire, 101, 102, 151n31
Hagman, Larry, 97, 111
Hancock, John Lee: *The Alamo*, 99–100
Happy Shahan's Alamo Village, 60, 61, 64; authenticity of, 60; as movie set, 8, 60, 61, 64; and reenactments, 67; as tourist attraction, 8, 60
Hardin, Stephen, 56, 70
Hart, Lynn: *The Best of Texas*, 35; revision of *Texas!*, 34–35
Hawai'i, Kingdom of, 2, 126n7
Hayes, Bill: "The Ballad of Davy Crockett," 103
Henrianna, TX, 33
Henson, Margaret Swett, 56
heroism: at Alamo, 11, 17, 18, 23, 27, 43, 56, 62, 64, 65, 70, 100, 129n12, 129–130n14; and Centennial, 73, 74; and Goliad, 22, 23, 24; importance of, in pageants, 42, 44, 47–48, 49, 50; and Republic of Texas, 45; and Texan identity, 51, 53, 54, 55, 90, 92, 115
Heston, Charlton, 21
Hill, Hank and Peggy. See *King of the Hill*
Hispanics: and Alamo, 9, 18–19, 40, 108; exclusion of, 11–12, 97; injustices towards, 38; political disenfranchisement, 106–108; population of, 126n16; and racial binary, 47; representations of, 50, 53, 81; Santa Anna as representative, 10, 62, 63; and Texan identity, 9, 107–108; in Texas Revolution, 40. *See also* Anglo/Mexican binary; Mexicans; Tejanos
historical dramas, 50, 68, 80; and Anglo male dominance, 11, 50, 51–52; importance of, 95; pedagogy of, 13, 59, 60; as performed outside, 32, 33, 35, 50, 51, 53; regional dramas, 134n7; and sacrifice, 37–38; and sesquicentennial, 53; about Texas Revolution, 38, 53–54. *See also specific dramas*

historical events, 29, 63, 74; dramatic representations of, 50, 53, 59; in pageants, 49; and performance of Texan identity, 1, 4, 13, 27, 33, 35, 37, 39, 100. *See also specific events*
historical markers, 12, 15, 28–31, 40, 74
historical plays. *See* historical dramas.
historical sites: as archival spaces, 14–15; as sites for the performance of identity, 1, 12–13, 32, 36
History and Legends of the Alamo and Other Missions in and Around San Antonio (De Zavala), 130n20
Hitchens, Christopher, 114
Hollywood, 11, 60, 99
Hooper, Tobe: *Texas Chainsaw Massacre*, 71
Horwitz, Tony: *Confederates in the Attic: Dispatches from the Unfinished Civil War*, 135n10
Houston, Sam, 9, 11, 83, 95, 98, 115, 122; and Battle of Gonzales, 43; and Battle of San Jacinto, 23, 45, 55; and Morgan, Emily, 57; as first president of Republic, 98, 100; representations of, 42, 48, 49, 53, 54; and Santa Anna, 45–47, 53; and Texian Army, 98, 126n15
Houston, TX, 7, 21, 71, 87–88, 97; as Centennial City, 29
Howard, Ed: *The Tuna Trilogy*, 72, 83
Huddle, William Henry: *The Surrender of Santa Anna*, 46–47, 137n37
Huntsville, TX: penitentiary, 125n3

illiteracy, 135n11; and survivor narratives, 9–10, 43
immigrants, 41, 50, 61, 62, 108
immigration, 22, 61, 107–108; of Scots-Irish, 114
The Immortal Alamo (1911), 60, 135n9
the Immortal Thirty-Two, 18, 25
Indian Paintbrush (pageant), 46
Institute of Texan Cultures (San Antonio), 24
interstate system, 79
Interstate 10, 7, 21
In the Shadow of the Alamo (Driscoll), 19
Iraq: invasion of, 113, 114
Israel, 96
Ivins, Molly, 75, 112, 114

Jackson, Andrew, 98
Japan, 129–130n14
Jasper, TX: departure from small town representation, 143n3
Joe (Travis's slave), 56–57
John Bull. *See* Bull, John
Johnson, Lyndon Baines, 62, 96, 115
Johnson Space Center, 27
Johnston, Albert Sidney, 48
Jones, Anson, 25
Jones, Preston: compared to Tennessee Williams and Eugene O'Neill, 82; *A Texas Trilogy*, 11, 13, 72, 78–83, 89, 94, 98
Judge, Mike: *King of the Hill*, 72, 75
justice, 96

Keillor, Garrison, 148
Kennedy, John F., 100
Kennedy Center's Bicentennial Humanities Program, 11, 78–79, 82
Kerr, Walter, 82
Kerry, John, 119
King of the Hill (television series), 8, 9, 10, 13, 72, 75–78; and Arlen, TX, 75, 77; and Bobby Hill, 75–77, 144n22, 144n25; and Cotton Hill, 75, 76; and diversity, 76, 77; and feminism, 76, 144n14; and gender conflicts, 77; and Hank Hill, 9, 10, 75–78, 80, 144n22; and liberalism, 77, 78; and masculinity, 75–76, 84; and Peggy Hill, 12, 75–78, 144n14; and race, 77; and regional identity, 78; and revolution-

ary pedagogy, 77–78, 144n22; and sexism, 76; and sexuality, 76, 77; supporting characters on, 75, 77; and Texan stereotypes, 76–77; and Texan values, 78
Kirschenblatt-Gimblett, Barbara, 4, 39
Kuftenic, Sonja, 121

Laffite, Jean, 53, 122
Lamar, Mirabeau B., 48
landscape, 30, 31, 33, 71, 79, 90, 129n10
La Pocha Nostra, 116
LaSalle, Rene-Robert de, 49
The Last Picture Show (1971), 75
Las Vegas, NV, 8
League of United Latin American Citizens. *See* LULAC
Lehrer, James: *Viva Max!* (novel), 141n95
liberty: associated with Alamo, 18; from Mexican oppression, 54–55; as Texan virtue, 48, 59
Life of Martin Van Buren, 102
Lily Dale (Foote), 89, 146n55, 147n56
Lind, Michael: on authenticity, 115; authority of, as Texan, 153n81; on Scots-Irish basis for Texan identity, 114–115
The Lion of the West (Paulding): and Colonel Nimrod Wildfire, 100–102; plot and characters of, 101–102; "Trip to New York" (British title); 102
Little Bighorn, Battle of, 16, 22
living history sites, 15
local authority, 73, 74, 87, 92. *See also* de Certeau, Michel
Lonesome Dove (McMurtry novel), 71
Lonesome Dove (television series), 75
"Lone Star": and Anglo male primacy, 97, 107–108; and authenticity, 95–96; as brand, 5, 95–98, 116; as commodity, 1, 27–28, 95, 120; as façade, 13, 23, 24, 28, 33; origin of, 126n15; and performance of Texan identity, 5, 97, 100; and Texas flag, 42; ubiquity of, 120–121
The Lone Star: A Symphonic Drama of the Texas Struggle for Independence (Green), 53–55, 59, 138n60
Lone Star beer, 97; and Shiner Bock, 149n11
Lone Star Iconoclast (Crawford): endorsement of Kerry, 119
Long, Walter: as Santa Anna, 61
Lord, Walter, 39
The Lost Colony (Green), 33
Louisiana State Museum, 25, 43
LULAC (League of United Latin American Citizens), 4, 40, 108, 152n62

machismo, 107; and nostalgia, 152n61
MacKaye, Percy, 40
Maine, 1, 126n12
March of the Immortals (pageant), 48
Margraff, Ruth: *Centaur Battle of San Jacinto*, 58, 59, 115–116, 153n83
marketing: of Alamo, 21–22; of history, 36; of Texan identity, 13, 27–28, 95–96; of Texas in Centennial Celebration, 74, 104–107
Martínez, Walter: *Alamo . . . The Price of Freedom*, 65
Martyrs of the Alamo (1915), 61
masculinity: and reenactments, 66; representations of, 48, 72, 75–76; subversion of, 42, 50; and Texan identity, 4, 50, 51–52, 56, 59, 69, 72. *See also* gender
Mayo, Frank: *Davy Crockett, Or, Be Sure You Are Right, Then Go Ahead*, 102
McAllister, George: *Alamo . . . The Price of Freedom*, 64
McCulloch, Samuel, 139n73
McLaren, Richard, 2, 9, 125nn3
McMurtry, Larry: *Lonesome Dove*, 71
memorabilia, 20, 36, 131n21

Merrill, Kieth: *Alamo . . . The Price of Freedom*, 64, 142n101
The Messenger of Defeat (Roselle), 44
Mexia, José (Senator), 61
Mexican Army, 22, 23, 37, 50–51, 74, 108
Mexican Constitution, 126n15, 130n17; abolishment of, 61
Mexicans: and the Alamo, 11, 19, 43, 53, 61; and Anglo/Mexican binary, 23, 43, 45, 47, 107–108; identity of, 8, 38, 69, 70; immigration of, into Texas, 107, 108; as loyalists, 54–55; political disenfranchisement and injustices towards, 107–108, 152n57; and reenactments, 68; representations of, 19, 48, 49, 50–51, 52, 59; as settlers, 40; and *Viva Max!*, 62–64
Mexico: and Catholicism, 99, 107; and freedom from Spain, 61, 98, 99; government of, 22, 37; rebellion of, against Santa Anna, 61, 62; representations of, 42, 48; and Santa Anna, 21, 37, 61; and slavery, 98; Texas as province of (Coahuila y Texas), 21, 22, 41, 98, 107, 126n15
Michener, James: *Texas*, 71
Mier Expedition, 29
Milam, Ben, 42
Mission San Antonio de Béxar, 52; outdoor theater, 51
Mission San Antonio de Valero, 14, 19, 20, 129n12, 130n20. *See also* the Alamo (mission)
Miss Mona. See *The Best Little Whorehouse in Texas*; Chicken Ranch (La Grange, TX)
monuments, 35–36; of Alamo, 17–18, 23, 28; of Goliad, 22–24, 31; of San Jacinto, 21–22, 23–24, 28, 31, 40; of Texas Revolution, 21
morality plays, 51–52
Morgan, Emily (West), 55–58, 70; and Battle of San Jacinto, 55, 57; and Confederacy, 57; and de Zavala, Emily, 56; and Emily Morgan Hotel, 55; as free woman of color, 56, 57; and Houston, Sam, 10, 55, 57; and Morgan, Captain James, 55, 56; as mulatto slave, 55; representation of in *Centaur Battle of San Jacinto*, 115–116; and Santa Anna, 55, 56; and sexuality, 56, 57–58; and Texas Revolution, 55, 56–57; in *William Bolleart's Texas*, 55; as "Yellow Rose of Texas," 55, 56, 118
mulattos, 10, 55, 57
Muse of History, 34, 48
museums, 5, 14, 15, 16, 26, 36, 91, 121; history of, 24; and primacy of Anglo representations in, 10; as spaces for performance of identity, 6, 12–13, 25, 28; types of in Texas, 24. *See also specific museums*
Musketeer Battle Club, 65
myth, 83; historical myth, 89–90

Nagashino, Battle of, 129–130n14
A Narrative of the Life of David Crockett of the State of Tennessee (Crockett), 100
national narratives, 14–15, 32, 36; Alamo and, 17, 20–21; battlefields and, 16; Bhabha, Homi K., on, 3, 118; Bob Bullock Museum and, 28; Goliad Massacre and, 22–24; performance of, 28, 33, 38; redefinition of, 3
NASA, 26
Natchitoches, LA, 25
National Cowboy Hall of Fame, 64, 142n101
National Historic Landmark, 23
Native Americans. *See* American Indians
native Texans, 16, 33–34, 50, 72, 87
Navarro, Antonio, 53
Necessary Roughness (1991), 72
New Haven, TX, 56
New Orleans, LA, 25, 138n49
New York Daily News, 82

New York Post, 82
New York Times, 14, 82, 85, 96, 119
Nocona, 34
Norman, Marsha, 90
Norris, Chuck: as Cordell Walker, 96, 111
nostalgia, 3, 46, 91, 152n61

Oatmeal, TX, 103
Odessa, TX: Jack Rabbit Rodeo and Roping, 74
Oklahoma, 33, 119, 134n7, 154n93
Old County Jail (Gonzales), 30
Old Gonzales Teacher's College, 30, 31
Olmos, Edward James: as Santa Anna, 61
Only We Who Guard the Mystery Shall be Unhappy (Kushner), 117–118
Orphan's Home Cycle (Foote), 72, 87–90, 146n55, 146–147n56; *Convicts*, 88–89; *Courtship* and *Cousins*, 146n55, 147n56; critical reception of *Cycle*, 89; *The Death of Papa*, 146n55, 147n56; and Harrison, TX, 72, 73, 87–88, 91, 93; and Horace Robedeaux, 87–90, 91, 146–147n56; *Lily Dale*, 89; representation of small town life in, 89; representation of socioeconomic change in, 88, 89; *Roots in a Parched Ground*, 87–88, 89; *Valentine's Day*, 146n55, 147n56; *The Widow Claire*, 89
the Other: Indians as, 70; Mexicans as, 70; representations of, 21, 48; and sexuality, 57
Our Lady of Loreto Chapel. *See* Presidio La Bahía (Goliad)
Outer Banks, NC, 33
"outsider" identity, 9–10

Page, Geraldine, 87
pageants, 50, 52, 53, 68, 80, 89; Alamo-as-event in, 44–45; allegorical figures in, 34, 41, 48, 49, 50; and Centennial Exposition, 32, 34, 40, 48, 49; children in, 44–45, 47, 49–50; focus of, 50; historical pageants, 12, 40–41, 48, 49–50; pageant movement, 134n8; pedagogy and 13, 38, 39, 41, 49–50, 60; post–World War I, 41; pre–World War I, 40; purpose of, 136n18; representations of American Indians in, 137–138n46; representations of Battle of San Jacinto in, 45–47; representations of Confederacy in, 136n20; stereotypes in, 49, 59; stock characters in, 34. *See also specific pageants*
Palo Duro Canyon State Park (Canyon, TX): *The Best of Texas*, 35; Pioneer Amphitheater, 32, 35; *Texas! A Symphonic Outdoor Drama of American Life*, 12, 15, 32–33, 34
Panhandle (Texas), 7, 32, 34, 35
Paris, Texas, 75
Parker, Fess: as Davy Crockett, 5, 7, 17, 103, 104, 111
Parker, Quanah, 32, 34
parody, 76, 83, 85, 86, 93, 94
patriotism, 26, 44, 55, 56, 106; and Battle of the Alamo, 17; and Davy Crockett, 103
Paulding, James Kirke (*The Lion of the West*), 100–101
Pearl Harbor, 16, 130n14
Peña, Aaron, 129n12
Perdue, Thelma Cade, 55, 57, 139n72
performance, 32, 33, 34, 35, 36; and reenactments, 65; of regionality, 69, 121, 122–123; of Texan identity, 3–5, 37, 38, 39, 40, 49–50, 52, 53, 100
Perley, Benjamin: *Reminiscences of Sixty Years in the National Metropolis*, 101
Perot, H. Ross, 115
Piedras Negras. *See* Eagle Pass/Piedras Negras
pilgrimages, 16, 129n12, 131n30
plantations, 56, 88, 147n56
Plymouth Plantation, 15

politics: and authenticity, 95–96; and branding, 111, 118–119; of Progressive Era, 40; and Texan identity, 9, 12, 13, 95–97, 148; and Texas Revolution, 98–99
Port Hudson, Battle of, 67
Port Isabel, TX, 97
Positively True Adventures of the Alleged Texas Cheerleader-murdering Mom (1993), 72
preservation, 3, 21, 24, 30
Presidio La Bahía (Goliad), 23, 50, 67, 68, 131n28, 139n73
Presidio La Bahía Living History Program, 131n30
Progressive Era, 40, 134n8
prostitution, 57–58; in *The Best Little Whorehouse in Texas*, 57; Dickinson, Angelina and, 57; Morgan, Emily, and, 55, 139n72
Provisional Government of the Republic of Texas, 98, 100

race, 12, 38, 43, 56–57, 58, 69, 88; and Anglo/Mexican binary, 43, 44, 45, 47, 55, 107–108; prejudice based on, 80–81; stereotypes about, 54, 59; tension based on, 47, 54, 61
racism, 10–11, 23, 40, 57, 72, 80
Ragsdale, William, 104
railroads, 34–35
range wars, 32
"reality effect," 135n13
Reconstruction, 41, 46, 128n1, 149n20
Red, White and Tuna (Sears, Williams, Howard), 85–86. See also *The Tuna Trilogy*
Reed, Rex, 11
reenactments, 13, 39, 135n10; and accuracy, 8, 39, 66, 67; of Alamo, 66, 142n110; Anglo heroism represented in, 11; of Civil War, 8, 66; of Coleto and Goliad, 67–69; "Come and Take It" celebration, 8, 67; as commemoration, 15, 40; didactic power of, 66; festivals, 67; Goliad Massacre, 50; Happy Shahan's Alamo Village, 8, 67; participants in, 39, 66; and pedagogy, 66–67; and regionality, 69; role of women in, 66; and spectators, 66, 67; of Texas Revolution, 8, 39; of twentieth-century wars, 67
regionality, 11, 69, 71, 72, 78, 82–83, 92, 121, 122; and cultural identity, 122–123
Registered Texas Historical Landmark (RHTL), 29
Reminiscences of Sixty Years in the National Metropolis (Perley), 101
Republic of Texas (1836–1845), 29, 31, 76, 77; Alamo as birthplace of, 137n36; citizenship in, 128n29; Constitution of, 128n29; and de Zavala, Lorenzo, 42, 53; establishment of 21, 45; flag of, 42, 126n15; government of, 23, 25; and Jones, Anson, 25; and Lamar, Mirabeau B., 48; and Navarro, Antonio, 53; and political conflicts, 98, 100; and proslavery faction, 57, 98; Provisional Government of the Republic of Texas, 98, 100; representations of, 42, 53–55, 149n18; Tejanos and, 61; and Texan identity, 2, 10, 24; in *William Bolleart's Texas*, 55
Republic of Texas (movement), 2, 125n2, 125n4, 126n5, 126n8. *See also* McLaren, Richard
Republic of Texas Museum, 13, 130n15
Richards, Ann, 25, 75
Rio Grande, 7
ritual behavior, 37–38
Rivercenter IMAX Theater, 64
Roanoke Island Colony, 33
Rogers, Roy, 112
Roosevelt, Franklin D., 26
Roots in a Parched Ground (Foote), 87–89, 146–147n56

Rose, Moses, 9, 43, 136n23; dramatic representations of, 52, 64, 70; and Zuber, W. P., 43
Roselle, Bessie Lee Dickey: *The Messenger of Defeat*, 44
Rove, Karl, 115
"runaway" Democrats: representation of, as Texians vs. Mexicans, 119, 154n93
Runaway Scrape, 22, 24, 29, 31, 131n25, 132n33

sacrifice: and Battle of the Alamo, 17, 18, 23, 56, 100; futility of, 23; sexual sacrifice, 58; and Texas Revolution, 30, 38, 39, 45, 59, 69
Sam Houston Oak, 31
San Angelo, TX, 79, 83
San Antonio, TX, 7–10, 17, 43, 71; and Alamo, 60, 62–63, 64, 122; Battle of San Antonio, 22; as Centennial City, 29; City Council of, 62; and Emily Morgan Hotel, 55–56; and Fiesta, 129n12; Latino community of, 65
San Antonio Light, 55
San Felipe, TX, 54, 138n60
San Jacinto, Battle of, 10, 21–22, 55, 57, 126n15; and American Indians, 58–59; battle cry at, 45; battle site of, 8, 10; pedagogical function of, 8, 16; reenactments of, 68; representations of, 45, 49, 53–55; and Texas Revolution, 8, 61; victory at, 23. *See also* Texas Revolution
San Jacinto Monument, 12, 21–22, 23, 24, 28, 31, 40, 131n22
Santa Anna, Antonio Lopez de, 37, 115, 131n25; and Battle of the Alamo, 23, 43; and Battle of San Jacinto, 22, 24; dramatic representations of, 42, 45–47, 48–49, 51, 52, 53, 54, 59, 64, 65, 116, 137n42; as "El Presidente," 49, 57; and Goliad Massacre, 22; as Hispanic, 10, 48–49; and Mexican Constitution, 61; and Morgan, Emily, 10, 55, 56; as "Napoleon of the West," 43, 48, 61; representations in film, 61, 99, 108; surrender of, 49; and Texas Revolution, 133n4; tyranny of, 21, 22, 61
Saturn V, 27
Savage, Kirk, 35
Scots-Irish culture, 114–115
Sears, Joe: *The Tuna Trilogy*, 72, 83, 84, 85
segregation, 107–108
Seguin (1982), 60–61
Seguín, Juan, 10, 23, 26, 60, 61, 62, 107
Seguin, TX, 97
settlers, 5, 17, 99; Anglos as, 21, 34, 35, 40, 107; Mexicans as, 40; Spanish as, 22, 40
Sharon, Ariel, 96
Sheridan, Philip, 14, 128n1
Shiga, Shigetaka, 129–130n14
Shiner Bock, 149n11
Shores, Del: *Daughters of the Lone Star State*, 81
slavery, 10, 41, 50, 55, 56, 57, 85, 88, 139n73; Mexico against, 98; representations of, 41
small towns: and celebrations, 73, 74–75; and Centennial, 74–75; dramatic representations of, 72, 87, 89, 90–94, 143n3; mass media representations of, 71–72; and nostalgia, 122; in *Orphan's Home Cycle* (Foote), 89; and otherness, 72; and politics, 95–96; stereotypes of, 72; and Texan identity, 74–75, 89, 90–94, 108–110, 119, 121; *A Texas Trilogy*, 79, 83; *The Tuna Trilogy*, 84–85, 86
Smith, Deaf, 42, 46, 54
Smith, Robert Penn: *Colonel Crockett's Exploits and Adventures in Texas "Written by Himself,"* 100
Smithsonian Magazine, 99
Smokey Mountains, 33

Spain: conquistadors from, 26, 53; Mexico under, 61, 98, 99; settlement of Texas by, 22, 44; Texas under, 41
spectacle, 8, 16, 35, 99; Bob Bullock Museum as, 25; "The Star of Destiny" as, 26–27
Spirit of Progress, 34, 80
"The Star of Destiny" (multimedia show), 26–27
"The Star-Spangled Banner," 102
Steinbeck, John, 37
stereotypes: of American Indians, 59; of Americans, 127n23; of genders, 56, of Mexicans, 38, 48–49, 53, 54, 61, 63, 141n98, 152n60; in pageants, 49; of races, 59; of Southerners, 84; of Texans, 63, 77–78, 91, 94, 109–110
stock characters, 34, 102; Bowery Boy Mose as, 102; "Kaintuk" as, 114; the "Kentuckian" as, 33, 102; noble savage Metamora as, 102; Yankee as, 114
Stoker, Bram: *Dracula*, 7
"The Story of Texas." *See* Bob Bullock Texas State Historical Museum
The Surrender of Santa Anna (Huddle), 46–47, 137n37

Tate, Bronson, 99
Taylor, Diana, 4
Tender Mercies (Foote), 87
Tejanos, 8; accounts of Alamo battle by, 43, 60–61; and *Alamo . . . The Price of Freedom*, 65; definition of term, 130n17; dramatic representations of, 50, 52, 53, 54, 59; political disenfranchisement of and injustices towards, 38, 61, 107; in representations of Texas Revolution, 9, 19, 40, 53, 59, 60, 61–62, 63; and *Seguin*, 60–61; in Texas Revolution, 23; and *Viva Max!*, 128n63. *See also* Hispanics, Mexicans
television: representations of small town life, 72. *See also titles of specific series and specials*
Tennessee: and Davy Crockett, 100, 104
Texas (Michener), 71
Texas: America Supersized (television special), 97, 114
Texas!! The Battle of San Jacinto (slide-show), 21–22
Texas, Land of the Strong (pageant), 44
Texas! A Symphonic Outdoor Drama of American Life (Green), 12, 32–35, 50, 53; and Armstrong, Calvin, 98, 112; and Hart, Lynn, 34–35
The Texas Chainsaw Massacre (Hooper), 71
Texas Declaration of Independence, 25, 47
Texas Department of Transportation: "Don't Mess with Texas," 95
Texas Historical Commission, 56
Texas House of Representatives, 119, 128n29
Texas Justice (television series), 96, 148n7
Texas Legislature: and the Alamo, 129n4
Texas Parks and Wildlife Department: and the Alamo, 129n4
Texas Rangers, 32, 48
Texas Revolution (1835–1836), 13, 26, 37–40, 82, 122; African Americans and, 56–57; Alamo and, 3, 16, 17, 19, 129n12; and American identity, 3; and Anglo-Tejano relations, 140n89; and "average" Texans, 73; battles of, 21, 22, 45; and borders, 7; causes of, 133n4, Declaration of Independence, 133n4; dramatic representations of, 41–42, 50, 53, 59, 98–99, 149n18; federalists and, 133n4; historical markers commemorating, 29, 30–31; immigration and, 133n4; Mexican Constitution, 133n4; and pedagogy, 50, 51, 58, 59, 60, 68, 69, 70, 72, 74, 77–78, 90, 93, 96, 112, 115, 120; politics of, 98,

100; recreations of, 21–22, 38, 39; reenactments of, 66–69; representations of ethnicities in, 18, 19, 23, 38, 40, 59; and revolutionary narrative, 50, 51, 59, 61–62, 70, 74; revolution-as-event, 70; Tejanos in, 60, 61–62; and Texas identity, 2, 3 7, 16, 23, 37–40, 48, 49–50, 59, 91, 104; women and, 57–58

Texas Senate, 105

Texas Sesquicentennial Celebration, 53, 55

Texas Spirit Theater. *See* Bob Bullock Texas State Historical Museum

Texas State Archives, 120

Texas State Capitol, 25, 26, 46

Texas State Historical Archives, 44

A Texas Trilogy (Jones), 11, 13, 72, 78–83, 84, 90; and authenticity, 82; and Bradleyville, 72, 73, 79, 81, 82, 83, 86, 91–92, 93, 96; on Broadway, 82–83; Claudine Hampton in, 80; Colonel Kincaid in, 79, 80, 81, 83, 89, 98; critical reception of, 11, 82–83, 89, 145n39; at Dallas Theater Center, 79, 82, 83; everyday people in, 80; in Kennedy Center's Bicentennial Humanities Program, 11, 78–79, 82; Knights of the White Magnolia as Ku Klux Klan, 80, 80–81, 98; and humor, 81–82; *The Last Meeting of the Knights of the White Magnolia*, 79; 146n42; *Lu Ann Hampton Laverty Oberlander*, 79, 80, 88; and militarism, 80; Mirabeau B. Lamar Military Academy in, 79, 98; *The Oldest Living Graduate*, 79, 80; racial prejudice in, 81–82; racial roles in, 80–81; and regional identity, 82–83; representation of small town life, 79, 83; and revolutionary pedagogy, 83; Texan stereotypes, 80; Whitehead, Robert, on, 145n39

Texas Under Six Flags: An Historical and Symbolic Pageant, Depicting in a Symbolic Way, in Story, Song, Dance and Tableaux, the History of the Lone Star State, 41–42, 46, 70

Texas Was Mine (pageant), 58

Texian Army, 21, 22, 23, 26, 42, 43, 45, 51, 55, 58, 61, 98; Tejanos in, 40, 52, 61; Texian rebels, 54

Texians, 8, 9–10, 18, 19, 33, 40, 48, 131n23

Thais (Terence), 57

theater, 6, 35; "extreme theater," 27; pedagogy of, 32; and performance of identity in, 127n20; regional theater, 83; stereotypes in, 127n23; stock characters in, 34

Thornton, Billy Bob: as Davy Crockett, 99, 104

Thorpe, Melvin J., 108–110. See also *The Best Little Whorehouse in Texas*; Chicken Ranch

Tolson, Michael, 55, 56

tourism, 8, 13, 28–29, 30, 36; advertisements for, 149n12; and tourists, 16, 26, 37, 38, 39, 50, 56, 63, 64, 72; and "walking the city," 72–73

traitors, 40, 52

Travis, William B., 90, 98, 111, 119; at Alamo, 18, 25, 60, 64; dramatic representations of, 47, 48, 49, 52, 59, 99; letter from the Alamo, written by, 42, 43–44, 44, 45, 47, 52; and line in the sand, 43, 47, 48, 50, 135n14

Treviño, Jesús, 60–61

Trio (British television station): and *Fat City*, 97; and *Texas: America Supersized*, 97; and Texas programming, 153n79

The Trip to Bountiful (Foote) 87

"Trip to New York." See *The Lion of the West*

Trollope, Mrs. Frances: *Domestic Manners of the Americans*, 101

Troutman, Johanna, 42, 126, 136

Truan, Carlos, 37

Trudeau, Gary: *Doonesbury*, 119, 154n92
Tucker, Richard: "Don't Mess with Texas," 95
The Tuna Trilogy (Sears, Williams, Howard), 72, 83–86, 90, 94; authenticity of, 86; branding of Texas in, 85–86; Charlene Bumiller in, 92; critical reception of, 85; and cross-dressing, 146n41; and gender, 86; *Greater Tuna* (1982), 71, 83–84, 85, 147n74; and HBO, 85, 86; humor in, 82, 84–85; and masculinity, 84; postmodernism in, 84; racial issues in, 86, 122; *Red, White and Tuna*, 85–86, 145n40; representation of women in, 84; and small town life, 84–85, 86; stereotypes in, 84, 86; a *Tuna Christmas* (1989), 85, 145n40; Tuna, TX, 72, 73, 90, 91, 92, 93, 96; whiteness in, 86
Turner, Victor, 6

U.S. Cavalry: and Alamo, 19, 22
U.S. Congress, 100
U.S. Department of Housing and Urban Development, 56
U.S. News and World Report, 2
Uncle Sam, 42
the Union (U.S.A.), 7, 42, 66, 98, 103, 121
University of Texas, 25; Longhorn Band, 97
Unto These Hills (drama), 33
Urban Development Action Grant (UDAG), 55, 56
Ustinov, Peter: in *Viva Max!*, 62, 63, 64

Valentine's Day (Foote), 146n55, 147n56
Vattimo, Gianni, 93, 122
Vergo, Peter, 24
Veteran's Day, 16
Vicksburg, Battle of, 67
Viesca, Agustín, 61
Vietnam Veteran's Memorial, 15
Vietnam War, 66
Village Voice, 85, 99
Villareal, Ricardo, 68
violence, 88–89; absence of, 44–45; Girard, René, on, 37–38, 121; as purifying, 38; as spectacle, 8
the Virginian, 112
virtues, 27, 32, 34, 49, 52, 59, 74, 78, 83, 97. *See also* freedom, heroism, justice, liberty
Viva Max! (Lehrer novel) 141n95; and DRT, 141n95
Viva Max! (1969 film), 62–64, 128n30, 141n99; Battle of the Alamo, 62; and DRT, 62–64; filming of, at Alamo, 62–63; Hispanics in, 63; reception of, 63–64; as satire, 62; stereotypes in, 63; Tejanos in, 63, 128n30

Walker, Texas Ranger (television series), 96, 111
"walking the city," 72–73, 79, 90
Walt Disney Studios. *See* Disney Studios
Warzecha, Newton, 67
Washington, D.C., 101, 105
Washington Lee, Rebecca: *Following the Lone Star: A Pageant of Texas*, 44–45
Washington Monument, 131n22
Washington-on-the-Brazos, 24; and Texas Declaration of Independence, 25; and Washington-on-the-Brazos State Park, 25
Washington Post, 82
Wayne, John: 3, 5, 8, 13, 17, 60, 63, 67, 99, 140n85, 150n23
We Are Texas (pageant), 46
West, Emily. *See* Morgan, Emily (West)
West Bank, 96
West Texas, 7, 79, 83
Westward the Course of Empire: The History of Texas from Exploration to Annexation (pageant), 44
Wharton, TX, 87, 146n52
Whig Party, 102

whiteness: and American identity, 146n51; and Driscoll, Clara, 19; in representations of the Battle of the Alamo, 19, 68; in representations of the Battle of San Jacinto, 21; subversions of, 42; and Texan identity, 5, 10–11, 50, 52, 53, 54, 56, 58, 59, 69, 72, 94, 95
White Noise (DeLillo), 69
"whitewashing" of history, 40, 54
The Widow Claire (Foote), 89, 146n55, 147n56
"Widows of Gonzales," 52, 53
Wildfire, Colonel Nimrod: based on Davy Crockett, 99, 100–102; character in *Lion in the West*, 100–102; Hackett, James, as, 101, 102; as stock "Kentuckian" character, 33, 102
William Bollaert's Texas (Bollaert), 55
Williams, Jaston: *The Tuna Trilogy*, 72, 83, 84, 85
Williams, Raymond, 121–122
Wilson, Ron, 14
Winfrey, Oprah, 113
Winter, Jessica, 99
women: and reenactments, 66; representations of, 12, 33, 50–51, 56, 69; as spectators, 52, 53, 54; and Texas identity, 4; in Texas Revolution, 57
World War II, 38, 130n14
World Wide Web: as site for subversion, 117–118

"Yellow Rose of Texas" (legend), 55, 56–57, 58, 70
"Yellow Rose of Texas" (song), 55, 56
Yelvington, Ramsey: *A Cloud of Witnesses*, 51, 52, 53
Yoakum, TX: Tom Tom Festival, 74
Young, Kevin, 70

Zuber, W. P., 43

CPSIA information can be obtained at www.ICGtesting.com
Printed in the USA
LVOW100010021211

257338LV00003B/8/P